7-7-65

MATHEMATICS FOR ELECTRONICS ENGINEERS & TECHNICIANS

by NORMAN H. CROWHURST

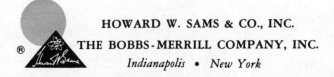

HOWARD W. SAMS & CO., INC.

THE BOBBS-MERRILL COMPANY, INC.

Indianapolis • *New York*

FIRST EDITION

FIRST PRINTING — SEPTEMBER, 1964

MATHEMATICS FOR ELECTRONICS ENGINEERS & TECHNICIANS

Library of Congress Catalog Card Number: 63-13905

Preface

Because of the rapid advance of electronics, no technican can expect to become thoroughly conversant with each new development; nor can he expect to master all the latest specialized mathematical techniques of electronics. Any book intending to inform him of the latest techniques would very likely be out of date by the time it was published. Together with this problem is the situation of the newly graduated engineer or technician, who must transform his knowledge of theory into capability in practice. To cope with these problems a book should do more than illustrate certain special instances; it must show the worker how to take well-established principles and apply them to his immediate problem, whatever it may be.

The programmed format of this book is designed to help the reader develop his intuition and initiative. For example, in mathematics one solution may be exclusively correct for a given problem, but in electronics many questions have unstated details which, under varying circumstances, result in more than one possible correct answer. Conversely, in some cases a solution may be academically correct, but unworkable for some reason not originally stated in the problem. By use of the programmed method it is possible to work with these types of problems, which are so common in practice and which instill that "have I thought of everything" philosophy so necessary in electronics.

The mathematics itself is not explained; this book is not about mathematics, but about how to use mathematics in electronics. If you need more explanation of the basic mathematics, there are several good textbooks available.

Although this isn't the first programmed book, it uses programming in a way that you may not have seen. So before you begin the text you should turn to page 7, "How to Use This Book." Good luck!

NORMAN H. CROWHURST

September 1964

Contents

How To Use This Book

The text begins with fairly basic material and builds an understanding by exploring more completely some of the familiar elements of electronics. It can be used either as a textbook or a handbook; an extensive index has been provided to assist you in using it as a handbook.

Each of the first four sections is self-contained and is to be followed from its first page through the various references until you are referred to the test questions which terminate each section. The last section, however, is a little different; it contains unconnected sequences which cover more advanced areas to show you how to apply what you have already learned.

For some questions you are expected to reason out the answer. In others you are expected to guess because not enough information has been given to allow you to arrive at a positive conclusion. Work in electronics is often aided by noting the similarity of new problems to old ones and knowing when such similarities are and are not meaningful. Guesswork such as this, followed by a more detailed analysis, develops the ability to quickly perceive all the necessary factors.

When working in electronics, you will seldom be presented with a problem to solve, along three or four suggested solutions from which you're asked to select the correct one. Instead, you'll be presented with the problem—generally minus half the facts—and left on your own to solve it as best you can. Thus programming is designed to develop that problem-solving ability. When a page break occurs, giving you an opportunity to try to figure out the next step for yourself, don't be in too much of a hurry to turn to the answer. There is great satisfaction as well as training value in discovering that you were on the right track, whether you were strictly correct or not. You will also be developing your initiative so that you can go ahead on your own after this book has taught you all it can.

Take your time and don't work against the clock. Gradually, as you develop a clearer insight into the methods that are most effective, you will find yourself progressing faster. You'll be ahead of where you would have been had you impatiently pushed ahead.

Now you may begin. First, turn to page 9. When you have read this, pick the method you think is right and turn to the appropriate page. You are on your way.

Section 1

OHM'S AND KIRCHHOFF'S LAWS

9-A. Many circuit calculations involve what is generally called "Ohm's law," although it really includes two principles attributed to Kirchhoff as well. A good example is the bridge circuit shown here. If the bridge is balanced, so that the voltages at the points marked A and B are equal, then no current flows through the bridging resistor, or arm (shown here as 5 ohms), and the calculation is simple. It is the nonbalanced condition, like that shown here, which complicates matters.

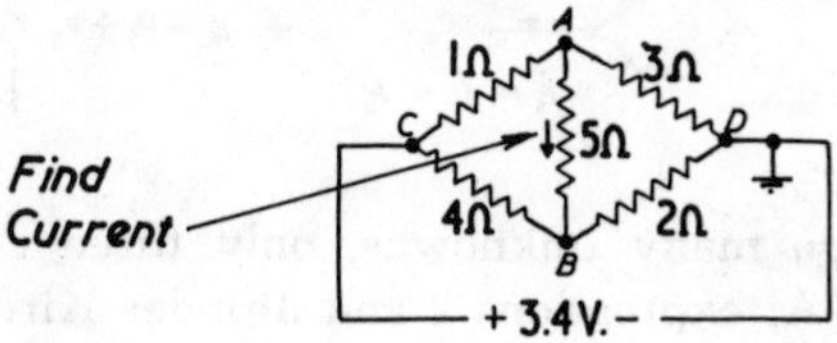

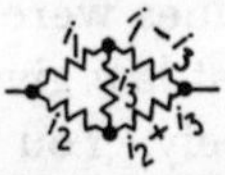

Method 1.

Voltage at A = $\frac{3}{4}$ of 3.4 V.

= 2.55 V.

Voltage at B = $\frac{1}{3}$ of 3.4 V.

= 1.133 V.

Voltage from A to B = 2.55 − 1.133

= 1.417 V.

Current in 5 Ω = 1.417 V ÷ 5

= .2833 A.

Method 2.

Current in CAD = $\frac{3.4}{4}$

= .85 A.

Current in CBD = $\frac{3.4}{6}$

= .567 A.

Current in AB = .85 − .567

= .2833 A.

Method 3.

1. $4i_2 = i_1 + 5i_3$

2. $3(i_1 - i_3) = 5i_3 + 2(i_2 + i_3)$

$5i_3 = -i_1 + 4i_2$ ⟨x2 & subtract⟩

$10i_3 = 3i_1 - 2i_2$

$0 = 5i_1 - 10i_2$ $5i_3 = i_1 - 2i_2$

$i_1 - i_3 = \frac{4}{5}i_1$ $i_2 + i_3 = \frac{7}{5}i_2 = \frac{7}{10}i_1$

$1i_1 + \frac{12}{5}i_1 = 3.4$ V. $i_1 = 1$ A.

$i_3 = \frac{1}{5}$ A.

Three methods of finding the current in the bridging arm of 5 ohms are given. Methods 1 and 2 happen to give the same answer, which may or may not be significant. Method 3 gives a different answer. Sometimes a wrong method will yield a right answer for one particular case. Which is the right method here? Method 1: turn to 13-A; method 2: turn to 14-A; method 3: turn to 10-A.

10-A. (From 9-A) *Correct.* This method uses the simplified version of Kirchhoff's laws. Five uses of Ohm's law are tabulated, one for each arm of the bridge, and four uses of Kirchhoff's first and second laws are given—for the first law, one for each junction; for the second, one for each loop. A fifth loop could be made (around the outer arms of the bridge), but this would be a combination of the first and second loops and hence would contain no new information.

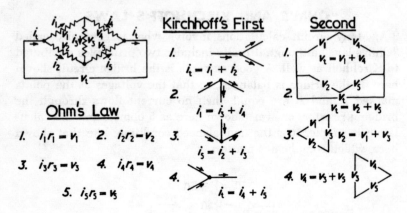

Rather than using so many unknowns, only three current-values were used on 9-A; expressions 2 and 3 under Kirchhoff's first law give the values for i_4 and i_5 as $i_1 - i_3$ and $i_2 + i_3$, respectively. You could then have three simultaneous equations, representing the first, third, and fourth uses of Kirchhoff's second law. But, again, a simplified method was used: the third and fourth equations (1 and 2 on page 9-A) were combined to eliminate i_3 and get a ratio between i_1 and i_2. This was substituted to obtain i_3 expressed as a ratio to either i_1 or i_2. Finally, the first use of Kirchhoff's second law provides a value for i_1, and from it the other unknowns, i_2 and i_3, are obtained. From this, if desired, all voltages and currents in the circuit can be calculated, and all the facts shown for Ohm's and Kirchhoff's laws may be checked.

In case you need to brush up on Kirchhoff's laws, turn to page 12-A. If you selected Method 3 the first time and have no difficulty with Kirchhoff's laws, turn to page 17-A.

KIRCHHOFF'S SECOND LAW

11-A. (From 15-A) This law states: *The algebraic sum of all the IR drops around a circuit is equal to the algebraic sum of the e.m.f.'s.*

The first law treats the currents entering and leaving points, whereas the second law treats the voltages between points. If the IR drops and e.m.f.'s are added, the sum will equal zero. Both of Kirchhoff's laws seem self-evident to us today. The first law merely says that all current must be continuous and cannot accumulate at a point; the second law means that as you progress around a circuit point by point, you eventually return to the starting potential.

KIRCHHOFF'S SECOND LAW

$$V_1 + V_2 + V_3 + V_4 + V_5 = 0$$

$$V_1 + V_2 + V_3 = V_4$$

As with the first law, you can assume that the current flows in either direction, whichever seems more convenient. Then all IR drops due to this current are taken as positive. Likewise, a source of e.m.f. that aids this current direction is considered positive, but any that opposes it is considered negative.

Kirchhoff's laws can best be understood when applied to calculate steady voltage and current (d.c.). However, which of the following statements is true?

1. They apply with equal validity to fluctuating currents (a.c.) at all times (turn to 16-B).
2. They are completely useless in relation to alternating currents (turn to 18-A).
3. They can be applied to alternating currents, provided that instantaneous values are used (turn to 17-A).

KIRCHHOFF'S FIRST LAW

12-A. (From 10-A) This law states: *In any branching network of wires the algebraic sum of the currents in all the wires that meet in any point is zero.* In its mathematical expression, this law assumes that all currents are of the same polarity, whether entering or leaving the point, *i.e.*, using either the conventional or electron concept of flow, consistently. If the assumption is that a current entering the point is positive (left-hand diagram), then a current leaving the point will have a negative sign. This is why the word *algebraic* is used in the statement of the law.

KIRCHHOFF'S FIRST LAW

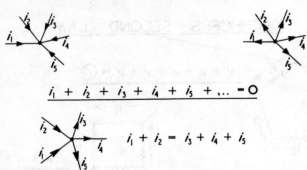

$$i_1 + i_2 + i_3 + i_4 + i_5 + \ldots = 0$$

$$i_1 + i_2 = i_3 + i_4 + i_5$$

In everyday use, it is simpler to spot which currents are entering the point and which are leaving, and then equate those entering with those leaving. This will avoid some of the involvement with negative signs. For example, in the top junction on page 9-A, it was assumed that current from C entered A, whereas the current to B and D was leaving A.

Suppose that an error is made in the assumption of direction of a current; then the calculation will (1) give an impossible answer (turn to 16-A); (2) give an answer with a minus sign (turn to 15-A).

12-B. (From 17-A) *Wrong.* It means there is no power at the four instants represented by the diagrams, but at other instants there is. Select again.

13-A. (From 9-A) *Wrong.* This method of calculation finds the voltage at points A and B when no current enters or leaves by the bridging arm (the 5-ohm resistor). If the bridge is balanced, the two voltages are equal, and no current flows; in this case the method is correct. But if the bridge is unbalanced, current will flow through the bridging arm, and voltages at both A and B change, because the current in all four main arms is changed by this bridging-arm current. Select another method.

13-B. (From 26-A) *Correct.* The solution of a differential equation is needed to prove this. As the diagram for discharge here shows, the rate of discharge decreases in proportion to the decrease of charge—this was evident from the facts on page 26-A.

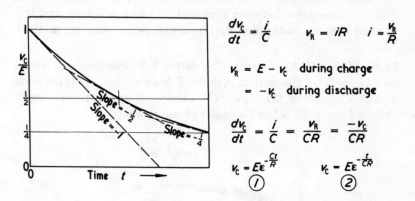

$$\frac{dv_c}{dt} = \frac{i}{C} \qquad v_R = iR \qquad i = \frac{v_R}{R}$$

$$v_R = E - v_c \quad \text{during charge}$$

$$= -v_c \quad \text{during discharge}$$

$$\frac{dv_c}{dt} = \frac{i}{C} = \frac{v_R}{CR} = \frac{-v_c}{CR}$$

$$v_c = E\varepsilon^{-\frac{Ct}{R}} \qquad v_c = E\varepsilon^{-\frac{t}{CR}}$$

$$① \qquad\qquad ②$$

When the charge is halved, the rate of discharge is halved. The curve is exponential: if it takes a certain time for the voltage to drop to half, it takes twice that time to drop to one-fourth its original value, three times that time to drop to one-eighth, and so on.

By the algebra shown here we deduce the differential equation that expresses these facts in terms of the resistance and capacitance values (where resistance is in ohms, and capacitance is in farads). Select that which you think is the correct solution. Answer: 1; turn to 19-B. Answer: 2; turn to 27-B.

14-A. (From 9-A) *Wrong.* Here the current in the two main branches is calculated without regard to any possible current through the bridging arm. Thus it is assumed that the current in the bridging arm is the difference between the two main currents. This obviously cannot be, because no account is taken of the value of the bridging arm (5 ohms). If this had an infinite value (open circuit), no current could flow through it. With zero value (short circuit) total current could be calculated by paralleling the arms CA and CB (⅘ ohm) and AD and BD (1⅕ ohms). The two parallel circuits in series make up 2 ohms, and hence the total current is $3.4/2 = 1.7$ amps, ⅘ of which (or 1.36 amps) flows through CA, while ⅖ (or 0.68 amp) flows through AD. The difference, $1.36 - 0.68 = 0.68$ amp, would flow through the short-circuited bridge, AB. With the resistance of the bridging arm at 5 ohms, some value between zero and 0.68 amp will flow, but this method does not determine that quantity. Select another method.

14-B. (From 21-A) *Correct.* The dotted construction here shows how phase '1' of the output is derived from a connection between phases Y and R of the input. The other two are correspondingly obtained from the other two sides of the triangle.

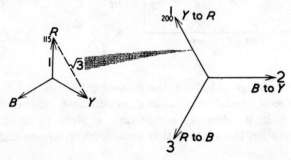

Note that the voltage is not twice the input phase voltage but the voltage times the square root of 3, as determined by the geometry of the vector diagram. Now turn to page 23-B.

15-A. (From 12-A) *Correct.* We assumed a positive sign for all currents and rearranged the equation only for convenience. In Kirchhoff's original law some of the currents always have a negative sign, which indicates that their direction is the opposite of that used as a reference. To check this fact, repeat the problem of page 9-A using the assumption that the current through the 5-ohm resistor is from *B* to *A*. You will find the answer will be *numerically* the same, but of opposite sign, i.e., $-\frac{1}{5}$ amp. Now turn to 11-A.

15-B. (From 17-A) *Wrong.* This needs figuring out instant by instant. Try another answer.

15-C. (From 21-A) *Wrong.* There are two ways in which the relationship shown at *A* could be achieved. The parallelogram completed in dashed lines shows how phase '1' of the output can be made by adding phases *R* and *Y* (Red and Yellow) of the input. The transformer arrangement shown at (1) will add pairs of phases numbered '1', '2', and '3'.

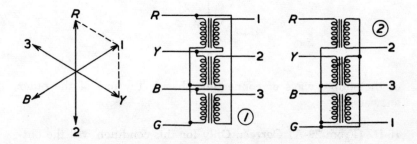

The alternative way is simply reversing the original three phases: blue reversed yields '1'; red reversed yields '2'; and yellow reversed yields '3'. This is shown at (2). Now try one of the other answers.

16-A. (From 12-A) *Wrong.* Turn to the other answer.

16-B. (From 11-A) *Wrong.* Kirchhoff's second law, as stated, applies to voltages and e.m.f.s acting around a loop or circuit, whatever the momentary cause of e.m.f.s. However, we find in studying a.c. that the voltages and currents measured are continuously changing, although they are given a nominal or measured value. Thus Kirchhoff's laws cannot be applied directly to a.c. conditions. Try another answer.

16-C. (From 21-A) *Wrong.* Presumably you had in mind a construction similar to that shown here, which does not represent any

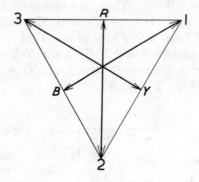

of the simple ways of connecting phases. Try one of the other answers.

16-D. (From 29-A) *Correct.* Only for this condition will the output voltage always be a small fraction of the input voltage. Note that for this reason an integrating circuit can never have the equivalent of the mathematical constant of integration, which would require an infinite time constant. Now turn to 33-A.

A.C. CIRCUITS

17-A. (From 10-A, 11-A) If your answer on page 11-A was number 3, your choice was correct. Both Ohm's law and Kirchhoff's laws are valid in a.c. calculations relating to conditions obtaining at any instant. But because it is often more convenient to use methods that tell what happens steadily instead of instant by instant, these laws are modified into forms that include the quantity known as reactance, so that a more complete picture can be covered in a single calculation.

In a d.c. transmission circuit (shown here in sketches numbered 1 to 4) power, as the product of voltage and current, can flow

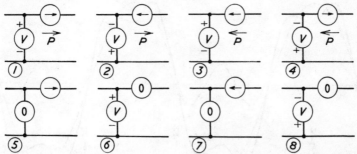

either way. If both voltage and current reverse their directions, the direction of power flow remains the same (1 and 2). If only current (or only voltage) is reversed, power is reversed (3 and 4). Thus, in alternating current, voltage and current can reverse together, so that power flow is the same way on both half-cycles (1 and 2, or 3 and 4). Now consider another kind of sequence (5 to 8). In this example, current flows one way at zero voltage; then there is voltage with zero current flow. After this, current flows the other way at zero voltage. This is followed by voltage the opposite way with zero current flow. Then the cycle repeats. Since power in electrical circuits is the product of voltage and current, and at each point shown from 5 through 8 either voltage or current is zero, which of the following is true?

1. This condition means that the circuit carries no power (turn to 12-B).
2. At these four instants there is no power, but on an average there is a power flow (turn to 15-B).
3. At other instants there is power flow, but the average flow is zero (turn to 19-A).

18-A. (From 11-A) *Wrong.* The fact that currents are fluctuating or alternating does not alter their basic relationships as laid down in Ohm's and Kirchhoff's laws. Kirchhoff's laws are applicable to a.c. with certain restrictions. Try another answer.

18-B. (From 23-B) *Correct.* The time that will be taken for the second-harmonic vector to reach the vertical, representing maximum, will be measured in terms of its own cycle, or frequency. Hence the phase angle on the vector diagram and on the time-based curve must be in terms of the second-harmonic frequency of rotation or repetition.

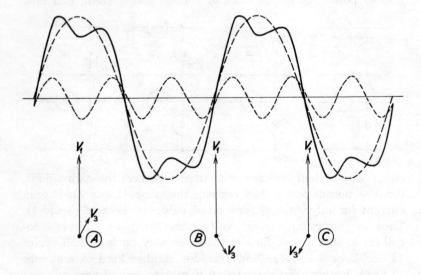

Now select the correct vector representation for the waveform shown on this page, *A*, *B*, or *C*. Answer: *A*; turn to 27-A. Answer: *B*; turn to 28-A. Answer: *C*; turn to 24-A.

19-A. (From 17-A) *Correct.* To verify this, we can draw the curves for the voltage and current fluctuation in an alternating current, known as sine waves. We have multiplied instantaneous values of voltage and current to find instantaneous power, and plotted the power curve, which in every case has twice the frequency of voltage or current.

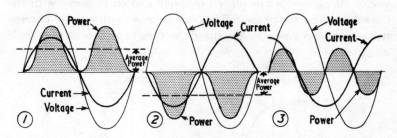

Where voltage and current are in phase (1), the power flow is always in a 'positive' direction, fluctuating between zero (when both voltage and current are zero) and maximum, when voltage and current are maximum. Where voltage and current are out of phase, or current opposes voltage at all times (2), the power flow follows the same form but the opposite direction.

In each case the power is represented by the shaded area between the power curve and the zero line. The horizontal line through the power curve gives the average power as half its peak value in each of these cases.

But in the case where voltage maxima coincide with current zeros and vice versa, the power curve has zeros whenever voltage *or* current is zero. In between, the power is positive when the voltage and current are in the same direction, and negative (or flowing in the opposite direction) when voltage and current are in opposite directions. As the area below zero is equal to that above it, the *average* power flow is zero—the momentary flows in opposing directions at twice the working frequency equalize to yield no net flow in either direction. Now turn to 20-A.

19-B. (From 13-B) *Wrong.* Don't guess—try the other answer!

20

VECTORS

20-A. (From 19-A) It would be very laborious to make all calculations pertaining to a.c. circuits by working everything out point by point with instantaneous values for the sine-wave curves. Now a sine wave can be regarded as a projection of the end of a rotating vector; thus, vectors displaced by angles to correspond with the time difference (or phase difference) between voltage and current waveforms can give a single, simple picture to represent the whole a.c. situation.

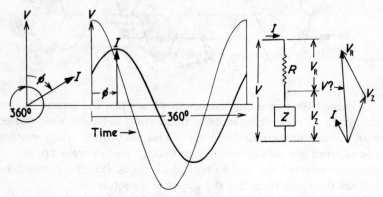

The vector is regarded as rotating in a counterclockwise direction. So an interval later in time (or delayed in phase) is represented by a clockwise displacement on a vector diagram that represents an instantaneous condition. Here the projection of the vectors horizontally represents magnitudes at the instant in time where the curves begin. When a time corresponding to the phase angle ϕ has elapsed, both vectors will have rotated so that the current arrow is vertical. Note that a complete cycle, or rotation, is 360°, as in conventional geometry or trigonometry. Thus, by imagining the two vectors at the left as rotating counterclockwise, we can generate both of the curves at the right or, in fact, any number of similar curves representing voltages and currents in a circuit.

At the right is shown a series combination of resistance and impedance, through which a current I is flowing. The vector diagram is drawn to show the current I and the voltages across the resistance and impedance (V_R is parallel to I, because they are in phase). Does the vector marked with a question mark against V represent the terminal voltage across the two elements in series? If so, see 22-A. If not, see 23-A.

POLYPHASE SYSTEMS

21-A. (From 22-A) Vector analysis is very useful in determining phase as well as magnitude relations in polyphase systems, of which the commonest are three-phase. Consider first a three-phase source which can be regarded as three 115-volt generators whose voltages are each displaced from one another by 120°. When using a common ground the system is known as *star-* or Y-connected. When loads are connected to the system between phase and ground, the whole system is Y-connected.

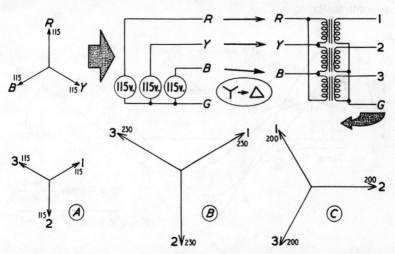

But loads may also be connected between lines, without any ground connection, forming another system known as *mesh-* or *delta-connected* (using the Greek capital "delta"). Now suppose that the 115-volt star system is connected to a three-phase transformer with delta-connected primaries and star-connected secondaries. Which vector diagram represents the output voltage of this group of 1:1 transformers—*A, B* or *C*? Answer: *A*; turn to 15-C. Answer: *B*; turn to 16-C. Answer: *C*; turn to 14-B.

21-B. (From 26-A) *Wrong.* You are probably confusing this value with the r.m.s. value of a current or voltage, which is explained on page 153-A.

22-A. (From 20-A) *Correct.* For verification, the curve representing a superposition of two voltage curves (having the same frequency) is plotted in full. Notice points a, b, c, and d, where the value of one of the curves (V_1 or V_2) being added is zero: at each of these points the resultant (V) crosses the other curve. Also notice the slopes of the component curves at the point where the resultant (V) is maximum. They are equal and opposite. Because the slope of a sine or cosine wave is a wave of equal frequency displaced $90°$, the magnitude of the slope can be represented on the vector diagram by dashed lines e and f, which are geometrically equal.

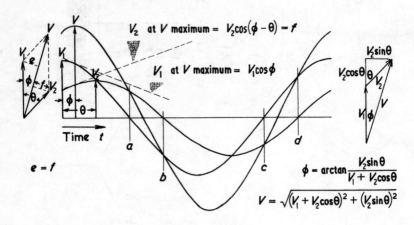

$$V_2 \text{ at } V \text{ maximum} = V_2\cos(\phi - \theta) = f$$

$$V_1 \text{ at } V \text{ maximum} = V_1\cos\phi$$

$$e = f$$

$$\phi = \arctan\frac{V_2\sin\theta}{V_1 + V_2\cos\theta}$$

$$V = \sqrt{(V_1 + V_2\cos\theta)^2 + (V_2\sin\theta)^2}$$

To relate the vector diagram more completely to its geometry, and also show how vectors can be resolved into components, the diagram at the right shows how to derive expressions for the magnitude of V and the phase angle ϕ from the original quantities, V_1, V_2, and θ. Now turn to page 21-A.

22-B. (From 30-A) *Wrong.* You probably made the mistake of comparing this with the solution on page 13-B but did not notice that the constant $-1/CR$ was a coefficient of the *variable* there, while in this case the corresponding constant, $-L/R$, was a coefficient of the *derivative* on page 30-A. Try the other answer.

23-A. (From 20-A) *Wrong.* See the other answer.

VECTORS FOR MORE THAN ONE FREQUENCY

23-B. (From 14-B) The vectors introduced on page 20-A all concerned the same frequency. These vectors could be regarded as a solid entity rotating counterclockwise. Vectors can be used to represent more than one frequency at the same time, by regarding them as rotating separately at their own rates. For example, here vectors are used to represent fundamental and second harmonic. Simply regard the second-harmonic vector as rotating twice as fast as the fundamental vector.

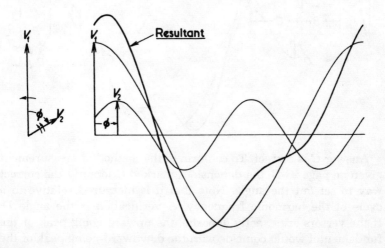

The component waves can be traced out by using the projection concept and the time-phase relationship. Now the question arises, do we measure off the angle ϕ along the time axis in terms of the fundamental cycle, or the second harmonic? If you say the fundamental, turn to 25-A. If you think it is the second harmonic, turn to 18-B.

23-C. (From 26-A) *Wrong.* You are probably confusing this with the average rectified value, which is explained on page 154-A.

24-A. (From 18-B) *Correct.* Answer *A* made the mistake of measuring the angle between the two sine waves at the points where they each cross the zero line. While this is a possible reference point for phase relationships, it is not the one used for vector presentation. Answer *B* had the proper angle, but measured in the wrong direction.

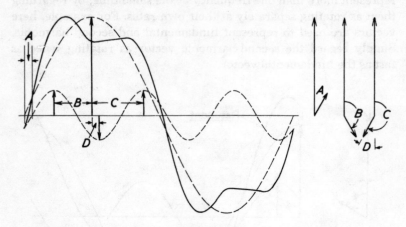

Answer *C* is correct. To conform to the method of measurement given on page 23-B, the dimensions marked *C* identify the correct way to set out the angle. Note that it is measured relative to a cycle of the harmonic frequency. A verification is the angle *D*. If the vectors are exactly opposite, the upward-going peak of the fundamental would coincide with the downward-going peak of the harmonic. The angle *D* is the difference from this condition. Now turn to 26-A.

24-B. (From 32-B) *Wrong.* It is conventional for an inductance to be regarded as a positive reactance and capacitance as a negative one. But this convention does not fit the formula at this point. Remember that the derivative of the cosine is minus the sine. Turn to the other answer.

25-A. (From 23-B) *Wrong.* Turn to the other answer.

25-B. (From 30-A) *Correct.* The solution, after transposing the constant so that $-R/L$ is a coefficient of the dependable variable, is similar to that on page 27-B.

Time constants are given by the product RC for resistance and capacitance circuits, or by the quotient L/R for inductance and resistance circuits. In the first case, resistance must be given in ohms and capacitance in farads, to give time in seconds. In the second, inductance must be given in henrys and resistance in ohms, to give time in seconds. Note that in the solution, the time constant is in the denominator of the exponent of ϵ in each case, with time t in the numerator. This exponent of ϵ is always the ratio of the actual time t to the time constant. Now turn to 28-B.

25-C. (From 29-A) *Wrong.* This would provide integration only for the components in the input representing the shortest time intervals, or the more rapid changes. Although this does not meet the requirement of an integrating circuit, it may often be more nearly what a practical electronic circuit needs, and thus it is not to be dismissed as useless. Now try the other answer.

25-D. (From 37-A) *Wrong.* You apparently noticed that the j times j part would bring about a minus, changing the normal product of plus times minus back to plus, but then you added a j. Having multiplied j by j to get a real product, the result is no longer imaginary. Try another answer.

26

RC TIME CONSTANTS

26-A. (From 24-A) For simpler electronics work, it may be satisfactory to use time-constant curves without explanation, but in more advanced work it is necessary to understand what a time constant is, and how it is derived.

Take the case of a capacitor being charged through a resistor. When the voltage across the capacitor is zero (at the instant E is applied) all the applied voltage (E) is across the series resistor, which thus controls the current (i). As the capacitor charges, the voltage across it increases, and that across the resistor drops by an equal amount. So the charging current drops in proportion to the voltage across the resistor.

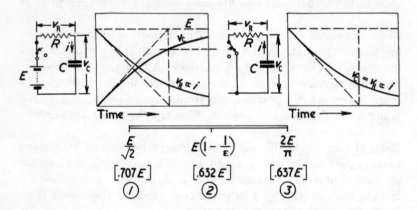

$$\frac{E}{\sqrt{2}}$$
$$[.707\,E]$$
①

$$E\left(1-\frac{1}{\varepsilon}\right)$$
$$[.632\,E]$$
②

$$\frac{2E}{\pi}$$
$$[.637\,E]$$
③

Similarly on discharge, when the switch is closed, the full charge voltage of the capacitor is put across the resistor and current flows at the rate fixed by Ohm's law. But as the capacitor discharges, the voltage across the resistor drops and the current reduces.

In these diagrams the sloping dashed lines represent what *would* happen if the charge or discharge current continued at the initial rate. The vertical dashed line marks the 'time constant' when charge or discharge would be fully accomplished if the current remained constant. But, because the rate does decrease, the charge is not fully attained in the period of the time constant. What is the fraction actually reached (in charge): (1), (2), or (3)? Answer: 1; turn to 21-B. Answer: 2; turn to 13-B. Answer: 3; turn to 23-C.

27-A. (From 18-B) *Wrong*. Try one of the other answers.

27-B. (From 13-B) *Correct*. The simplest way to solve this is to write the expression in a general form, as shown here, using A

Write $v_c = A\varepsilon^{at}$: $\qquad \dfrac{dv_c}{dt} = Aa\varepsilon^{at} = av_c = \dfrac{-v_c}{CR}$ $\qquad$ so $\quad a = -\dfrac{1}{CR}$

When $t = 0$, $\quad \varepsilon^0 = 1$, $\quad v_c = E$ (discharge case) $\qquad$ so $\quad A = E$

$$\underline{\text{Solution}} \quad v_c = E\varepsilon^{-\frac{t}{CR}}$$

and a as constants for which we need solutions. Differentiating, and substituting the original dependent variable, shows a to be equal to $-1/CR$. From the starting condition, we find that the integration constant A is just the starting voltage E. Now turn to 30-A.

27-C. (From 28-B) *Correct*. In each case the function relating the output voltage to the drop across the series element (capacitor in the first case and resistor in the second) is the time constant of the combination: CR or L/R. Thus by making this smaller than any rate of change encountered by the circuit, the output voltage will always be a small fraction of the input voltage, which is the condition required. Now turn to 29-A.

27-D. (From 33-A) *Wrong*. Note that for an inductance, voltage is a function of the derivative (rate of change) of current, whereas for a capacitance it is the other way around—current is a function of the derivative of voltage. Try the other answer.

28

28-A. (From 18-B) *Wrong.* Try one of the other answers.

DIFFERENTIATING CIRCUITS

28-B.(From 25-B) The formula derived on page 13-B can be rearranged to show that the voltage across the resistance is a linear function of the derivative (or rate of change) of the voltage across the capacitor. Similarly, the formula derived on page 30-A can be rearranged to show that the voltage across the inductance is a linear function of the derivative of the voltage across the resistance.

In practical circuits there must be an input and output, arranged so that the output is a function of the input. Each of the two statements of the previous paragraph relates to voltages, each of which must be some function of the input voltage. The output voltage can be made proportional to an approximate derivative

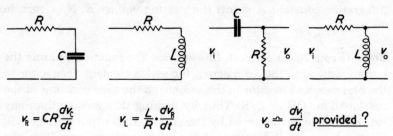

$$v_R = CR \frac{dv_C}{dt} \qquad v_L = \frac{L}{R} \cdot \frac{dv_R}{dt} \qquad v_o \triangleq \frac{dv_i}{dt} \quad \underline{\text{provided ?}}$$

of the input voltage by selecting component values so that the voltage across one of the elements is always small compared to the other. In this way the small voltage is approximately proportional to the derivative of the input voltage, because the input voltage is very nearly identical to the larger voltage, which is across the other element.

Which of the following is a sufficient condition for this approximation to be good?

1. The voltage across the resistance must always be small compared to that across the capacitance or inductance (turn to 31-A).
2. The voltage across the resistance must always be large compared to that across the capacitance or inductance (turn to 32-A).
3. The time constant of the combination must always be equivalent to a shorter time than that taken for the quickest rates of change the circuit will encounter (turn to 27-C).

INTEGRATING CIRCUITS

29-A. (From 27-C) Reversing the configuration of the circuits of Page 28-B and integrating the associated formulas shows that the voltage across one element is proportional to the time-integral of the voltage across the other element.

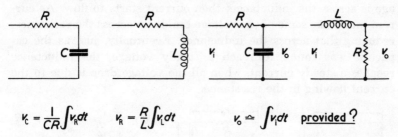

$$v_c = \frac{1}{CR}\int v_R dt \qquad v_R = \frac{R}{L}\int v_L dt \qquad v_o \simeq \int v_i dt \quad \underline{\text{provided}}?$$

It is evident that the output voltage will be proportional to the time-integral of the input voltage if the output voltage is always small compared to the input voltage. This also requires which one of the following conditions?

1. A time constant for the combination that is long compared to the longest interval over which voltage is to be integrated (turn to 16-D).
2. A time constant for the combination that is longer than the time taken for the fastest rates of change that occur (turn to 25-C).

29-B. (From 37-A) *Correct.* Taking this by parts: plus (+) times minus (−) gives minus (−); j times j gives -1; putting both together, minus times minus gives plus. Or using the geometrical

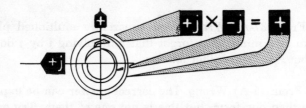

construction, $+j$ represents $90°$, $-j$ represents $270°$ (or $-90°$), so adding the two angles gives $360°$ (or $0°$) representing the real plus-direction. Now turn to 38-B.

RL TIME CONSTANTS

30-A. (From 27-B) When a steady current is flowing, a pure inductance has no voltage across it; a voltage across it is due to *changing* current. When a voltage is applied across a resistance and inductance in series, at first no current flows and all the voltage is across the inductance; then current starts to flow. As current increases, some of the voltage builds up across the resistance, reducing that across the inductance. Eventually, just as the capacitor was found to reach a steady voltage, the inductance reaches a steady current, when all the voltage drop is due to the current flowing in the resistance.

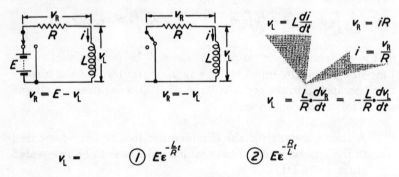

$$v_L = L\frac{di}{dt} \qquad v_R = iR$$

$$i = \frac{v_R}{R}$$

$$v_R = E - v_L \qquad v_R = -v_L \qquad v_L = \frac{L}{R}\cdot\frac{dv_R}{dt} = -\frac{L}{R}\cdot\frac{dv_L}{dt}$$

$$v_L = \qquad \textcircled{1}\ E\varepsilon^{-\frac{L}{R}t} \qquad \textcircled{2}\ E\varepsilon^{-\frac{R}{L}t}$$

When the resistance and inductance are short-circuited, at first the same current continues to flow, with the same voltage across both resistance and inductance now opposing current flow. The current starts to drop, dying away with the same time constant with which it built up.

The solution for the voltage across the inductance during either build-up or decay is (1) or (2). Which one is it? Answer: 1; turn to 22-B. Answer: 2; turn to 25-B.

30-B. (From 37-A) *Wrong.* You apparently multiplied plus by minus to give minus, but forgot that multiplying j by j does not give j, but -1. Try another answer.

30-C. (From 45-A) *Wrong.* The correct answer can be expressed in more than one form, but this is not one of them. Try another answer.

31-A. (From 28-B) *Wrong.* This would be right for the capacitance and resistance combination, but not for the inductance and resistance combination. Select another answer.

31-B. (From 46-A) *Correct.* Here are shown two possible values for R, one smaller than reactances at resonance and one larger. In either case, as the vector diagram shows, the length of the voltage vector for the resistance does not change as the reactances change, so the resultant vector follows the dashed lines, which are parallel to the reactance vector direction. The shortest length of the resultant is, in each case, when the reactance resultant is zero, leaving pure resistance.

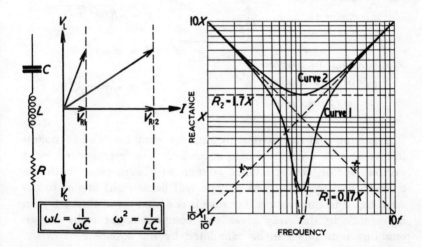

The curves to logarithmic scale show how the reactance curves (which continue in dashed lines off the bottom, near the center) are almost identical with the resultant until they get nearly down to the resistance value (horizontal dashed lines, marked R_1 and R_2). At this point, the resultant curve (Curves 1 and 2) just touches the resistance value at f.

Resonance still occurs when the reactances are equal, so the frequency of resonance is still given by ω^2 equals $1/LC$. Now turn to 50-A.

32

32-A. (From 28-B) *Wrong.* This would be right for the inductance and resistance combination, but not for the capacitance and resistance combination. Select another answer.

IMPEDANCE

32-B. (From 35-A) Any impedance can be resolved into components of resistance and reactance, just as if it consisted of resistance either in series or in parallel with a reactance which may be inductive or capacitive.

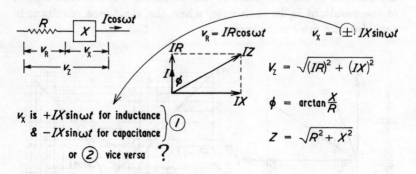

Assuming that the current through the combination has magnitude I and is a cosine function, and thus is represented by a vertical vector, the resistance voltage will be in phase with the current, and the reactance voltage will be at right angles to the current, or in quadrature, because it is a sine term. Resolving an impedance in this way gives two components at right angles, enabling impedance to be calculated by the square root of the sum of the squares of resistance and reactance, and the phase angle is the angle whose tangent is X/R. (Note that *arctan* and similar terms are used with this significance in this book, in preference to the symbol $\tan^{-1}$.)

Now, as an exercise in identifying phase for the expression for voltage, one of the signs (+ or −) is for inductive reactance, the other for capacitive reactance. Which is which? Answer: 1; turn to 24-B. Answer: 2; turn to 34-A.

REACTANCE

33-A. (From 16-D) Ohm's law was originally stated for d.c.; to make it applicable to a.c. it is necessary to use a quantity known as *reactance*. Impedance will later be described as a more general opposition to current flow, but here we must introduce vectors in order to "add" inductive and capacitive oppositions to current flow. Reactance is thus a specific property, applying only to pure capacitance and pure inductance.

By definition, the voltage across an inductance is the value in henrys multiplied by the rate of change of current in amperes per second. If we assume current to be a single-frequency sine wave, with peak value I and frequency f, a formula for voltage V can be derived. It is a cosine wave. The relation between the amplitudes of the voltage and current, V/I, is the reactance of the inductance, just as resistance is V/I directly. For resistance this is true at every instant. With reactance, it is the relation of peak values, which do not occur at the same instant, but 90° apart along the sine-wave cycle.

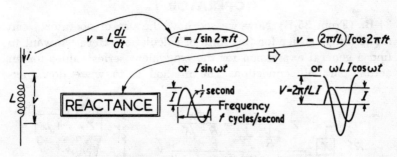

Reactance of an inductance is $2\pi fL$
Reactance of a capacitance is:

① $\dfrac{1}{2\pi fC}$ ② $2\pi fC$

Which is the correct formula for the reactance of a capacitance? Try to figure it for yourself. Answer: 1; turn to 35-A. Answer: 2; turn to 27-D.

33-B. (From 38-B) *Wrong.* You apparently added the two resistances and then took the inductive reactance as a further series element. Try another answer.

34-A. (From 32-B) *Correct.* The easiest way to be sure about this is to draw out the vectors for the + case, which we have done here. This results in a clear relationship where voltage lags cur-

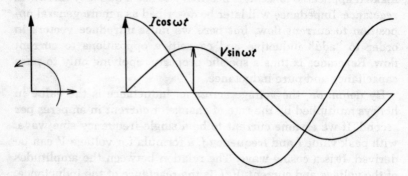

rent (or current leads voltage), which is the relationship for a capacitance. Now turn to 36-A.

OPERATOR *j*

34-B. (From 35-B) Now we see how the use of operator *j* can make things easier for this kind of calculation. Here we want to find a general expression for the equivalent series values for an actual parallel connection. The method is to write down ex-

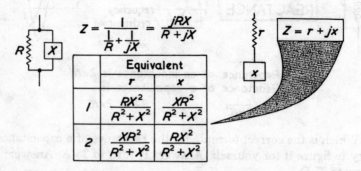

pressions for each form and then equate the real parts for resistance and the imaginary parts for reactance. Which would you think is the correct pair of answers? Answer: 1; turn to 42-A. Answer: 2; turn to 37-B.

35-A. (From 33-A) *Correct.* Here the relationship between capacitance (C) and capacitive reactance is developed in the same way as was done for inductance (page 33-A). The symbol for inductive reactance is a capital X with the subscript L. For capacitive reactance it is a capital X with the subscript C.

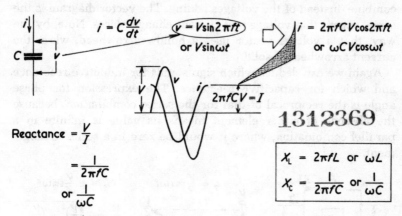

Reactance $= \dfrac{V}{I}$

$= \dfrac{1}{2\pi f C}$

or $\dfrac{1}{\omega C}$

1312369

$$X_L = 2\pi f L \text{ or } \omega L$$
$$X_C = \frac{1}{2\pi f C} \text{ or } \frac{1}{\omega C}$$

As inductive reactance is proportional to inductance and frequency, so capacitive reactance is inversely proportional to capacitance and frequency. A direct proportion can be gained by using the reciprocal of reactance, or *susceptance*, which we shall study later.

When a resistance is included in a circuit, the opposition which is presented to current flow by resistance, inductance, and capacitance must be given as *impedance*. For a discussion of this, turn now to page 32-B.

35-B. (From 41-A) *Correct.* Although this seems simple enough, it's the kind of thing where a slip can easily be made. Now turn to 34-B.

35-C. (From 45-A) *Wrong.* Although the correct answer can be expressed in more than one form, this is not one of them. Try another answer.

35-D. (From 53-A) Each of the transformers a, b, and c connects between phase and neutral; so each needs a 230-volt primary. Each of the transformers d, e, and f connects between phases; so each needs a 400-volt primary. This was explained on 21-A.

IMPEDANCE OF PARALLEL ELEMENTS

36-A. (From 34-A) Impedances may consist of elements in parallel, or be resolved that way, instead of series combinations. In this case the same voltage is across both elements and the currents combine, instead of the voltages adding. The vector diagram is the same, except that voltage and current change places. Note, by the way, that a voltage vector uses a hollow arrowhead, while the current arrowhead is solid.

Again we can deduce which sign stands for inductive reactance and which for capacitive reactance. The expression for phase angle is the reciprocal of that for the series combination, because the absence of either element means its value is infinite in a parallel combination, where it would be zero in a series arrangement.

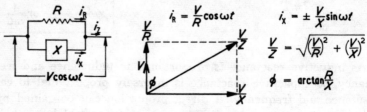

$$i_R = \frac{V}{R}\cos\omega t \qquad i_x = \pm\frac{V}{X}\sin\omega t$$

$$\frac{V}{Z} = \sqrt{\left(\frac{V}{R}\right)^2 + \left(\frac{V}{X}\right)^2}$$

$$\phi = \arctan\frac{R}{X}$$

i_x is $+\frac{V}{X}\sin\omega t$ for inductance

$\&\ -\frac{V}{X}\sin\omega t$ for capacitance

① $\quad Z = \dfrac{RX}{\sqrt{R^2 + X^2}}$

② $\quad Z = \sqrt{R^2 + X^2}$

But which is the correct expression for impedance in this case? Answer: ①; turn to 38-A. Answer: ②; turn to 40-A.

36-B. (From 38-B) *Wrong.* You apparently took a parallel combination, but regarded the reactance as in parallel with the total resistance, instead of only part of it. Try another answer.

36-C. (From 39-C) *Wrong.* Try the other answer.

THE OPERATOR *j*

37-A. (From 38-A) In calculations connected with reactances, impedances, and the voltages and current associated with them, the operator *j* can save a lot of work. It is a symbol with the significance of the square root of minus one. In mathematical treatments, this is given the symbol *i*, but in electronic work *j* is used to avoid confusion with *i*, which represents current. Its usefulness derives from the fact that geometrically it can be regarded as signifying a rotation through 90°, just as a minus sign signifies a rotation through 180°.

In this way, as a minus times a minus makes a plus, because two 180° angles make up 360°—a complete revolution back to the starting point—so +*j* times +*j* makes a minus, because two 90° angles make up 180°. As plus is opposite minus, so +*j* and −*j* are opposite. In making calculations, as we shall see, the operator *j* provides a convenient way of keeping resistive and reactive components separated. Mathematically, they take the form of real and imaginary components (the latter being those of having *j* as a factor). So the four quadrants are divided up into positive and negative real quantities and positive and negative imaginary quantities.

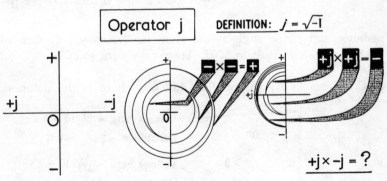

Operator j   DEFINITION: $j = \sqrt{-1}$

$+j \times -j = ?$

What would you expect the product of +*j* times −*j* to be? Answer: −*j*; turn to 30-B. Answer: +1; turn to 29-B. Answer: +*j*; turn to 25-D.

37-B. (From 34-B) *Wrong.* Presumably that was an inspired guess, and your inspiration wasn't too good this time. So, it's the other answer.

38-A. (From 36-A) *Correct.* In case you ran into difficulty deriving it, here is what proves to be comparatively simple algebra.

$$\frac{1}{Z} = \sqrt{\frac{1}{R^2} + \frac{1}{X^2}} \qquad Z = \frac{1}{\sqrt{\frac{1}{R^2} + \frac{1}{X^2}}} = \sqrt{\frac{R^2 X^2}{R^2 + X^2}}$$

$$= \frac{RX}{\sqrt{R^2 + X^2}}$$

Now turn to 37-A.

IMPEDANCE CALCULATIONS

38-B. (From 29-B) To see what is involved in impedance calculations, try this one. Which of the three answers given for im-

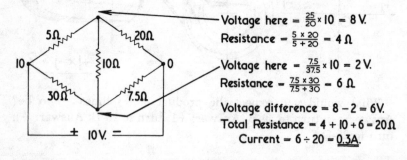

$X_L = 75\Omega$ 28Ω 100Ω

$$Z = \begin{cases} ① & 80\,\Omega \quad \phi = \arctan.75 \\ ② & 148\,\Omega \quad \phi = \arctan.586 \left[\frac{75}{128}\right] \\ ③ & 65\,\Omega \quad \phi = \arctan 1.71 \left[\frac{128}{75}\right] \end{cases}?$$

pedance and phase angle is the right one? Answer: 1; turn to 41-A. Answer: 2; turn to 33-B. Answer: 3; turn to 36-B.

38-C. (From 54-A) If you had difficulty, here is the solution.

5Ω   20Ω   10   100Ω   0   30Ω   7.5Ω   ± 10 V.

Voltage here $= \frac{25}{20} \times 10 = 8$ V.
Resistance $= \frac{5 \times 20}{5 + 20} = 4\,\Omega$

Voltage here $= \frac{7.5}{37.5} \times 10 = 2$ V.
Resistance $= \frac{7.5 \times 30}{7.5 + 30} = 6\,\Omega$

Voltage difference $= 8 - 2 = 6$ V.
Total Resistance $= 4 + 10 + 6 = 20\,\Omega$
Current $= 6 \div 20 = \underline{0.3A}$.

39A. (From 41-A) *Wrong.* The reactance is in shunt with the 100-ohm resistance, so when its value is zero, the 100-ohm resistance would not be left in the circuit. Try another answer.

39-B. (From 44-A) *Wrong.* So try the other answer.

EQUIVALENT IMPEDANCES

39-C. (From 52-A) The next question is what the equivalents are for capacitances. As you get more advanced in electronics calculations, it's often helpful and time-saving to spot the patterns into which formulas fall. So giving questions like the one on this page, for which you are not fully prepared, not only provides a little interesting guess work, but helps train you to spot the patterns—which is why it is done.

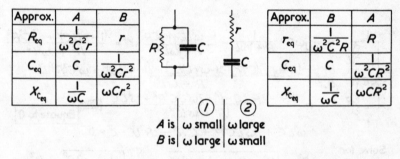

Approx.	A	B
R_{eq}	$\dfrac{1}{\omega^2 C^2 r}$	r
C_{eq}	C	$\dfrac{1}{\omega^2 C r^2}$
$X_{C_{eq}}$	$\dfrac{1}{\omega C}$	$\omega C r^2$

Approx.	B	A
r_{eq}	$\dfrac{1}{\omega^2 C^2 R}$	R
C_{eq}	C	$\dfrac{1}{\omega^2 C R^2}$
$X_{C_{eq}}$	$\dfrac{1}{\omega C}$	$\omega C R^2$

	①	②
A is	ω small	ω large
B is	ω large	ω small

Here at the left are worked out the approximate relationships for very small and very large values of ω for equivalent parallel values of a circuit that is really series, and at the right for equivalent series values of a circuit that is really parallel. Columns are headed A and B. Is the correct identification (1) A for small values of ω, B for large values, or (2) vice versa? Answer: 1; turn to 43-A. Answer: 2; turn to 36-C.

40-A. (From 36-A) *Wrong.* This, you will notice, is the same expression as that on page 32-B for the series combination and thus cannot be right for the parallel one: the same elements in series and in parallel cannot yield the same impedance. Try the other answer.

40-B. (From 41-A) *Wrong.* For the infinite value of reactance, you've somehow added in the actual reactance value (which you are assuming is now infinite). Try another answer.

40-C. (From 50-A) If you've tried some of the other answers before this one, you'll be finding that resonance can mean more than one thing as soon as you leave the simple arrangements of 50-A. This one gives the frequency at which the impedance of the circuit is a *maximum* (its admittance is a minimum). It is

$$Y = j\omega C + \frac{1}{R + j\omega L} = \frac{1 - \omega^2 LC + j\omega CR}{R + j\omega L} \quad \bigg| \quad Y^2 = \frac{(1 - \omega^2 LC)^2 + \omega^2 C^2 R^2}{R^2 + \omega^2 L^2}$$

$$\frac{dY^2}{d\omega^2} = \frac{(R^2 + \omega^2 L^2)\{C^2 R^2 - 2(1 - \omega^2 LC)LC\} - \{(1 - \omega^2 LC)^2 + \omega^2 C^2 R^2\}L^2}{(R^2 + \omega^2 L^2)^2}$$

$$= \frac{C^2 R^4 - 2R^2 LC - L^2 + 2\omega^2 L^2 C^2 R^2 + \omega^4 L^4 C^2}{(R^2 + \omega^2 L^2)^2}$$

Equate to 0

$$\omega^4 L^4 C^2 + 2\omega^2 L^2 C^2 R^2 + C^2 R^4 - 2R^2 LC - L^2 = 0$$

Solve for

$$\omega^2 = -\frac{R^2}{L^2} \pm \sqrt{\frac{R^4}{L^4} - \frac{R^4}{L^4} + \frac{1}{L^2 C^2} + \frac{2R^2}{L^3 C}} = \pm \sqrt{\frac{1}{L^2 C^2} + \frac{2R^2}{L^3 C} - \frac{R^2}{L^2}}$$

$$= \frac{1}{LC}\left[\sqrt{1 + \frac{2R^2 C}{L}} - \frac{R^2 C}{L}\right]$$

derived by finding the expression for admittance. As you are only concerned with magnitude you don't need to rationalize it. And you can avoid radicals by using the expression for admittance squared. To make the working easier differentiate Y^2 with respect to ω^2 and equate the resulting expression to zero. If Y^2 is a minimum, Y will be too. Now, if you've already tried 43-B and 51-A, turn to 47-A.

41-A. (From 38-B) *Correct.* Here we take it step by step. The first step is to convert the parallel combination of 100 ohms resistance and 75 ohms reactance into a series equivalent, which proves to be 36 ohms resistance and 48 ohms reactance. Now add the 28 ohms resistance, to make a total resistance component of 64 ohms. The whole network has an impedance of magnitude 80 ohms and phase angle arctan .75.

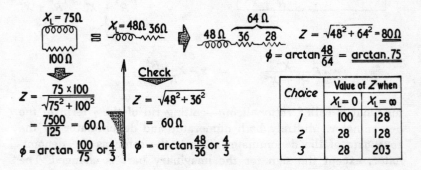

A check on this kind of problem, which will determine whether the answer is within range, is to eliminate the reactance in two ways. Write the reactance alternatively equal to zero and infinity and see what resistance values result. Which is the correct pair here? Answer: 1; turn to 39-A. Answer: 2; turn to 35-B. Answer: 3; turn to 40-B.

41-B. (From 47-A) *Wrong.* Under certain very limited circumstances, an iron-core inductor can be approximately represented as an inductance with a resistance in parallel, or shunt. But even then, there will be a resistance element in series, due to winding resistance. So the simple combination of inductance in parallel with resistance is not an accurate representation of any practical component. Turn to the other answer.

42

42-A. (From 34-B) *Correct.* Whether that was a good guess or you figured it out, here is how it's done. First note the procedure

$$\frac{jRX}{R+jX}\left[\otimes \frac{R-jX}{R-jX}\right] = \frac{jRX(R-jX)}{R^2+X^2} = \frac{RX^2+jXR^2}{R^2+X^2}$$

$$\boxed{\begin{aligned}(R+jX)(R-jX) &= R^2-(jX)^2\\ &= R^2+X^2\end{aligned}}$$

$$= \underset{\underset{\textstyle r}{\uparrow}}{\frac{RX^2}{R^2+X^2}} + j\underset{\underset{\textstyle jx}{\uparrow}}{\frac{XR^2}{R^2+X^2}}$$

$$r = R\frac{X^2}{R^2+X^2} \qquad\qquad x = X\frac{R^2}{R^2+X^2}$$

for what is called *rationalizing*—getting rid of the j term in the denominator. Multiply both numerator and denominator by the *conjugate* of the denominator. This is the same as the denominator, except the sign for the imaginary part is changed. The denominator is $R + jX$, so you multiply 'top and bottom' by $R - jX$. If the denominator had been $R - jX$, you would have multiplied both by $R + jX$.

This makes the denominator the sum of the squares of the real and imaginary parts, while the numerator now has real and imaginary parts. Identifying these with the corresponding parts, r and jx from 34-B, we have the expressions for the equivalents. Rewritten as shown, the result is easier to remember. In each case the equivalent value is the actual value, multiplied by an expression composed of terms that are the actual values squared. Now turn to 44-A.

42-B. (From 46-A) *Wrong.* Impedance is a combination of resistance and reactance at all frequencies except resonance, in this case. Is this always true? For the moment try the other answer.

42-C. (From 48-A) *Correct.* Now turn to page 53-A.

43-A. (From 34-C) *Correct*. Here is the complete derivation on which the approximate values are based. For the parallel circuit write the expression for admittance, and rationalize its reciprocal to find impedance. For the series circuit write the expression for impedance and rationalize its reciprocal to find admittance. For

$$Y = \frac{1}{R} + j\omega C$$

$$Z = \frac{R - j\omega C R^2}{1 + \omega^2 C^2 R^2}$$

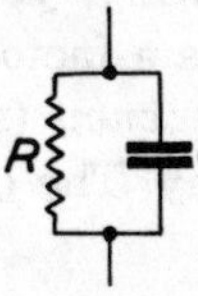

$$Z = r + \frac{1}{j\omega C}$$

$$Y = \frac{\omega^2 C^2 r + j\omega C}{1 + \omega^2 C^2 r^2}$$

$$r_{eq} = \frac{R}{1 + \omega^2 C^2 R^2} \quad C_{eq} = \frac{1 + \omega^2 C^2 R^2}{\omega^2 C R^2} \quad R_{eq} = \frac{1 + \omega^2 C^2 r^2}{\omega^2 C^2 r} \quad C_{eq} = \frac{C}{1 + \omega^2 C^2 r^2}$$

the series equivalent of a parallel circuit, equate the two expressions for impedance, real and imaginary parts. For the parallel equivalent of a series circuit, equate the two expressions for admittance, real and imaginary parts. Now turn to 45-A.

43-B. (From 50-A) This answer will usually be accepted as correct. If resonance is defined as the frequency where the impedance or admittance is purely resistive, this answer fits, as

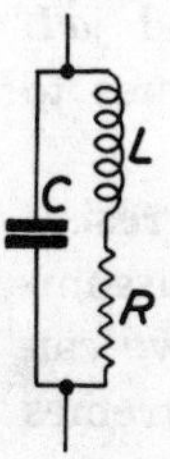

$$Y = j\omega C + \frac{1}{R + j\omega L} = \frac{1 - \omega^2 LC + j\omega CR}{R + j\omega L}$$

$$= \frac{(1 - \omega^2 LC + j\omega CR)(R - j\omega L)}{R^2 + \omega^2 L^2}$$

$$= \frac{R + j\omega CR^2 - j\omega L + j\omega^3 L^2 C}{R^2 + \omega^2 L^2}$$

Imaginary part zero:

$$\omega CR^2 - \omega L + \omega^3 L^2 C = 0$$

So $\omega = 0$ or

$$\omega^2 L^2 C = L - CR^2$$

$$\omega^2 = \frac{1}{LC} - \frac{R^2}{L^2}$$

$$= \frac{1}{LC}\left[1 - \frac{R^2 C}{L}\right]$$

it appears here. But if resonance is taken to mean the frequency at which impedance is a maximum (or admittance a minimum) this answer is not correct (for some purposes, this may be the practical significance of resonance, if not the one usually given in academic definitions). Check one of the other answers.

EQUIVALENT IMPEDANCES

44-A. (From 42-A) The working on page 34-B was general, using a reactance that could be of either kind. Now assume a specific reactance, and see how frequency enters the picture. Just as you did on page 33-A and following, you can write frequency as f, in which case there is always a factor 2π associated with it; or you can use ω for *angular frequency* (sometimes called *pulsatance*), which is 2π times frequency. The one symbol ω is simpler to write than $2\pi f$.

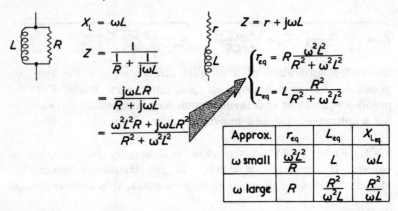

$$X_L = \omega L$$

$$Z = \frac{1}{\frac{1}{R} + \frac{1}{j\omega L}}$$

$$= \frac{j\omega L R}{R + j\omega L}$$

$$= \frac{\omega^2 L^2 R + j\omega L R^2}{R^2 + \omega^2 L^2}$$

$$Z = r + j\omega L$$

$$\begin{cases} r_{eq} = R\dfrac{\omega^2 L^2}{R^2 + \omega^2 L^2} \\[2mm] L_{eq} = L\dfrac{R^2}{R^2 + \omega^2 L^2} \end{cases}$$

Approx.	r_{eq}	L_{eq}	$X_{L_{eq}}$
ω small	$\dfrac{\omega^2 L^2}{R}$	L	ωL
ω large	R	$\dfrac{R^2}{\omega^2 L}$	$\dfrac{R^2}{\omega L}$

You use exactly the same method as on pages 34-B and 42-A. Then, by equating the real and imaginary parts to r and $j\omega L$ respectively, we get expressions for equivalent series values to the actual parallel configuration.

We can go a step further. Notice that both equivalent resistance and equivalent inductance vary with frequency. By assuming frequency (ω) to be very small, and then very large, we can see how these quantities depend on frequency at the extremes of the frquency range. For low frequencies, resistance is proportional to frequency squared, and inductance is virtually constant. For high frequencies, resistance is constant, and inductance is inversely proportional to frequency squared (or reactance inversely proportional to frequency, instead of its more usual direct proportion).

Suppose we take equivalents the opposite way—is the way they depend on frequency the same (turn to 39-B) or vice versa (turn to 52-A)?

44-B. (From 53-A) The answer is (2) 0.3A, derived as on 9-A.

A.C. CIRCUIT SOLUTION

45-A. (From 43-A) Calculating what happens in a specific circuit is one thing, but electronics calculations are just as often concerned with finding a circuit to fit specific requirements. A good example of this is the a.c. bridge in its various configurations.

$$\frac{Z_1}{Z_2} = \frac{Z_3}{Z_4}$$

At $\omega = 0$ $\frac{R_1}{R_2} = \frac{R_3}{r_4}$

At $\omega \neq 0$

① $\frac{L}{C} = R_1 R_2$ ② $\frac{L}{r_4} = R_1 C$ ③ $\frac{L}{C} = R_3 r_4$

?

This one is of a type characterized by a balance that is independent of frequency. Other bridges may be critical of frequency for obtaining balance, according to purpose. It is useful for measuring air-core inductors, where the loss is entirely due to winding resistance, which may be regarded as in series with the inductance. An inductance with a magnetic core will possess core losses, which more nearly approximate a shunt or parallel resistance in effect, so this bridge would not balance independently of frequency when measuring that type.

The conditions for balance are just the same, basically, as for the d.c. bridge, using the ratio of the arms. At zero frequency (which is d.c.) C is an open circuit and L is a short circuit, so the bridge must balance on resistance values alone. Which is the correct second condition for it to balance at various a.c. frequencies? Answer: 1; turn to 30-C. Answer: 2; turn to 49-A. Answer: 3; turn to 35-C.

45-B. (From 48-A) *Wrong.* If you substitute Z's for R's, the formula works out just as validly. So the principle works, on an instantaneous basis, like Ohm's and Kirchhoff's laws, or, using reactance and impedance values, with a consideration of phase, the principle can be used either by means of vectors or the j operator (see 34-B). Now turn to the other answer.

SERIES RESONANCE

46-A. (From 49-A) Combining the two kinds of reactance, inductance and capacitance, produces the effect known as resonance, at the frequency where the two reactances are equal. In the series combination, shown here, the current is the same through both, and the voltages are in opposition. When the reactances are unequal, the terminal voltage is the difference between them. So the terminal impedance is the difference between the reactances, which becomes zero at resonance.

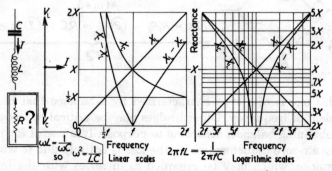

Here f represents the frequency of resonance, and other frequencies are plotted as ½f (or .5f), 2f, etc. The symbol X is used for the reactance of each (L and C) at resonance, so that other values of reactance are plotted as ½X (or .5X), 2X, etc. Using a specific value at an important or critical point like this as a reference value for other values is known as *normalizing*. By using this method, the curves or calculations apply equally to any case, whatever the frequency and whatever the reactance at resonance.

Using linear reactance and frequency scale results in curves that are not symmetrical. But using logarithmic scales for both frequency and reactance results in symmetry, because the curves for both kinds of reactance are then linear. Equating the expressions for the two reactances and rearranging, we find the expression for resonance frequency is ω^2 equals $1/LC$. This is where angular frequency is very convenient.

All of this assumes that there is no resistance in the circuit. Inserting resistance in series prevents impedance from being zero at resonance. Instead it is: (1) a combination of reactance and resistance (turn to 42-B); (2) pure resistance equal to the series value (turn to 31-B).

Q-FACTOR AND RESONANCE

47-A. (From 40-C) If you've read each of the pages 43-B, 51-A, and 40-C you can see that resonance can have a rather ambiguous significance. Sometimes these different expressions have values that are nearly identical, and sometimes they are quite different. This relationship is easily expressed in terms of Q. Note that the expression L/CR^2, although it does not contain ω, is the product of the two reactances divided by resistance squared— or the square of the ratio between either reactance and resistance at resonance. This quantity, X/R, is defined as Q.

$$X_L = \omega L \qquad X_c = \frac{1}{\omega C} \qquad X_L X_c = \frac{\omega L}{\omega C} = \frac{L}{C} = X^2 \qquad \frac{L}{CR^2} = \frac{X^2}{R^2}$$

$$\frac{X}{R} = Q \qquad \frac{L}{CR^2} = Q^2 \qquad \frac{R^2 C}{L} = \frac{1}{Q^2}$$

		Suppose $Q = 10$
② $\frac{1}{LC}\left[1 - \frac{R^2 C}{L}\right] = \frac{1}{LC}\left[1 - \frac{1}{Q^2}\right]$		$= \frac{0.99}{LC}$
③ $\frac{1}{LC}\left[1 - \frac{R^2 C}{4L}\right] = \frac{1}{LC}\left[1 - \frac{1}{4Q^2}\right]$		$= \frac{0.9975}{LC}$
④ $\frac{1}{LC}\left[\sqrt{1 + \frac{2R^2 C}{L}} - \frac{R^2 C}{L}\right] = \frac{1}{LC}\left[\sqrt{1 + \frac{2}{Q^2}} - \frac{1}{Q^2}\right]$		$= \frac{1}{LC}\left[\sqrt{1.02} - .01\right]$
		$= \frac{0.99995}{LC}$

Making this substitution into the expressions on 50-A, 43-B, 51-A, and 40-C we see why $1/LC$ was taken out as a factor. To show the practical significance, values have been given when $Q = 10$. Often much higher values are encountered, which will make the values for different resonant effects much closer together. Occasionally smaller values of Q are encountered, resulting in a more definite separation of these effects. The effect derived on 51-A is described more fully in relation to the complex plane (see page 115-B).

The series circuit corresponding to the parallel one we have just investigated is shown at the bottom. Which of the following statements is correct?

1. This circuit represents the behavior of an iron-core inductor in a series resonant circuit (turn to 41-B).
2. This circuit never represents a practical circuit with sufficient accuracy to be of value (turn to 52-C).

48

THEVENIN'S PRINCIPLE

48-A. (From 52-C) Here we shall discuss a principle that is of great value in making electronics calculations. First it will be demonstrated with simple resistances. The principle is understood best by this simple example, rather than trying to put it into a formal statement.

A source of voltage, V_1, has a voltage divider, R_1 and R_2, connected across it, which in the absence of any load produces a voltage V_2 across the R_2 part of the divider. Now if a load (R_3) is connected to this divider, the voltage and current in it will be the same as if it were connected to a source voltage of V_2, with an internal impedance consisting of R_1 and R_2 in parallel.

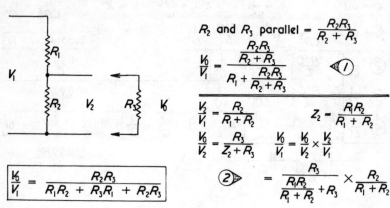

$$R_2 \text{ and } R_3 \text{ parallel} = \frac{R_2 R_3}{R_2 + R_3}$$

$$\frac{V_0}{V_1} = \frac{\dfrac{R_2 R_3}{R_2 + R_3}}{R_1 + \dfrac{R_2 R_3}{R_2 + R_3}} \quad ①$$

$$\frac{V_2}{V_1} = \frac{R_2}{R_1 + R_2} \qquad Z_2 = \frac{R_1 R_2}{R_1 + R_2}$$

$$\frac{V_0}{V_2} = \frac{R_3}{Z_2 + R_3} \qquad \frac{V_0}{V_1} = \frac{V_0}{V_2} \times \frac{V_2}{V_1}$$

$$\frac{V_0}{V_1} = \frac{R_2 R_3}{R_1 R_2 + R_3 R_1 + R_2 R_3}$$

$$② \quad = \frac{R_3}{\dfrac{R_1 R_2}{R_1 + R_2} + R_3} \times \frac{R_2}{R_1 + R_2}$$

To prove this, the voltage ratio V_0/V_1 has been calculated directly (1) from the series-parallel resistance configuration. Also an expression for V_2 has been found and a value for the ratio V_0/V_1 in terms of the voltage V_2 and the source impedance at the junction (2). If you simplify expressions (1) and (2), you will find they both reduce to the one enclosed in the box.

Having proved that this works in a general way for simple resistance circuits, the question is whether the same principle works when the voltage is alternating and the elements include reactance elements. If you think so, turn to 42-C. If you think not, turn to 45-B.

49-A. (From 45-A) *Correct.* Here is a complete derivation of the conditions for balance. The final expression has two imaginary terms in the numerator at the left side, and none on the right. Since one is positive and the other negative, they must be equal for balance. This leads to the second condition in the form given at (2) on page 45-A.

$$\frac{Z_1}{Z_2} = \frac{Z_3}{Z_4} \qquad Z_1 = \frac{R_1 - j\omega C R_1^2}{1 + \omega^2 C^2 R_1^2} \qquad Z_2 = R_2$$

$$Z_3 = R_3 \qquad Z_4 = r_4 + j\omega L$$

$$Z_1 Z_4 = Z_2 Z_3 \qquad \frac{(R_1 - j\omega C R_1^2)(r_4 + j\omega L)}{1 + \omega^2 C^2 R_1^2} = R_2 R_3$$

$$L = C R_1 r_4 \text{ or } \frac{L}{r_4} = C R_1$$

$$\frac{R_1 r_4 + \omega^2 L C R_1^2 + j\omega L R_1 - j\omega C R_1^2 r_4}{1 + \omega^2 C^2 R_1^2} = R_2 R_3 \quad \blacksquare(\omega = 0) \quad R_1 r_4 = R_2 R_3 \text{ or } \frac{R_1}{R_2} = \frac{R_3}{r_4}$$

$$\blacksquare(\omega \to \infty) \quad \frac{L}{C} = R_2 R_3 = R_1 r_4$$

Of the real part, both the numerator and denominator on the left side have a term without ω and a term in ω^2. Making ω zero reduces the expression to the first condition, applicable for d.c. Making ω approach infinity, the other terms can be neglected from both numerator and denominator, and the ω^2 factor can be cancelled, leaving an expression $L/C = R_2 R_3$. Applying the first condition yields the second condition again in its first form, thus providing a verification. Now turn to 46A.

49-B. (From 53-A) If you had trouble, here is the answer.

$$Z_1 = R_1 + \frac{1}{j\omega C} \qquad Z_2 = R_2 \qquad Z_3 = R_3 \qquad \frac{1}{Z_4} = \frac{1}{R_4} + \frac{1}{j\omega L}$$

$$Z_1 = \frac{Z_2 Z_3}{Z_4} \qquad R_1 + \frac{1}{j\omega C} = R_2 R_3 \left[\frac{1}{R_4} + \frac{1}{j\omega L}\right] \quad \underline{\text{Real part}} \ R_1 = \frac{R_2 R_3}{R_4} \text{ or } \boxed{\frac{R_1}{R_2} = \frac{R_3}{R_4}} ①$$

$$\text{Imaginary part } \frac{1}{j\omega C} = \frac{R_2 R_3}{j\omega L} \quad \text{As } R_2 R_3 = R_1 R_4 ① \quad \frac{L}{C} = R_1 R_4 \text{ or } \boxed{C R_1 = \frac{L}{R_4}} ②$$

Answer to both (*a*) and (*b*) is <u>YES</u>

49-C. (From 54-A) For this question, (1) is the value at which the parallel circuit is reactanceless; (2) is the value at which the parallel circuit has maximum impedance; (3) is the value of resonance (by any definition) in the series circuit. Identification of the formulas is on 47-A.

PARALLEL RESONANCE

50-A. (From 31-B) Shown here is the correspondence between series and parallel connected resonance circuits, by taking voltages in series to correspond with currents in parallel, and conductance, susceptance and admittance as the reciprocals respectively of resistance, reactance and impedance. Note the very precise similarity between the two sets of formulas as arranged.

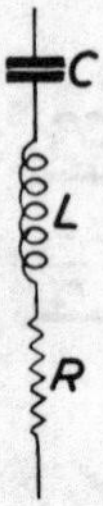

$$X_c = \frac{1}{j\omega C}$$

$$X_L = j\omega L$$

$$R$$

$$V = I\left[R + j\omega L + \frac{1}{j\omega C}\right]$$

$$\omega L = \frac{1}{\omega C} \qquad \omega^2 = \frac{1}{LC}$$

$$Z = R + j\omega L + \frac{1}{j\omega C}$$

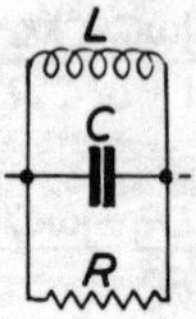

$$B_L = \frac{1}{j\omega L}$$

$$B_C = j\omega C$$

$$G = \frac{1}{R}$$

		Reciprocals	
Conductance	$G = \frac{1}{R}$		Resistance
Susceptance	$B = \frac{1}{X}$		Reactance
Admittance	$Y = \frac{1}{Z}$		Impedance

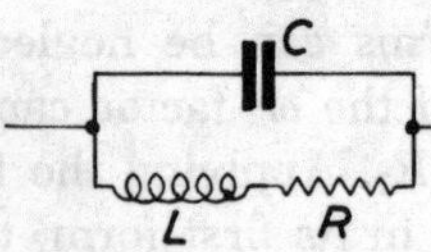

$$I = V\left[G + j\omega C + \frac{1}{j\omega L}\right]$$

$$Y = G + j\omega C + \frac{1}{j\omega L}$$

$$\omega^2 = \begin{cases} \underset{(1)}{\frac{1}{LC}} \qquad \underset{(2)}{\frac{1}{LC}\left[1 - \frac{R^2C}{L}\right]} \qquad \underset{(3)}{\frac{1}{LC}\left[1 - \frac{R^2C}{4L}\right]} \\ \text{or} \quad \frac{1}{LC}\left[\sqrt{1 + \frac{2R^2C}{L}} - \frac{R^2C}{L}\right] \;(4) \end{cases}$$

This works, provided a resistance in series for the series circuit is compared with a resistance in parallel for the parallel circuit (but regarding the latter as a conductance). Suppose, however, the parallel circuit has resistance in series with the inductance element (a condition often encountered). Which is the correct expression for the resonance frequency now? Answer: 1; turn to 52-B. Answer: 2; turn to 43-B. Answer: 3; turn to 51-A. Answer: 4; turn to 40-C.

50-B. (From 54-A) The formula for capacitive reactance (where C is in farads) is given on page 35-A. From this formula the correct answer is 1,000 ohms.

51-A. (From 50-A) This answer is sometimes given for the resonant frequency of *this* circuit, and it has a rather special meaning The easiest way to arrive at it is to isolate the circuit and apply Kirchhoff's second law in a differential equation. An expression is written for current, i, with arbitrary constants A and a, whose value is then sought. After substitutions are made, it is found

$$iR + L\frac{di}{dt} + \frac{1}{C}\int i\,dt = 0 \quad \text{Solution} \quad \boxed{i = A\varepsilon^{at}} \quad \text{Find } A \text{ and } a$$

$$iR = AR\varepsilon^{at} \qquad L\frac{di}{dt} = AaL\varepsilon^{at} \qquad \frac{1}{C}\int i\,dt = \frac{A}{aC}\varepsilon^{at} \quad \boxed{\begin{array}{c} A \text{ common} \\ \text{factor} \end{array}}$$

$$\boxed{R + aL + \frac{1}{aC} = 0} \qquad La^2 + Ra + \frac{1}{C} = 0$$

Write $\alpha = \dfrac{R}{2L}$ $\quad \boxed{\omega^2 = \dfrac{1}{LC} - \dfrac{R^2}{4L^2}}$

$$a = -\frac{R}{2L} \pm \sqrt{\frac{R^2}{4L^2} - \frac{1}{LC}} \quad \text{or}$$

Solution is:
$$i = A\left(\varepsilon^{[-\alpha+j\omega t]} + \varepsilon^{[-\alpha-j\omega t]}\right)$$

$$-\frac{R}{2L} \pm j\sqrt{\frac{1}{LC} - \frac{R^2}{4L^2}}$$

$$= A\varepsilon^{-\alpha t}\cos\omega t \quad \text{where} \quad \text{or} \quad \omega^2 = \frac{1}{LC}\left[1 - \frac{R^2C}{4L}\right]$$

that A is a common factor and, in fact, represents the constant of integration needed for the last term. Practically, it represents the starting amplitude of the wave. Now solve for a, getting a quadratic solution. This has a radical part which, when R is small enough for resonance to occure (corresponding to Curve 1 on 31-B), will be imaginary. The expression represents a decaying cosine (or sine) wave, of frequency given by expression (3) on page 50-A. Now try one of the other answers.

51-B. (From 54-A) Answer (3) is correct; here is the solution.

$$Y = \frac{1}{2028} + \frac{j}{845} \qquad Z = \frac{1}{\frac{1}{2028} + \frac{j}{845}}$$

$$= \frac{845 \times 2028}{845 + j2028} = \frac{845 \times 2028\,(845 - j2028)}{845^2 + 2028^2}$$

$$845 = 5 \times 13^2$$
$$2028 = 12 \times 13^2$$
$$5^2 + 12^2 = 13^2$$
$$13 \times 13^2 = 2197$$

Real part $= \dfrac{2028 \times 845^2}{2197^2} = \dfrac{2028 \times 5^2}{13^2} = 12 \times 5^2 = \underline{300\,\Omega}$

Imaginary part $= \dfrac{845 \times 2028^2}{2197^2} = \dfrac{845 \times 12^2}{13^2} = 5 \times 12^2 = \underline{720\,\Omega}$ $\Big\}$ Answer ③

52-A. (From 44-A) *Correct.* Here it is all worked out, the same as for the opposite case, which we did on page 44-A. For con-

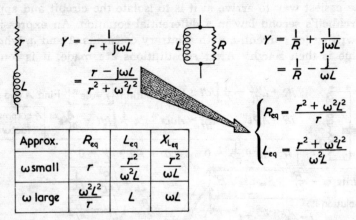

$$Y = \frac{1}{r + j\omega L}$$

$$= \frac{r - j\omega L}{r^2 + \omega^2 L^2}$$

$$Y = \frac{1}{R} + \frac{1}{j\omega L}$$

$$= \frac{1}{R} - \frac{j}{\omega L}$$

$$\begin{cases} R_{eq} = \dfrac{r^2 + \omega^2 L^2}{r} \\[2mm] L_{eq} = \dfrac{r^2 + \omega^2 L^2}{\omega^2 L} \end{cases}$$

Approx.	R_{eq}	L_{eq}	$X_{L_{eq}}$
ω small	r	$\dfrac{r^2}{\omega^2 L}$	$\dfrac{r^2}{\omega L}$
ω large	$\dfrac{\omega^2 L^2}{r}$	L	ωL

verting this way, it is easier to work in terms of the real and imaginary parts of *admittance*, which is the reciprocal of impedance. The symbol for admittance is Y. Turn to 39-C.

52-B. (From 50-A) *Wrong.* This may come close to all of the expressions in practical value, but it is incorrect. Try one of the others.

52-C. (From 47-A) *Correct.* Now turn to page 48-A.

52-D. (From 54-A) The formula for reactance of an inductance is given on page 33-A; from this the correct answer is 120 ohms.

52-E. (From 53-A) The product of resistance in ohms and capacitance in farads gives the time constant in seconds (see 13-B); so the answer is 1 second.

53-A. TEST QUESTIONS ON SECTION 1

1. The drawing shows an unbalanced bridge. Calculate the current in the vertical arm. It is (1) 0.147 A, (2) 0.3 A, or (3) 0.75 A? After identifying your answer, turn to 44-B.

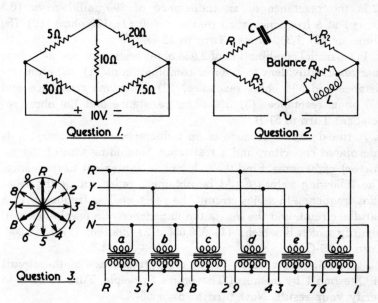

Question 1.

Question 2.

Question 3.

R 5 Y   8 B   2 9   4 3   7 6   1

2. This bridge is different from the one discussed in the section. Find whether the conditions for balance are (a) the same at all frequencies or (b) the same as for the other bridge. If in difficulty, turn to 49-B.

3. The drawing here shows a circuit for providing twelve-phase voltages for rectification, from a three-phase supply. Check the identification of vectors and, assuming the secondaries provide the correct voltage needed by the rectifier system (not shown) and that the three-phase circuit is 230 volts from each phase to neutral (N), find the primary voltages for which each transformer must be wound. For the answer, turn to 35-D.

4. Measuring the voltages between points round a circuit, designated by points $ABCDE$, the readings are: AB, 3.5 v.; BC, 3.75 v.; CD, −1.25 v.; DE, −4.35 v. Should the voltage measured from EA be (1) −1.65; (2) +1.65; or (3) 12.85? Turn to 54-B.

5. Is the time constant of a resistance of 250,000 ohms combined with a capacitance of 4 microfarads (1) 1 second, (2) 6.25 seconds, or (3) 0.16 second? Turn to 52-E.

54

6. Is the reactance of a capacitor of 4 microfarads, at a frequency such that ω is 250 (which is approximately 40 cycles) (1) 62.5 ohms, (2) 1,000 ohms, or (3) 1,600 ohms? Turn to 50-B.

7. Is the reactance of an inductance of 300 millihenrys (0.3 henry) at a frequency such that $\omega = 400$ (1) 120 ohms, (2) 750 ohms, or (3) 1,330 ohms? Turn to 52-D.

8. Is a parallel combination of 2,028 ohms resistance and 845 ohms reactance equivalent to a series combination of (1) 250 ohms resistance and 595 ohms reactance, (2) 275 ohms resistance and 570 ohms reactance, (3) 300 ohms resistance and 720 ohms reactance? Turn to 51-B.

9. A tuned circuit consists of an inductance of 0.25 henry, a 4-microfarad capacitor, and a resistance (including that of the inductor) of 50 ohms. Find the value of ω^2 equivalent to resonance. The following values could be obtained, representing the resonant frequency in series circuit, the reactanceless frequency of a parallel circuit, and the maximum impedance of a parallel circuit. Identify which is which: (1) 960,000; (2) 999,166; (3) 1,000,000. Turn to 49-C.

10. Calculate the current in the center resistance of the circuit of Question 1 by means of Thevenin's Principle. Turn to 38-C to verify your result. Now turn to page 55-A.

54-B. (From 53-A) The total, adding round the loop and taking signs into account, must add up to zero (Kirchhoff's second law). Thus the correct answer is (1) −1.65.

Section 2

TRANSFER CHARACTERISTICS

55-A. Many electronics calculations are concerned with some aspect of transfer characteristics which refer to the relationship between input and output of a circuit or network. You may be concerned with how this relationship changes with frequency, amplitude, or time. Here we will assume that frequency in some way affects the input-output relationship (or transfer characteristic) of a network.

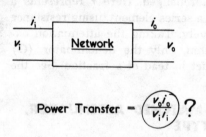

Voltage Transfer	$= \dfrac{v_o}{v_i}$
Current Transfer	$= \dfrac{i_o}{i_i}$
Mutual Admittance (Conductance)	$= \dfrac{i_o}{v_i}$
Mutual Impedance (Resistance)	$= \dfrac{v_o}{i_i}$

All as frequency variables

Power Transfer $= \left(\dfrac{v_o i_o}{v_i i_i} \right)$?

Transfer can be measured in terms of voltage output related to voltage input; current output related to current input; current output related to voltage input (usually used for tube circuits) or voltage output to current input (sometimes used for transistor circuits). It would be defined in terms of the quantities shown here, and the transfer characteristic in those terms would be specified as a more or less complicated function of frequency.

Sometimes, instead of either voltage transfer or current transfer, the characteristic of a network is needed in terms of power. Is power transfer the quantity shown ringed with a question mark? If you think so, turn to 56-A; if not, turn to 58-A.

55-B. (From 57-A) *No.* You correctly perceived that X would be in a shunt position in the overall equivalent, but you do not have the correct combination of input and output impedances. Try again.

56

56-A. (From 55-A) Academically this answer is wrong. Strictly speaking, the ratio between the products of voltage and current at input and output would be the *VA* (volt-amp) *transfer*. To be a true power transfer, each product of voltage and current should include a power factor (cosine of the angle between the voltage and current vectors at that point). However, in many electronic applications, the actual power has little significance. A tube circuit, for example, is more often capable of a certain volt-amp output, rather than the power output specified (*e.g.*, a pentode capable of 5 watts output will give 5 VA if there is a phase difference between output voltage and current—not 5 watts). For this reason, the words "power transfer" are often used in electronic applications where they are academically incorrect, and "VA transfer" would be a better choice. Turn to 58-A.

56-B. (From 67-A) *Wrong.* This is the same form as for voltage transfer—with the elements interchanged. Here r represents a shunt element and G represents a series element, using resistance and conductance units respectively. Taking the attenuation expression from the second column, only the denominator (G) needs inverting to give a product instead of a fraction. See the other answer.

TWO-WAY IMPEDANCE-MATCHED ATTENUATOR, PI-TYPE

56-C. (From 76-A) This is the dual form of the T-type (see 72-A) and uses a similar design approach. In principle, where the T-type uses series arms at input and output to provide matching, and a

	①	②	③	④
$a =$	$\dfrac{k^2-1}{2k}$	$\dfrac{2k}{k^2-1}$	$\dfrac{k-1}{k+1}$	$\dfrac{k+1}{k-1}$
$b =$	$\dfrac{k-1}{k+1}$	$\dfrac{k+1}{k-1}$	$\dfrac{k^2-1}{2k}$	$\dfrac{2k}{k^2-1}$

shunt arm to attenuate by current division (although this is not such a simple segregation of function as occurs in the L-pad) the π-type reverses things. A series arm provides basic voltage division, while shunt arms at each end provide impedance matching. Which one of the pairs of values for a and b is correct? Answer: 1; see 73-A. Answer: 2; see 77-A. Answer: 3; see 75-A. Answer: 4; see 76-B.

57-A. (From 70-A) One of the simplest networks is a simple element in series between input and output, as shown here. Consider the input to have a source resistance or impedance r and an open-circuit voltage e. The input voltage delivered to the network is v_i, and the output, delivered to the terminating load R, is v_o. Here you are working in terms of voltage transfer. The important aspect of the transfer characteristic, when frequency response is considered, is how the presence of the network, in this case X, changes it.

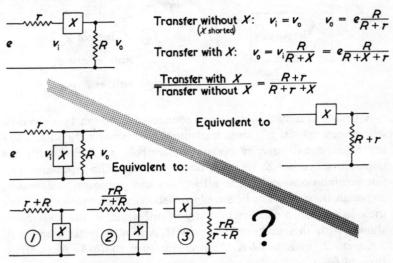

Transfer without X: $v_i = v_o$ $v_o = e \dfrac{R}{R+r}$
(X shorted)

Transfer with X: $v_o = v_i \dfrac{R}{R+X} = e \dfrac{R}{R+X+r}$

$\dfrac{\text{Transfer with } X}{\text{Transfer without } X} = \dfrac{R+r}{R+r+X}$

Equivalent to:

Equivalent to

Note that we have used simple algebraic signs, which would only be correct as simple algebra if X is a resistance. But the statements are still correct if X is a reactance (which is more commonly the case), by writing $\pm jX$, and including its frequency-dependent function. Or, if X should be an impedance (in which case Z is substituted for it), it becomes a complex quantity in the algebraic expressions. When this fact is recognized, the expressions are universally true.

Notice that the algebra enables the whole circuit to be simplified to an equivalent circuit, consisting of a series component "X" and a shunt component composed of R plus r in series combination.

Now turn to the shunt case, where the simple element X is in shunt with input and output. Which is the correct equivalent now? Answer: 1; turn to 55-B. Answer: 2; turn to 61-A. Answer: 3; turn to 58-B.

58-A. (From 55-A) If you answered "no," you were academically correct. The formula gave what would correctly be called VA (volt-amp) transfer, and the correct one should include a power factor (cos ϕ) term in both numerator and denominator, for the output and input phase angles respectively. But as 56-A mentions, the expression given often has more practical significance than the true or academic power transfer.

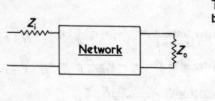

Transfer characteristic affected by:

① Z_0 but not Z_i
② Z_i but not Z_0
③ Both Z_i and Z_0
④ Neither Z_i nor Z_0

A practical network is always connected between two circuits, which may consist of tubes, transducers, or other networks. They are represented here by resistance symbols, identified with the impedance symbol Z. Usually, but not always, the input and output terminations will be, to all intents and purposes, resistances, although they may not be simple resistances. Sometimes one may include reactance elements. In any event, which of the statements shown with this diagram is correct? Answer: 1; turn to 60-A. Answer: 2; turn to 62-A. Answer: 3; turn to 70-A. Answer: 4; turn to 66-A.

58-B. (From 57-A) *Wrong.* You correctly derived the value combination of input and output impedance, which is parallel instead of series, but you chose the wrong configuration. Try again.

58-C. (From 65-A) *Wrong.* Here you have inverted values, a for b, and vice versa. Notice that two changes occur to the elements so identified: each changes from series to parallel, and from resistance to conductance. The direction of transfer (from left to right) and reflection of impedance (from right to left) remain the same. Try another answer.

59-A. (From 75-B) *Correct.* The easiest way to obtain it is to square both numerator and denominator of the expression for k, real and imaginary part separately, to obtain the square of the magnitude of each. If you rationalize first and then find the magnitude by squaring real and imaginary parts of the numerator, the result is the same. This method is more direct.

In short, the answer means that, without resistive elements in the lattice network, attenuation is zero at all frequencies. For this reason, it is called an *all-pass* network. But it produces a phase response which, as we have shown here, is the same as

$$db = 10 \log_{10}\left[\frac{1+x^2}{1+x^2}\right] = 10 \log 1 = 0 \qquad \text{Zero attenuation at all frequencies}$$

$$k = \frac{1+jx}{1-jx} = \frac{1-x^2+j2x}{1+x^2} \qquad \phi_t = \arctan\frac{2x}{1-x^2}$$

2 roll-offs: $(1+jx)(1+jx) = 1-x^2+j2x$; $db = 10\log_{10}(1+2x^2+x^4) = 20\log_{10}(1+x^2)$

that produced by two simple roll-off networks in cascade. Although the latter have a very definite attenuation response, the lattice duplicates the phase response but without the attenuation. This property makes it a useful element in making phase compensation without the attenuation that normally accompanies such phase response. Now turn to 93-A.

59-B. (From 104-A) Using the standard designation we established at 101-A, and the approximate formula on 82-C for x much less than 1, the value of x^2 is $(2,120/38,000)^2$, or 0.0031. For the 3-db point to be at 2,120 cycles, $(2a/c)^2$ must be the reciprocal of this value, or 322, the square root of which is very close to 18, making $a/c = 9$. From the formula on 101-A the corresponding value of b/c to produce a null is 9/8, or 1.125. Using the starting point given in the question, with ω as 238,500, the values are: a, 180K and 23.3 micromicrofarads; b, 22.5K and 186.5 micromicrofarads; c, 20K and 210 micromicrofarads. To get a close null these values need careful selection. This design assumes the network is driven from zero source-resistance, or constant voltage. If a practical circuit has a source resistance large enough to be considered finite, then it will contribute to the roll-off and must be taken into account, in addition to the resistance a. The ratio a/c will have to be correspondingly reduced, and b/c adjusted to retain a null condition.

60

60-A. (From 58-A) This statement is not universally correct, but it may be used practically, under two specific conditions:

1. If the network is designed to present a constant impedance at its input, its characteristic will be unaffected by the input terminating impedance. However, any network designed to present a constant input impedance will only do that provided the output impedance is a specific value. So, even in this case, the transfer characteristic is unaffected by input impedance for only one value of output impedance. Other values of output impedance not only affect the characteristic directly but cause the input impedance to affect it also.
2. If the input reference is the actual voltage or current (or combination of the two) measured at the input to the network. In practice this will be affected by the input impedance of the network, which will also have a characteristic, in conjunction with the terminating impedance at the input. So the condition never completely represents practical performance, except in special case (1). Try one of the other answers.

60-B. (From 93-A) *Correct.* Here we equate the coefficients of x^2 and x^4 to zero, to leave only the term in x^6 in the db expression. Then equating the coefficient of x^6 to 1, to meet the nor-

$$x^2: \; 2bc = (a+c)^2 \quad x^4: \; b^2c^2 = 2abc(a+c) \; \Rightarrow \; bc = 2a(a+c), \; (a+c)^2 = 4a(a+c)$$

$$x^6: \; abc = 1 \quad \tfrac{8}{3} \cdot 3a^3 = 8a^3 = 1 \; \Leftarrow c \quad 3b = 2(1+3)a \Leftarrow \frac{a+c = 4a \quad c = 3a}{b = \tfrac{8}{3}a}$$

$$\boxed{a = \tfrac{1}{2} \quad b = \tfrac{4}{3} \quad c = \tfrac{3}{2}}$$

$$y = Y_o \frac{1 - \tfrac{2}{3}x^2 + j\tfrac{4}{3}x}{1 - 2x^2 + j2x - jx^3} = Y_o\left[\frac{1}{1+x^6} - j\frac{2x + x^3 + 2x^5}{1+x^6}\right]$$

$$k = 1 - 2x^2 + j2x - jx^3$$

$$\phi_t = \arctan\frac{2x - x^3}{1 - 2x^2}$$

malizing requirement, we have values for a, b, and c. Substituting these into the expression for k, we get the expression for phase transfer. When $x = 1$, the tangent is -1, and the angle is 135 degrees, half the ultimate of 270 degrees. The expression for admittance simplifies to a real part and an imaginary part that follow the pattern. Substituting $1/x$ for x and adding, as represented by connecting the complementary network in parallel, the real part adds up to 1, and the imaginary parts cancel, being identical but of opposite sign. Now turn to 95-A.

61-A. (From 57-A) *Correct.* Good going if you inferred this intuitively. Here the algebraic derivation is presented. When we

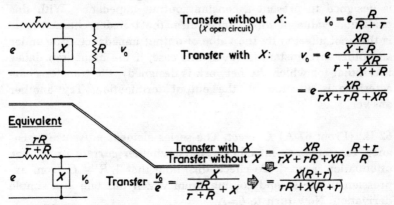

Transfer without X:
(*X* open circuit)
$$v_0 = e\,\frac{R}{R+r}$$

Transfer with X:
$$v_0 = e\,\frac{\frac{XR}{X+R}}{r + \frac{XR}{X+R}}$$
$$= e\,\frac{XR}{rX + rR + XR}$$

Equivalent

$$\frac{\text{Transfer with } X}{\text{Transfer without } X} = \frac{XR}{rX+rR+XR}\cdot\frac{R+r}{R}$$

Transfer $\dfrac{v_0}{e} = \dfrac{X}{\frac{rR}{r+R}+X}$ $\Rightarrow$ $= \dfrac{X(R+r)}{rR+X(R+r)}$

consider the complete circuit and its equivalent, we find that the transfer characteristic simplifies to the identical expression in each case. Now turn to 67-A.

61-B. (From 101-A) *Correct.* Here we show the vector relations for these cases. At the left is a case where c is less than the parallel combination of a and b, resulting in phase-reversed output. The formula gives the value of phase-reversed output, which is always at least 14 db below the input voltage level.

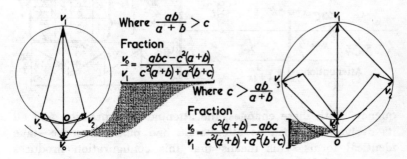

Where $\dfrac{ab}{a+b} > c$

Fraction
$$\frac{v_0}{v_1} = \frac{abc - c^2(a+b)}{c^2(a+b)+a^2(b+c)}$$

Where $c > \dfrac{ab}{a+b}$

Fraction
$$\frac{v_0}{v_1} = \frac{c^2(a+b)-abc}{c^2(a+b)+a^2(b+c)}$$

We have also indicated the locus of the vector, showing that this is always a circle. This will be proved later from the formula given. But, before we turn to that, is the response-shaping independent of values of a, b, and c, provided they are in one of the correct relationships that produce a null (see 84-C), or does the response change, aside from null, according to whatever combination of values achieves the null (see 82-C)?

62-A. (From 58-A) This answer is correct only for one special case: where the network, with a chosen value of input impedance, is designed to present a constant output impedance. With this particular value of input impedance, the transfer characteristic is then not affected by the value of output impedance. But under any other circumstances (even this case, if the input impedance is not that for which the network is designed), the transfer characteristic is affected by the output termination. Try another answer.

62-B. (From 67-A) *Correct.* The series element must use resistance, reactance, or impedance units, whether current or voltage attenuation is used. To check this, note that $1/R = G$ from expression in the second column, from which this one is a simple derivation. Now turn to 65-A.

62-C. (From 78-C) *Correct.* Notice that, while we make similar substitutions for f_x, those for x are the inverse of the ones on the right-hand side of page 73-B, because in this configuration the reactances each produce opposite results relative to fre-

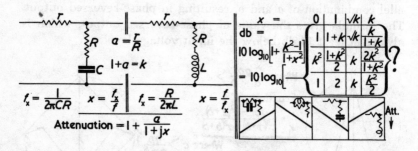

quency. With these changes, the attenuation expression and all its derivations—such as attenuation and phase response—take identical forms. This means that this configuration produces responses of shape identical to the other, merely by interchanging reactance types. At the bottom right we have indicated this variety.

At the top right we have listed four important values of x with their relevant values for db attenuation in terms of k. Which is the correct group? Answer: top line; see 76-C. Answer: middle line; see 84-B. Answer: bottom line; see 87-B.

63-A. (From 65-A) *Correct.* Here we have followed the same method of derivation, with slight differences in writing, which makes the result even more brief. Note that we have regarded the *b* element together with the output termination as providing the voltage attenuation, as the same current flows through both, while the *a* element equalizes impedance back to its correct value. If you refer back to the network on page 65-A you will see the same thing could be done with it by considering current attenuation, instead of voltage attenuation, and then taking the *b* element to provide the current division, while the *a* element equalizes impedance. This similarity, apparent by exchanging current for voltage, series for parallel, and impedance for admittance, is called *duality.*

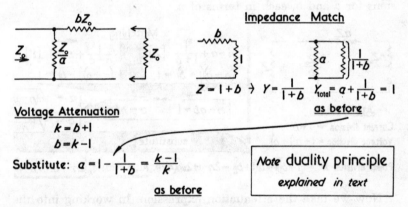

Voltage Attenuation

$$k = b + 1$$
$$b = k - 1$$

Substitute: $a = 1 - \dfrac{1}{1+b} = \dfrac{k-1}{k}$

as before

Note **duality principle**
explained in text

If your choice was wrong, note carefully how this principle of duality was used. Formulas sometimes given for these circuits use impedances, reactances, and resistances only. In this case, other forms may be encountered.

In these circuits, termination with Z_o at the output causes the input to "look like" Z_o, but the reverse is not true. The same circuits can be used to make the output "look like" Z_o by using the correct (Z_o) input termination. The condition is:

1. The network is just transposed, left to right (see 69-A).
2. Switch values, between *a* and *b*, for the configuration shown (see 71-A).

63-B. (From 73-B) *Wrong.* If you figured this out, then your ratio was correct, but you made a mistake in direction. Try another answer.

ASYMMETRICAL MATCHING PADS

64-A. (From 75-A, 76-A) The simplest matching pad, to ensure correct matching both ways between different impedances, uses an L-configuration. To design it, we assume the input impedance is n times the output impedance. With this assumption, we obtain two expressions for the impedance match, one "looking" each way. From the input, it is an impedance expression. From the output, it is an admittance expression. These are each transposed to similar form, multiplied out (not shown, but check the result, if you're unsure of them), and terms are combined to give the much simpler expressions, $n - ab = 1$ and $a = nb$. From these, by substituting one in the other, we derive expressions for a and b, each in terms of n.

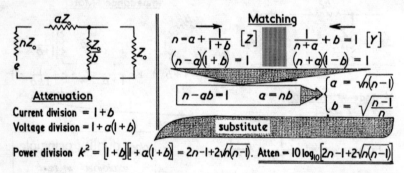

Attenuation

Current division $= 1 + b$

Voltage division $= 1 + a(1 + b)$

Power division $k^2 = [1 + b][1 + a(1 + b)] = 2n - 1 + 2\sqrt{n(n-1)}$. Atten $= 10 \log_{10}[2n - 1 + 2\sqrt{n(n-1)}]$

Now we take the attenuation expression. In working into the same impedance, or where the reflected impedance equals the terminating impedance, we can use either the voltage or current attenuation, because both will be the same. Where impedances differ, we have to take power attenuation, because voltage and current attenuation differ. Taking the current division at the output end, and voltage division from input to output, we multiply the two together to get the power attenuation. The attenuation in db is ten times the log to the base ten of this expression, into which we have substituted the impedance relationships to give attenuation in terms of the impedances being matched.

This is the basic (or minimum) attenuation for matching the impedance ratio, n. For greater attenuations, the network can be extended to an asymmetric T or π. If this is done, the result is (see 78-A), or is not (see 83-A), the same (except for the number of elements involved) as adding the basic L derived here to a T or π configuration.

IMPEDANCE-MATCHED ATTENUATOR, L-TYPE

65-A. (From 62-B) The principles just discussed are applied first to the simplest attenuator networks. Here the input impedance of the attenuator is to be made the same as its output terminating impedance and its attenuation is to be k. The quantity $20 \log_{10} k$ will give the attenuation in db. Here we normalize everything to the operating impedance Z_0. The output shunt resistor has b times the conductance $1/Z_0$ and the input series resistor has a times the resistance Z_0. Using this normalizing value as a unit, the conductance of the output pair is $1 + b$. Their impedance (or resistance) is the reciprocal of this, and the total input impedance is found by adding a, which makes the total up to the normalizing value 1 again to meet the impedance-matching condition.

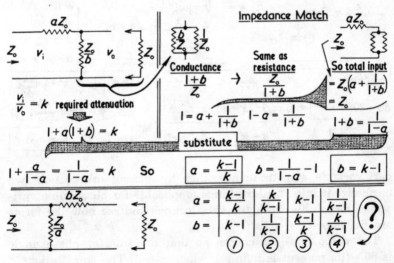

Now, writing the attenuation as 1 plus the product of series impedance and total shunt conductance, we equate the expression to k for attenuation. Substituting for $1 + b$ from the impedance expression, we obtain an expression for a in terms of k. Finally, we substitute into an expression for b in terms of a (taken from the impedance condition) to get an expression for b in terms of k.

Now let's reverse the network, keeping the same normalizing convention. Which is the correct pair of expressions for a and b? Answer: 1; see 63-A. Answer: 2; see 68-A. Answer: 3; see 58-C. Answer: 4; see 87-A.

66-A. (From 58-A) *Wrong*. There are some circuits called "constant impedance networks," and they are sometimes supposed to have properties of the kind implied by this answer. Such networks have special characteristics, which we shall discuss more fully later, but this is not one of them. Try one of the other answers.

COUPLING NETWORKS

66-B. (From 81-B) The network shown here is similar to the low-pass configuration, but with far greater variety of practical variations. It represents the basic form of a variety of coupling arrangements. Starting with the attenuation expression, k, we factor it into a fixed or non–frequency-dependent part and a

$$k = 1 + \left(r + j\omega L\right)\left(\tfrac{1}{R} + j\omega C\right)$$

$$= 1 + \tfrac{r}{R} - \omega^2 LC + j\omega\left(\tfrac{L}{R} + rC\right)$$

$$= \underbrace{\left[1 + \tfrac{r}{R}\right]}_{\text{Fixed loss}}\underbrace{\left[1 - \omega^2\tfrac{RLC}{R+r} + j\omega\left(\tfrac{L}{R+r} + \tfrac{RrC}{R+r}\right)\right]}_{\text{Variable with frequency}}$$

Write:
$$\omega_\phi^2 = \frac{R+r}{RLC}$$
$$d^2 = \frac{L}{CRr}$$
$$a = \frac{R}{r} \qquad x = \frac{\omega}{\omega_\phi}$$

$$\omega^2\frac{RLC}{R+r} = x^2 \quad \bullet \quad \frac{\omega L}{R+r} = \frac{xd}{\sqrt{1+a}} \quad \bullet \quad \frac{\omega CRr}{R+r} = \frac{x}{\sqrt{1+a}} \quad \bullet \quad k = \left[\frac{1+a}{a}\right]\left[1 - x^2 + jx\left(\frac{d+\frac{1}{d}}{\sqrt{1+a}}\right)\right]$$

$$db = 20\log_{10}\left[\frac{1+a}{a}\right] + 10\log_{10}\left[1 - 2x^2 + x^4 + x^2\frac{\left(d+\frac{1}{d}\right)^2}{1+a}\right]$$

$$\phi = \arctan\frac{d+\frac{1}{d}}{\sqrt{1+a}} \cdot \frac{x}{1-x^2}$$

$$1 + \frac{r}{R} \qquad \left[1 + \left\{\frac{\left(d+\frac{1}{d}\right)^2}{1+a} - 2\right\}x^2 + x^4\right]$$

Write
$$D = \frac{d+\frac{1}{d}}{\sqrt{1+a}}$$

when $x = 1$?

part variable with frequency; then by making substitutions we normalize it into standard forms, applicable for all possible variations. Carefully check the substitutions and see how the forms are developed.

The value of ω_ϕ is chosen so that the transfer phase angle is 90° (its tangent is infinite) when $x = 1$. The substitutions d and D are made, successively, to simplify the overall expression. A little study will show that the amplitude, or db expression, bears a unique relationship to the phase expression, regardless of the combination of values of d and a that produces them, because each uses the same resulting expression that simplifies in one case to D^2 and in the other to D.

We made the reference frequency for x such that the transfer phase angle is 90° for $x = 1$, but how does this relate to the amplitude response? Is this point always at the 6 db/octave slope point (see 87-C), or do the 90° phase shift and 6 db/octave slope points only coincide under certain circumstances (see 98-A)?

67-A. (From 61-A) In designing networks the formulas and equations to be solved are often much easier to handle if we use attenuation instead of transfer. This is merely a matter of inverting the ratio, or taking the reciprocal. Using the latter form and taking a series element r for voltage transfer or attenuation, you obtain an expression identical in form with that for a parallel source element g, using reciprocal elements for current transfer or attenuation. Taking this a step further, by using con-

				$G = \frac{1}{R}$, $g = \frac{1}{r}$
Transfer	$\dfrac{v_o}{v_i} = \dfrac{R}{R+r}$	$\dfrac{i_o}{i_i} = \dfrac{G}{G+g}$	$\dfrac{v_o}{v_i} = \dfrac{1}{1+rG}$	
Attenuation	$\dfrac{v_i}{v_o} = \dfrac{R+r}{R}$	$\dfrac{i_i}{i_o} = \dfrac{G+g}{G}$	$\dfrac{v_i}{v_o} = 1+rG$	$\dfrac{i_i}{i_o} = \begin{cases} 1+rG \quad (1) \\ \text{or} \\ 1+gR \quad (2) \end{cases}$
	$= 1 + \dfrac{r}{R}$	$= 1 + \dfrac{g}{G}$		

ductance, admittance, or susceptance units for shunt elements and using resistance, impedance, or reactance units for series elements, the voltage attenuation expression is simplified to $(1 + rG)$.

For current attenuation in the same network reversed, what is the expression? Answer: 1; see 56-B; Answer: 2; see 62-B.

67-B. (From 72-A) *Wrong.* This expression takes the first two elements and the second element with the terminating load as separate voltage dividers without any interaction. It assumes the second two do not load down the voltage division by the first two, because they are in parallel with the b element. This could only be correct if a buffer stage were inserted at this point, to prevent the interaction. This loading effect must be taken into account. Try another answer.

67-C. (From 80-A) You may have thought the ratio was the same as for the bridged-T. But the similarity between the two types does not extend that far. Note that in the bridged-T one element of the network is across null points. This does not happen in the lattice, except for one particular value, which gives infinite attenuation, and thus the terminating impedance is across null points. Try another answer.

68-A. (From 65-A) *Wrong*. These values are the reciprocals of the correct ones, probably arrived at because you failed to notice that shunt values are always normalized to conductance or admittance, while series values are normalized to resistance or impedance. Try another answer.

68-B. (From 77-B) *Correct*. Note that the expression for open-circuit (O.C.) impedance is the reciprocal of that for the short-circuit (S.C.) impedance. This means that the reflected impedance due to incorrect matching, providing it is a two-way-type network, is the same, regardless of type. This also means it is immaterial whether the attenuation is obtained all in one step or by means of more than one network (for the same impedance) in series or cascade.

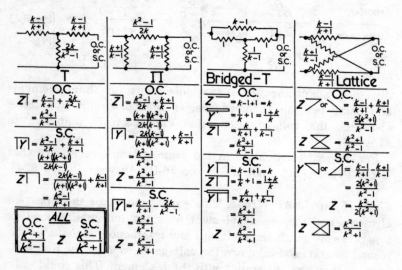

This identity does not hold for the one-way types, as you can easily check. Networks for two-way matching between different impedances can be made from L-pads in conjunction with any of these types to make up more than the minimum attenuation for the impedances involved (see 64-A), or they could be built up from first principles similar to those used to derive the T- and π-pads (see 72-A). Fairly obviously the lattice type does not lend itself to asymmetrical design; but could the bridged-T type be developed for asymmetrical use? If you think so, see 78-B; if not, see 82-B.

69-A. (From 63-A) *Correct.* To clarify the whole picture of L-pad matching, we have redrawn the pads here, with normalized values, using the formulas of page 65-A for both input and output matching. In the two left-hand examples, proper termination at the output makes the input present the correct value. In the two right-hand examples, using the correct input impedance makes the source "seen" at the output correct.

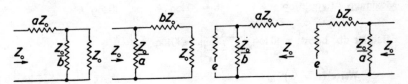

The theoretical attenuation will obtain only when the networks are correctly matched at their terminated end. In this case the attenuation figure obtains, regardless of the impedance at the other end (input for the left two and output for the right two). Just remember that the attenuation figure compares the transmission without the network interposed to that with it in circuit. Now turn to 72-A.

69-B. (From 83-C) This is merely a matter of applying the capacitive-reactance formula. Reference for the 3 db-up point, x on 78-C, is where reactance of C_1 is equal to r (at 2,000 cycles) and reactance of C_2 is equal to R (at 200 cycles).

$$\frac{1}{\omega C_1} = 9.16 \cdot 10^5 \text{ at } 2000 \text{ c/s.} \qquad \omega = 1.258 \cdot 10^4 \qquad C_1 = 87 \text{ μμF.}$$

$$\qquad\qquad\qquad\qquad\qquad\qquad\qquad\qquad\qquad Preferred \atop values \; \frac{82}{.015}$$

$$\frac{1}{\omega C_2} = 5.46 \cdot 10^4 \text{ at } 200 \text{ c/s.} \qquad \omega = 1.258 \cdot 10^3 \qquad C_2 = .0146 \text{ μF.}$$

Having solved a problem such as this, practical values should be sought that will give acceptably close approximations. For r, 1 meg will make sure that the step is not less than 20 db, which will allow R to be 56K and still maintain enough boost. As r is higher than calculated, C_1 should be correspondingly smaller (in the same ratio, approximately), so a value of 82 micromicrofarads should serve. For C_2 a value of 0.015 microfarad will be close enough, although both R and C_2 err in a direction that will reduce the lift very slightly.

70-A. (From 58-A) Correct under all normal circumstances. Turn to 57-A.

70-B. (From 73-B) *Correct.* By dividing the actual attenuation into the maximum attenuation, we get a new expression, still using x as the variable for frequency, for boost instead of attenuation.

Maximum Attenuation $= k$ $db = 20 \log_{10} k$ or $10 \log_{10} k^2$

Effective db "boost" $= 10 \log_{10}\left[\dfrac{k^2}{1 + \dfrac{k^2 - 1}{1 + x^2}}\right] = 10 \log_{10}\left[\dfrac{k^2(1 + x^2)}{k^2 + x^2}\right]$

Write $\boxed{z = \dfrac{k}{x}}$

$= 10 \log_{10}\left[1 + \dfrac{(k^2 - 1)x^2}{k^2 + x^2}\right]$

$= 10 \log_{10}\left[1 + \dfrac{k^2 - 1}{\dfrac{k^2}{x^2} + 1}\right] = 10 \log_{10}\left[1 + \dfrac{k^2 - 1}{1 + z^2}\right]$ When $z = 1$

$x = k$

To change phase normalizing frequency to form: X_c or $X_L = \dfrac{r}{k} = \dfrac{r}{1 + \dfrac{r}{R}}$

$\phi_t = \arctan b \dfrac{y}{1 + y^2}$ make $y = \left|\, z\, \right|\, \sqrt{xz}\, \left|\, \sqrt{\dfrac{x}{z}}\, \right|$?

$\qquad\qquad\qquad\qquad\qquad\quad\; \textcircled{1}\quad\; \textcircled{2}\quad\; \textcircled{3}$

$= \dfrac{rR}{r + R}$

Now we substitute $z = k/x$ into this, which converts the expression to its original form (on 73-B), but using the variable z instead of x. Note that writing $z = k/x$ establishes a ratio k between the reference frequencies and also inverts the relation to frequency (because x is in the denominator).

Substitution further shows that, to meet these substitution requirements, reactance of the capacitor or inductance must be equal to the parallel combination of R and r.

So we have two usable normalizing reference frequencies and levels for attenuation or boost response. What about the phase-transfer response? In the form given on 73-B every curve (for different values of k) would have a different shape. For a normalized presentation, the arctan expression should be capable of being factored into two parts, one of which contains only the "independent variable," which we will now call y, while the other contains the whole amplitude (of phase variation) expression. Which is the correct change of reference, to obtain y? Answer: 1; see 85-D. Answer: 2; see 74-C. Answer: 3; see 78-C.

71-A. (From 63-A) *Wrong.* So it must be the other one.

71-B. (From 84-B) *Correct.* This is deduced, stage by stage, by Thevenin's Principle. In the series network, R_2 is in parallel with R_o, and this combination has R_i in series with it, to make up the equivalent R. In the shunt network, R_i is in series with R_1, and this combination gets R_o in parallel to make up the effective value of r.

Now we turn to apply the same method used for step equalizers to equalizer networks that give the peak and hole (or absorption) responses. Instead of using just one reactance, L or C, both are used, in series or parallel resonant configuration, yielding two peaking circuits (top) and two absorption circuits (bottom).

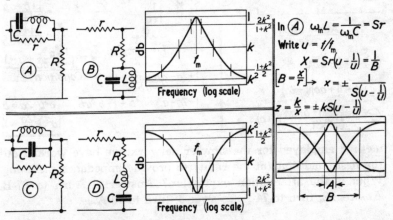

Any values of L and C that resonate at the right frequency would produce a peak or hole at that frequency, but problems usually require a specific "width" or "sharpness" (one is the reciprocal of the other) to the response. To develop a basis for working, take the peaking circuit (A) and write the reactance of each element at resonance (use the subscript m for "middle") as S times r. From this we can write an expression for X, the combined reactance of the two elements, and a substitution expression to apply the attenuation formulas of step networks to this circuit, giving x in terms of u—which is frequency normalized to the middle frequency. Now, before we apply the same method to the other three circuits, does the sharpness factor as we have derived it relate to dimension A (see 85-B) or dimension B (see 88-A) on the curves?

TWO-WAY IMPEDANCE-MATCHED ATTENUATOR, T-TYPE

72-A. (From 69-A) Where impedance match is required only one way (see 63-A), one resistor provides the voltage or current division ratio, and the other provides the impedance match, resulting in design that is relatively simple. To provide two-way matching, three resistance elements are needed. If the impedances are symmetrical, two resistors will be equal, so we again have a solution for two unknowns. Using the same normalizing

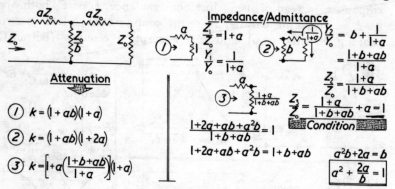

method employed for the simpler network, we have worked out the first condition (at the right) to provide impedance matching. What is the attenuation expression? Answer: 1; turn to 67-B. Answer: 2; turn to 74-A. Answer 3; turn to 76-A.

72-B. (From 95-A) *Wrong.* This would work tolerably well for wide bandpass networks. But for networks to give narrow bandpass or any band-stop characteristics, the second one will not give the correct termination for the first. In the band-stop combination, the first network must be operating in the attenuating band of the second, where its impedance will either be rising or falling from its nominal value, and thus will be incorrect for terminating the first. Note that these networks provide constant resistance input through cutoff and beyond only *when used in complementary pairs.*

For the bandpass, with a narrow-pass range, the same thing is true. The impedance at the input of the second network will already be starting to deviate from its designed value as a termination for the first network. For passbands of more than about two octaves width, the method is quite acceptable.

73-A. (From 56-C) *Wrong.* Try another answer.

STEP (SHELF) EQUALIZERS

73-B. (From 74-B) After attenuators the next logical derivation is step (or shelf) equalizers. Here at the left is shown the simple series network of 57-A, where the series element is either a capacitor or an inductance. By normalizing to the frequency where the reactance of the element is equal to the resistance (represented by the conditions stated underneath) the response, as a complex attenuation and in db and phase, is reduced to the same simple expressions.

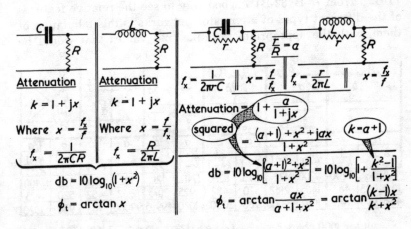

Attenuation

$$k = 1 + jx$$

Where $x = \dfrac{f_x}{f}$

$$f_x = \dfrac{1}{2\pi CR}$$

Attenuation

$$k = 1 + jx$$

Where $x = \dfrac{f}{f_x}$

$$f_x = \dfrac{R}{2\pi L}$$

$$db = 10 \log_{10}(1 + x^2)$$

$$\phi_t = \arctan x$$

$$f_x = \dfrac{1}{2\pi C} \qquad x = \dfrac{f}{f_x} \qquad f_x = \dfrac{r}{2\pi L} \qquad x = \dfrac{f_x}{f}$$

$$\dfrac{r}{R} = a$$

Attenuation $= 1 + \dfrac{a}{1 + jx}$

(squared) $= \dfrac{(a+1) + x^2 + jax}{1 + x^2}$

$$k = a + 1$$

$$db = 10 \log_{10}\left[\dfrac{(a+1)^2 + x^2}{1 + x^2}\right] = 10 \log_{10}\left[1 + \dfrac{k^2 - 1}{1 + x^2}\right]$$

$$\phi_t = \arctan \dfrac{ax}{a + 1 + x^2} = \arctan \dfrac{(k-1)x}{k + x^2}$$

One form of step uses a series resistor with either a capacitor or inductor in parallel. By normalizing response to the frequency at which the reactance of this element is equal to the resistance it parallels (r), we derive expressions for complex attenuation, db, and phase responses. Note that to obtain these identical expressions, x is varied sometimes directly and sometimes inversely with frequency, according to which element is used.

The maximum attenuation in each case is k, or, expressed in db, $20 \log_{10} k$. This means that by regarding the lower or attenuated level as reference, instead of the higher or unattenuated level, you can view the response as a "boost" instead of a "cut." To utilize this reference, we use the frequency where the reactance of the capacitor or inductance element is: (1) equal to R instead of r (see 79-A); (2) equal to $R + r$ instead of r (see 63-B); (3) equal to the parallel combined value of R and r instead of r (see 70-B).

74-A. (From 72-A) *No.* This expression first treats the voltage division between the first two elements, which is a possible approach. But then, for the second voltage division, it assumes the source resistance at the junction of the first is merely the first a element and omits the effect of the b element. If this method were used, by Thevenin's Principle (see 48-A), taking the b element into account as well, the correct answer would be obtained, although this is not the method used to get the correct expression on 72-A. Select one of the other answers.

ATTENUATOR TYPES

74-B. (From 78-B, 82-B) A good way to see the relative features of the different types of attenuator networks is this tabulation of them, with the appropriate formulas and values that would be

a	b	a	b	a	b	a	b	a	$1/a$	a	$1/a$
$\frac{k-1}{k}$	$\frac{1}{k-1}$	$\frac{k}{k-1}$	$k-1$	$\frac{k-1}{k+1}$	$\frac{2k}{k^2-1}$	$\frac{k+1}{k-1}$	$\frac{k^2-1}{2k}$	$k-1$	$\frac{1}{k-1}$	$\frac{k-1}{k+1}$	$\frac{k+1}{k-1}$
108.8	8200	9200	122	57.5	8280	17400	121	122	8200	57.5	17400
685	462	1465	2162	520	482	1925	2075	2162	462	520	1925
990	10.1	1010	99000	980	20.002	1020	49995	99000	10.1	980	1020

(Row labels: 1 db, 10 db, 40 db)

All for 1000 ohms Z_o 1 db $k = 1.122$ 10 db $k = 3.162$ 40 db $k = 100$

used for representative attenuation figures (1 db, 10 db, and 40 db). All these networks are designed for a terminating impedance of 1,000 ohms. This is not a much-used practical impedance, but forms a convenient normalizing value. For a 500-ohm network all values would be exactly half, for example. Checking these values by the formulas will also serve to make sure that you understand their significance. When you've digested this information, turn to 73-B.

74-C. (From 70-B) *No.* You probably have the right idea. The reference frequency for phase response is the geometric mean between the two possible amplitude or attenuation reference frequencies. But you did not notice that for x and z, one is always directly and the other always inversely proportional to frequency. Try another answer.

75-A. (From 56-C) *Correct.* These are exactly the same expressions as those on page 76-A. The difference is that we have followed our method of using conductance values for shunt elements and resistance values for series elements. Many presentations on this subject use resistance values throughout, which leads to the reciprocal values for a in the π-network, while the value for the b element in the T-network will be reciprocal. This system of design enables the same formula to be used for each circuit of a dual pair, as we first noticed in the L-pad design (see 63-A).

If you are not satisfied about this relationship, it is suggested that for verification you follow the same method of deduction used for the T-circuit. Now turn to 64-A.

75-B. (From 94-A) By using pure reactance elements, we can see the essential difference between bridged-T and lattice networks for filtering or equalization purposes. Here we are using a simple inductance for one element and a capacitance for the other, selecting values such that the matching condition is met in each case (see 77-B and 80-A).

The bridged-T network is simple, giving simple expressions for attenuation in db with frequency (normalized by x) and transfer phase response. The expression for k is different for the lattice network. Which is the correct expression to go in the square brackets of the attenuation-in-db formula? Answer 1: see 97-A; answer 2: see 59-A; answer 3: see 91-B.

75-C. (From 95-A) This method is approximately correct and will work for pass- or stop-bands that are relatively wide—a couple of octaves or more. But if it is used for narrow-band filters, the band will always turn out wider than it is calculated, because the series combination of reactances is always less than each by itself, and the parallel combination of susceptances is always less than each by itself. Turn to 81-B for the correct method.

76-A. (From 72-A) *Correct.* This expression is obtained by using as the first factor the actual voltage division that occurs across the first (left-hand) a element and the rest of the network, including the loading effect of the second (right-hand) a element and the output termination. The second factor is the simple voltage division from this point to the output termination. Multiplying the two factors out, as shown here, simplifies the expression somewhat. Then the expression for b in terms of a, obtained from the impedance match condition, is substituted for b, making it possible to simplify the expression for k into relatively simple terms of a. This is then transposed to give a in terms of k.

$$k = \left[1 + a\left(\frac{1+b+ab}{1+a}\right)\right](1+a)$$
$$= 1 + 2a + ab + a^2 b \qquad \boxed{\text{substitute}} \qquad a^2 + \frac{2a}{b} = 1 \qquad b(1-a^2) = 2a \qquad \boxed{b = \frac{2a}{1-a^2}}$$

$$= 1 + 2a + b(a + a^2) = 1 + 2a + \frac{2a^2}{1-a} = \frac{1+a-2a^2+2a^2}{1-a} = \frac{1+a}{1-a} \qquad \boxed{a = \frac{k-1}{k+1}}$$

$$\boxed{b = \frac{2a}{1-a^2} = \frac{2\left(\frac{k-1}{k+1}\right)}{1 - \frac{(k-1)^2}{(k+1)^2}} = \frac{2\left(\frac{k-1}{k+1}\right)}{\frac{4k}{(k+1)^2}} = \frac{k^2-1}{2k}}$$

Finally this expression is substituted into the expression for b in terms of a to give the expression for b in terms of k. This again proves to be relatively simple.

From this point, you may turn either to 56-C, which shows the duality equivalent of this network in the π configuration, or to 64-A, which extends this method to attenuators for two-way matching where the impedances are not identical.

76-B. (From 56-C) *Wrong.* These are reciprocals of the correct values. You probably erred because you have not accustomed yourself to using conductance units for shunt elements. Try another answer.

76-C. (From 62-C) *Wrong.* To start with, when $x = 0$, attenuation is a maximum, not a minimum, which is represented by the equation $\log_{10} 1 = 0$. Then the order of the remaining values shows error: after a value of 1 for $x = 0$, the value for $x = 1$ is highest, and that for $x = k$ (k always being greater than 1) is lowest; the values must be progressive. Try another answer.

77-A. (From 56-C) *Wrong.* Try another answer.

77-B. (From 80-A) *Correct.* If this gave you much trouble, here is our method. Because the network is balanced, we can take some short cuts, instead of considering the whole network. First, by Thevenin's Theorem (see 48-A) we find the current in the output termination. Here z_o' is the source resistance, looking back with zero input impedance, v_o' is the output voltage without the termination connected, and v_o and i_o the actual voltage and current in the output termination. The quantity i_o' is the total input

$$\tfrac{1}{2}v_o' = v_1\frac{\frac{1}{a}}{a+\frac{1}{a}} - \tfrac{1}{2}v_1 = v_1\left[\frac{1}{a^2+1} - \frac{1}{2}\right] = \tfrac{1}{2}v_1\left[\frac{1-a^2}{1+a^2}\right]$$

$$\tfrac{1}{2}z_o' = \frac{a \cdot \frac{1}{a}}{a+\frac{1}{a}} = \frac{a}{1+a^2} \quad\|\quad \tfrac{1}{2}z_o = \frac{a}{1+a^2} + \frac{1}{2} = \frac{(1+a)^2}{2(1+a^2)}$$

$$i_o = \frac{v_o'}{z_o} = v_1\left[\frac{1-a^2}{1+a^2}\right]\left[\frac{1+a^2}{(1+a)^2}\right] = v_1\left[\frac{1-a}{1+a}\right] \begin{array}{l}\text{Output}\\ \text{Current}\end{array}$$

$$\tfrac{1}{2}i_o' = \frac{v_1}{a+\frac{1}{a}} \qquad i_o' = 2v_1\frac{a}{1+a^2}$$

$$i_{01} = i_o\frac{\frac{1}{a}}{a+\frac{1}{a}} = i_o\frac{1}{1+a^2} \quad\Big\| \quad i_{02} = i_o\frac{a}{a+\frac{1}{a}} = i_o\frac{a^2}{1+a^2}$$

$$i_{01} - i_{02} = i_o\left[\frac{1-a^2}{1+a^2}\right] = v_1\left[\frac{1-a}{1+a}\right]\left[\frac{1-a^2}{1+a^2}\right] = v_1\frac{(1-a)^2}{1+a^2}$$

Input Current

$$i_1 = i_o' + (i_{01} - i_{02}) = v_1\left[\frac{2a}{1+a^2} + \frac{(1-a)^2}{1+a^2}\right] = v_1 \quad \underline{\text{verifying matching requirement}}$$

Attenuation $\quad k = \dfrac{i_1}{i_o} = \dfrac{1+a}{1-a}$ $\qquad\boxed{a = \dfrac{k-1}{k+1}}$

current without the output load connected. The output load draws extra current through the a element and draws current in opposition to the main component through the $1/a$ element, these elements being represented by i_{01} and i_{02}. This enables us to write an expression for i_1, the total input current. This simplifies to v_1 because the whole calculation is normalized to the output termination, and the input impedance equals the designed output termination. By evaluating the ratio between input and output current, we deduce the expression for k in terms of a and thus for a in terms of k, which was the one you selected.

Now, are all the two-way impedance-matching networks the same (see 68-B) or different (see 84-A) in their effect when they are not correctly terminated? If you want to see for yourself before you look at the answers, try calculating the input impedance of each when it is (a) unterminated, or open-circuited, and (b) terminated in a short circuit.

78-A. (From 64-A) *Correct.* The only way the result could differ, if the attenuation and matching are the same, is in mismatch reflection, which is dealt with in 77-B. Now turn to 80-A.

78-B. (From 68-B) *Wrong.* It is easy to check. Try solving for the values to replace the series T-arms, maintaining the condition that the output series T-arm is at null, and you'll find both conditions (forward and back, along with attenuation) cannot be achieved simultaneously. Turn to 74-B.

78-C. (From 70-B) *Correct.* Here is the correct sequence of substitution, in case you ran into difficulty. Also, we have drawn a complete graph of the response, particularly for the capacitor circuit. Frequency is plotted to logarithmic scale in the usual

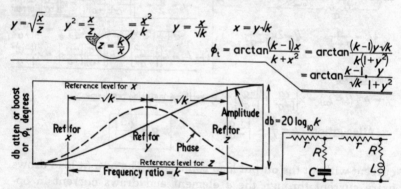

$$y = \sqrt{\frac{x}{z}} \qquad y^2 = \frac{x}{z} = \frac{x^2}{k} \qquad y = \frac{x}{\sqrt{k}} \qquad x = y\sqrt{k}$$

$$\left(z = \frac{k}{x} \right)$$

$$\phi_t = \arctan\frac{(k-1)x}{k+x^2} = \arctan\frac{(k-1)y\sqrt{k}}{k(1+y^2)}$$
$$= \arctan\frac{k-1}{\sqrt{k}}\frac{y}{1+y^2}$$

$$db = 20\log_{10}k$$

manner, increasing from left to right. This clarifies the relationship between the various references for normalizing. Note that the phase reference, as well as being the geometric mean between the two attenuation or amplitude references, is the point at which phase-transfer response reaches a maximum angle.

Now we turn to consider the other basic step-network, shown at the bottom right for capacitive and inductive elements. For the db response the attenuation and boost reference frequencies are respectively the frequencies at which the reactance is equal to:

1. R and the combination $R + r$ (see 62-C).
2. r and the combination of R and r in parallel (see 85-A).
3. R and r in parallel, and R (see 79-B).

79-A. (From 73-B) *Wrong.* If you substitute $x = 1$ into the expression, and use a value of k such as 10 (20-db step) you'll find that attenuation is within 3 db of maximum at the attenuation reference frequency. If the reactance is a capacitor, the slope is up (less attenuation) with increasing frequency. So the boost reference frequency will be higher than the attenuation reference frequency (the reverse occurs with inductance). But as R is 9 times r (for $k = 10$), the frequency where reactance is equal to R instead of r will be lower, not higher. The same argument can be followed through for inductance. Try another answer.

79-B. (From 78-C) *Wrong.* The value R is one of them, but it is at the other end. The parallel combination has nothing to do with this configuration, although it is a shunt step-circuit. Try another answer.

79-C. (From 85-C) The real point here is whether the phase responses at f_1, f_3 and at f_4, f_6 are identical or different. They are identical. If you refer back to the basic steps (see 78-C), you will find that substituting y equal to either $\sqrt{k}$, or its reciprocal will

$$\phi = \arctan \frac{k-1}{\sqrt{k}} \cdot \frac{y}{1+y^2} \text{ where } y = \frac{x}{\sqrt{k}} \text{ and } x = \frac{1}{S\left(u - \frac{1}{u}\right)}$$

$$= \arctan S(k-1)\frac{u - \frac{1}{u}}{S^2 k\left(u - \frac{1}{u}\right)^2 + 1}$$

When $u - \frac{1}{u} = 0$ $\left[\text{at } f_m\right]$ $\phi_t = \arctan 0 = 0$

When $u - \frac{1}{u} = \frac{1}{S\sqrt{k}}$ $\left[\text{at } f_2 f_5\right]$ $\phi_t = \arctan \pm \frac{\frac{k-1}{\sqrt{k}}}{1+1}$

When $u - \frac{1}{u} = \frac{1}{S}$ $\left[\text{at } f_1 f_6\right]$ $\phi_t = \arctan \pm \frac{k-1}{k+1}$

$$= \arctan \pm \frac{k-1}{2\sqrt{k}}$$

When $u - \frac{1}{u} = \frac{1}{Sk}$ $\left[\text{at } f_3 f_4\right]$ $\phi_t = \arctan \pm \frac{\frac{k-1}{k}}{\frac{1}{k}+1}$

$$= \arctan \pm \frac{k-1}{k+1}$$

yield identical values of ϕ_t. Here we've followed the derivation through to the complete phase expression for the peaking or absorption networks (the only difference is reversal of sign), to show that the expression for phase angle is the same as that in the prototype step-networks, justifying curve AA on 85-C.

Now, which is correct: for peaking circuits the transfer phase angle represents advance below the peak and delay above, and vice versa for absorption circuits (see 89-A); or, for peaking circuits the transfer phase angle represents delay below the peak and advance above, and vice versa for absorption circuits (see 80-C)?

80

BRIDGED-T AND LATTICE TYPES

80-A. (From 78-A) Now we consider two types that have features useful for applications (examples at 75-B and 91-A) other than simple attenuation. The bridged-T type has a very simple derivation. If you use the value relationship shown, the voltage division ratios at the T center and at the output, due to the bridge and output termination, are the same. This means there is no voltage or current in the output arm of the T. Once a relationship is established at which this holds true, the impedance calculation

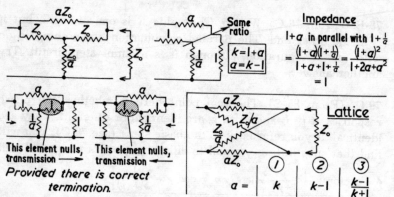

This element nulls, transmission →
This element nulls, transmission ←
Provided there is correct termination.

is simple to check, and the attenuation even simpler. Note that the null condition across the T arms depends on which way transmission takes place. Also note that the value of these arms is equal to the working impedance, Z_o. To verify this, assume that these arms have an arbitrary value, say, b. You will find that the attenuation and impedance conditions can only be satisfied simultaneously by making $b = 1$. Finally note that correct matching, as with other networks, only occurs with correct termination at the other end.

The lattice network is similar in that a pair of elements have values multiplied by a and a pair have values divided by the same factor. The bridged-T has one element each. But is the value of a for the lattice the formula identified as 1 (see 82-A), 2 (see 67-C), or 3 (see 77-B)?

80-B. (From 84-B) *No.* That must have been a guess; so try the other answer.

80-C. (From 79-C) *No,* it was the other one.

81-A. (From 93-A) *No.* The answer was 'yes.'

81-B. (From 95-A) *Correct.* The difference in derivation consists of taking the other element into account. The combined reactance of each series pair must be correct at each design frequency, whether band-pass or band-stop, while the combined susceptance (or reactance) of each parallel pair must also be correct at these two frequencies.

Since the effect of two reactances in series, or two susceptances in parallel, is to make the combined value change more rapidly with frequency than a single reactance, the characteristics are similar to those of individual low- and high-pass networks, but with the frequency scale compressed according to the interaction

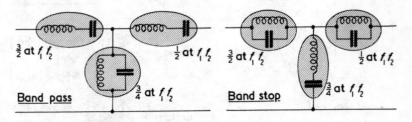

relationship determined by the ratio between f_1 and f_2. This means that to give a constant-resistance input a band-pass network cannot be combined with a low-pass or high-pass network whose cutoff is the same as one of the band-pass design frequencies, although it may approximate the condition. However, a succession of band-pass filters of this type may be connected in series or parallel (the latter for the type shown here) and will then provide a constant-resistance input, provided each has the same width ratio and is correctly terminated.

Note, however, that such a succession of filters will have an overall phase characteristic that rotates through several cycles. Each element of the type shown will rotate phase through three-quarters of a cycle and be displaced three-quarters of a cycle from the output of its neighbor. Now turn to 66-B.

81-C. (From 102-A) *No.* See the other answer.

82

82-A. (From 80-A) *No.* This answer had to be a guess. Try one of the other answers.

82-B. (From 68-B) *Correct.* It may not be too obvious. See 78-B if you want to know how to check the conclusion. Now turn to 74-B.

82-C. (From 61-B) *Correct.* Here's the transfer formula developed from the basic formula, merely by substituting $x = f/f_c$ (f_c is the critical frequency), and simplifying. Assuming this is for a null case (the formula becomes much more difficult to handle

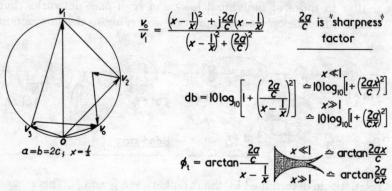

$$\frac{v_o}{v_i} = \frac{\left(x - \frac{1}{x}\right)^2 + j\frac{2a}{c}\left(x - \frac{1}{x}\right)}{\left(x - \frac{1}{x}\right)^2 + \left(\frac{2a}{c}\right)^2}$$

$\frac{2a}{c}$ is "sharpness" factor

$$db = 10\log_{10}\left[1 + \left(\frac{\frac{2a}{c}}{x - \frac{1}{x}}\right)^2\right]$$

$x \ll 1 \quad \simeq 10\log_{10}\left[1 + \left(\frac{2ax}{c}\right)^2\right]$

$x \gg 1 \quad \simeq 10\log_{10}\left[1 + \left(\frac{2a}{cx}\right)^2\right]$

$$\phi_t = \arctan\frac{\frac{2a}{c}}{x - \frac{1}{x}}$$

$x \ll 1 \quad \simeq \arctan\frac{2ax}{c}$

$x \gg 1 \quad \simeq \arctan\frac{2a}{cx}$

$a = b = 2c; \quad x = \frac{1}{2}$

for the other cases, beyond just the critical relation given on 61-B), we substitute for b so that only one pair of relative values occurs in the final form.

The term that recurs in the formulas, $2a/c$, can be regarded as a "sharpness" factor. The larger the value of this factor, the sharper the response curve shaping, in both db and phase. Note also the approximations when x is either much smaller or larger than 1. These can be a help in combining the complete absorption of one frequency with a roll-off, to obtain de-emphasis in radio reception, for example.

The expression for v_o/v_i is an equation for a circle, whatever value the factor $2a/c$ has. This merely changes the rate at which the point moves round the circle with change in value of x.

The dual form of the twin-T circuit uses two π networks. These are combined (1) in series at input and output—see 98-B; (2) in parallel at input, series at output—see 101-B; (3) in series at input, parallel at output—see 87-D.

83-A. (From 64-A) *Wrong.* See the other answer.

83-B. (From 87-C) *No.* The point at which peak occurs is controlled partly by the value of R (on page 66-B) and partly by the value of r. So the value of peak frequency is a function not only of R but of both quantities. It should therefore be evident that reflection of a resistance load due to L, C, and R coincident with peak response including r can only occur for certain relationships between r and R relative to L and C. See the other answer.

83-C. (From 103-A) Simple substitution of any values in a ratio of $9:1$ for r and R will not produce the required result because, as we showed on 84-B, source and load resistances affect the overall response characteristic. For the high-frequency boost, the value of R is modified; for the low-frequency boost, it is r that

$$\underline{k=10} \qquad \text{For high end} \quad k = 1 + \frac{r}{\dfrac{10^6 R}{10^6 + R} + 5 \cdot 10^4} = 1 + \frac{(10^6 + R)r}{5 \cdot 10^{10} + 1.05 \cdot 10^6 R}$$

$$\text{For low end} \quad k = 1 + \frac{(5 \cdot 10^4 + r)10^6}{(r + 1.05 \cdot 10^6)R} \longrightarrow \begin{cases} 10^6 r + Rr = 9[5 \cdot 10^{10} + 1.05 \cdot 10^6 R] \\ 5 \cdot 10^{10} + 10^6 r = 9[rR + 1.05 \cdot 10^6 R] \end{cases}$$

$$Rr = 5 \cdot 10^{10} \qquad r - 9.45R = 4 \cdot 10^5 \qquad \text{Solve for } r \text{ \& } R \qquad \begin{cases} r = 9.16 \cdot 10^5 \\ R = 5.46 \cdot 10^4 \\ \text{(Positive roots)} \end{cases}$$

Verification

Equivalent R for high end:

$$\frac{5.46 \cdot 10^4 \times 10^6}{5.46 \cdot 10^4 + 10^6} + 5 \cdot 10^4 = 10.17 \cdot 10^4 \simeq \frac{r}{9} \checkmark$$

Equivalent r for low end:

$$\frac{9.66 \cdot 10^5 \times 10^6}{9.66 \cdot 10^5 + 10^6} = 4.92 \cdot 10^5 \simeq 9R \checkmark$$

Preferred values:

$r = 910K.$

$R = 56K.$

is modified. Use these formulas and solve as simultaneous equations for r and R (actual values, according to the circuit on 103-A, not the values shown on 62-C and 73-B).

To verify these results, substitute into the formulas to find the equivalent R for the high end, which should be 1/9 the value of r; and the equivalent value of r for the low end, which should be 9 times the value of R. Within the limits of approximate calculation, these check, so proceed to calculate the values of C_1 and C_2. If you have difficulty in deciding how to do this, turn to 69-B.

84

84-A. (From 77-B) *Wrong*. It is true the one-way matching networks do not reflect equal mismatch for the same amount of attenuation, regardless of type, but the two-way types do. See the other answer.

84-B. (From 62-C) *Correct*. These values are important, because they are the attenuations at the three reference frequencies (given here in terms of x) and at $x = 0$. The attenuation at $x = 0$ is the full ultimate attenuation of the step. Attenuation at $x = 1$ is often erroneously taken as the 3-db point from maximum attenuation. It does correspond in a way with the 3-db and 45°

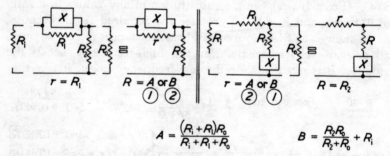

$$A = \frac{(R_i + R_l)R_o}{R_i + R_l + R_o} \qquad\qquad B = \frac{R_2 R_o}{R_2 + R_o} + R_i$$

point of the simple cutoff (left side of 73-B). In large steps (more than 20 db) the attenuation is close to 3 db from maximum, but in smaller steps it is markedly less. The attenuation at $x = \sqrt{k}$ is the mid-point, half the ultimate ($\log_{10} k$ is half of $\log_{10} k^2$). The attenuation at $x = k$ corresponds to the 3-db point in a cutoff response, but it is always less than 3 db, although it comes close for large steps.

Now we turn to applying step networks to practical circuits. Here we have each configuration, using R_1 and R_2 in place of r and R respectively, and the network is inserted between input and output impedances of R_i and R_o respectively. To apply the formulas of 62-C, 70-B, 73-B, and 78-C, we need to convert these values into equivalent r and R respectively. Below the two configurations we have indicated the obvious correspondences: $r = R_1$ at the left, and $R = R_2$ at the right. Which is the correct identification of values A and B for the remaining values, (1) or (2)? Answer: 1; see 80-B. Answer: 2; see 71-B.

84-C. (From 61-B) Wrong this time. You can be excused for making this mistake, because you haven't yet been given the formula for the response aside from null. So try the other answer.

85-A. (From 78-C) *Wrong.* This was the combination for the series step-circuit of 73-B, but it is incorrect here. Try another answer.

85-B. (From 71-B) *Wrong.* This is a possible basis for sharpness or width reference, but it is not the one we have used. See the other answer.

85-C. (From 88-A) *Correct.* In an equation of this type, it does not matter what value k has. So if one solution is taken for a value that is $\sqrt{k}$, then the solution for an identical equation using k will double all the exponents of k in the solution. That is, $\sqrt{k}$ becomes k, and k becomes k^2. Notice also that we have taken a solution (last line, right, 88-A) that allows u to be positive in every case. This was done by using plus or minus the sum of u and its reciprocal in the original equation (71-B), with the meaning that the positive sign applies for values of u greater than unity and the negative sign for values smaller than unity. Switching this around in the solution, the surd term of the quadratic solution is always positive, and the other term, whose sign is normally fixed (either $+$ or $-$) has alternative signs ($\pm$).

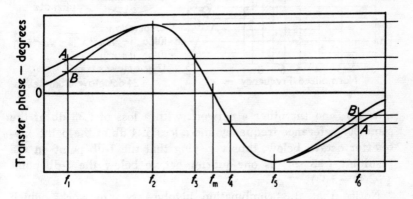

Now we have a universalized form for the attenuation or amplitude aspect of the response with these networks. How about phase response? Which is correct, *AA* (see 79-C) or *BB* (see 86-A)?

85-D. (From 70-B) *No.* Try the substitution and you will see that it does not result in the required form. Try another answer.

86

86-A. (From 85-C) *Wrong.* See the other answer.

86-B. (From 88-A) Why not? The change is a simple substitution. See the other answer.

86-C. (From 91-A) *Wrong.* One pair of values is right, but, for the other, you inverted the value of S. Try again.

86-D. (From 92-B) *Correct.* The method of derivation is the same as for the simpler network. Now $(1 + x^8)$ can be factored into the two expressions shown, one of which represents a peaking network with its peak 3 db at one-quarter octave below reference frequency (the 90° point at +2.33 db at reference fre-

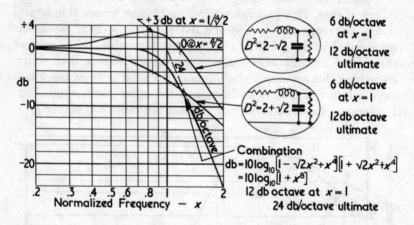

quency), and the other a network with a loss of 5.33 db at the same 90° reference frequency and a loss of 4 db at the point one-quarter octave below, thus verifying that the 1-db point on the resultant (+3 −4) is one-quarter octave below the 3-db point (+2.33 −5.33).

Notice that this combination involves two networks which involve essential interaction (see 100-A). For more involved response synthesis, we shall merely outline the most direct method, because the number of possible combinations becomes virtually endless. Turn to 90-B.

87-A. (From 65-A) *Wrong*. This answer has a double inversion. Try one of the others. There are many variables for such a relatively simple circuit, but it is worth making a little effort to make sure you understand how it works.

87-B. (From 62-C) *Wrong*. The sequence looks good, progressing from smaller values to larger—at least if k is greater than 2. But it is inverted, because *maximum* attenuation, not zero, occurs at $x = 0$. Also the values at $x = 1$ and $x = k$ are not precisely 3 db from zero and ultimate attenuation, which would be true for the values given here. Try another answer.

87-C. (From 66-B) Correct, for this particular network, although this does not form a precedent for more complicated networks. To prove this we merely differentiate the expression for amplitude k^2 (it is easier to use this, because we eliminate j) with respect to x, using logarithmic units for each, which is implied by

$$\frac{d \log k^2}{d \log x} = \frac{d \log k^2}{d \log x^2}\left(\frac{d \log x^2}{d \log x}\right) = \frac{2x\,[(D^2-2)+2x^2]}{1+(D^2-2)x^2+x^4}$$

$$k^2 = 1 + (D^2-2)x^2 + x^4$$

$$\log x^2 = 2\log x \quad \text{So} \quad \frac{d \log x^2}{d \log x} = 2$$

When $x = 1$
$$\frac{d \log k^2}{d \log x} = \frac{2D^2}{D^2} = 2$$

When $x^2 = \frac{2-D^2}{2}$?

6 db/octave

the "db/octave" unit of slope. Since $d \log k^2/d \log x$ evaluates to 2 when $x = 1$, the slope at this point is 6 db/octave, independent of the value of D and of how that value of D is derived from d and a.

Now we take another special value of x: that which, for values of D^2 less than 2 (which means the response contains a peak), gives a slope of zero (and therefore is the peak frequency). Does this have a unique relationship to phase response, such as that the impedance looking to the right from r is resistive at this point (see 83-B), or does this coincidence only occur under certain circumstances (see 102-A)?

87-D. (From 82-C) *Wrong*. Draw the circuit, and try to figure out what happens when you parallel the outputs. Starting with series inputs, the outputs are naturally in series. Paralleling them will short-circuit the output.

88-A. (From 71-B) *Correct.* Factor S relates the reactance value to the series element r (Circuit A of 71-B); and where reactance is equal to r, attenuation is within 3 db of maximum. For the other boost or peaking circuit (B), S relates to R, but the same reference is true for level. For hole or absorption circuits, the logical relations of S (at left here) are to points within 3 db of

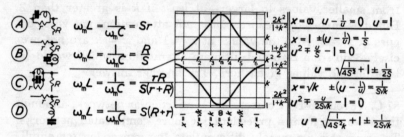

$$ (A) \quad \omega_m L = \frac{1}{\omega_m C} = Sr $$

$$ (B) \quad \omega_m L = \frac{1}{\omega_m C} = \frac{R}{S} $$

$$ (C) \quad \omega_m L = \frac{1}{\omega_m C} = \frac{rR}{S(r+R)} $$

$$ (D) \quad \omega_m L = \frac{1}{\omega_m C} = S(R+r) $$

$$ \frac{2k^2}{1+k^2} \quad x=\infty \quad u-\tfrac{1}{u}=0 \quad u=1 $$

$$ k \qquad x=1 \quad \pm(u-\tfrac{1}{u})=\tfrac{1}{S} $$

$$ \frac{1+k^2}{2} \qquad u^2 \mp \tfrac{u}{S}-1=0 $$

$$ u=\sqrt{\tfrac{1}{4S^2}+1}\pm\tfrac{1}{2S} $$

$$ \frac{1+k^2}{2} $$

$$ k \qquad x=\sqrt{k} \quad \pm(u-\tfrac{1}{u})=\tfrac{1}{S\sqrt{k}} $$

$$ \frac{2k^2}{1+k^2} \qquad u^2 \mp \tfrac{u}{2S\sqrt{k}}-1=0 $$

$$ u=\sqrt{\tfrac{1}{4S^2 k}+1}\pm\tfrac{1}{2S\sqrt{k}} $$

flat (farthest from hole). Thus, comparing with the step (78-C) the reference *level* for x is the top of the peak or the bottom of the dip, where x has a value of infinity. Reference turnover is nearest flat (farthest from peak or dip). At the right are expressions for the 7 critical frequencies relative to these curves, which correspond with the step circuit's 3 critical frequencies. The mid-frequency we designate f_m; the remaining six, in pairs, correspond to $x = 1$, $x = \sqrt{k}$ and $x = k$. We have found expressions for u (frequency normalized to f_m) for values $x = 1$ and $x = \sqrt{k}$. For the points representing $x = k$, would you substitute k for $\sqrt{k}$ and k^2 for k? If so, see 85-C; if not, see 86-B.

88-B. (From 104-A) Derivation of formulas used for this example is found on 93-A and 95-A. Using these factors, values are

$Z_o = 16$ ohms $\omega = 6280$ $\omega L_1 = 24$ohms	$L_1 = \underline{3.82 \text{ mH}}$	
$\omega L_2 = 12$ ohms	$L_2 = 1.91$mH.	$L_3 = 1.27$mH.
$\dfrac{1}{\omega C_1} = 24$ohms $C_1 = \underline{6.6\mu F.}$ $\omega L_3 = \dfrac{1}{\omega C_3} = 8$ ohms		
$\dfrac{1}{\omega C_2} = 12$ohms	$C_2 = \underline{13.3\mu F.}$	$C_3 = \underline{19.9 \mu F.}$

L.P. L_1 C_2 L_3 / C_1 L_2 C_3 H.P.

calculated from simple reactance formulas. In practice, values can be rounded out to convenient values, and the low-pass unit can include the voice-coil inductance in L_3, if it feeds a dynamic speaker. But deviation should not be too large (not more than, say, 5%) in this circuit. Bigger deviations are permissible in the simpler circuits.

89-A. (From 79-C) *Correct*. This can be figured out in a variety of ways. In coupling circuits that produce low-frequency cutoff, the transfer phase is leading (the output is advanced in phase compared to the input), while in circuits that produce high-frequency cutoff, the transfer phase is lagging. From this we may deduce that an upward-sloping amplitude response (attenuation reducing with increasing frequency) is accompanied by phase advance, whereas a downward-sloping one is accompanied by phase delay. Is this always true? (See last paragraph of 100-A.)

Alternatively, more detailed figuring will verify the truth of this in each case, by giving the phase response for each network. Now turn to 91-A.

89-B. (From 90-B) *Correct*. Real values, or values with correct signs, will only occur if the requirements substituted into the problem involve making the turnover "sharper" than the maximal flatness curve of that order (highest power of x^2 in the expression). If the requirements are exceeded anyway by the maximal flatness curve, then the latter will give better performance than the requirements used for substitution. Turn to 101-A.

89-C. (From 103-A) The correct answer is (2) 263 and 4,750 ohms. The attenuation factor was $k = 20$. Answers (3) and (4) used a value of $k = 400$, taking db $= 10 \log_{10} k$, instead of db $= 20 \log_{10} k$, which is the correct formula here, because we are dealing with voltage ratio, not power ratio. Answers (1) and (3) made the mistake of taking reciprocal expressions for quantities a and b. The relevant material will be found on 63-A, 65-A, and 74-B.

89-D. (From 103-A) The correct answer is (4) 153 micromicrofarads. This again is a question of using the right value for source resistance, which as shown in the previous answer (99-A) was 37.5K. The effective circuit impedance that the total circuit capacitance shunts is the parallel combination of this and the 470K resistor, which calculates to 34.8K. For frequency to be 30 kc, ω is 188,400. Substituting to find C gives the answer of 153 micromicrofarads.

90

90-A. (From 91-A) *Wrong.* Somehow, you inverted the value of S, which in this case is fractional, because the width at the points 3 db up (off the scale range shown) is several octaves. Try another answer.

90-B. (From 86-D) Here we show the general method of synthesizing response by combining networks. We use mathematical calculation to select responses that complement one another, approximately, up to a certain point. Any peaking circuit, whether using two or more reactances, will have a particular slope-amplitude relationship, as will each non-peaking circuit, as represented at one point by A and B for each respectively.

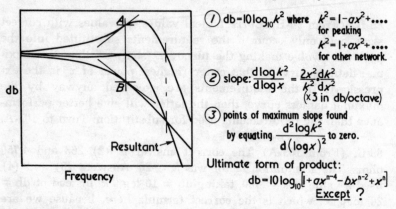

① $db = 10 \log_{10} k^2$ where $k^2 = 1 - ax^2 + \ldots$
 for peaking
 $k^2 = 1 + ax^2 + \ldots$
 for other network.

② slope: $\dfrac{d \log k^2}{d \log x} = \dfrac{2x^2}{k^2} \dfrac{dk^2}{dx^2}$
 (×3 in db/octave)

③ points of maximum slope found by equating $\dfrac{d^2 \log k^2}{d (\log x)^2}$ to zero.

Ultimate form of product:
$db = 10 \log_{10}[1 + ax^{n-4} - bx^{n-2} + x^n]$
<u>Except</u> ?

First select a form that ensures that the terms in x^2 have complementary coefficients (equal, with one positive and one negative). Then derive the slope expression, and equate the positive slope of the B curve to the maximum negative slope (upward) of the A curve, and also equate attenuation to boost at the same points. When these three conditions are applied, the ultimate form of the product expression will be that shown, with an exception that we will mention in a moment.

Having digested this, you may wish to apply it to narrow-band circuits (see 250-C). Alternatively, by inverting positions, the networks can be used for high-pass responses (low cutoffs) merely by using $1/x$ for frequency-normalizing in 66-B, 86-D, 87-C, 92-B, 100-A, 102-A. The exception is when the solution does not yield values for constants a and b which have the signs shown. In this case; (1) the signs should be changed to those shown (96A), or (2) the nearest approach is the maximal flatness curve (89-B).

BRIDGED-T EQUALIZER DESIGN

91-A. (From 89-A) As an example in using the formulas for peak and hole networks, as well as the bridged-T attenuator (see 80-A and 88-A), we'll design a circuit, shown here, to give a peak 24-db high (from broad-band reference level), with a center frequency of 800 cycles (taking ω as 5,000 will serve) and an octave to each half-attenuation point of 12 db. The network is to be inserted in a 600-ohm line, so that it will provide constant resistance matching both ways.

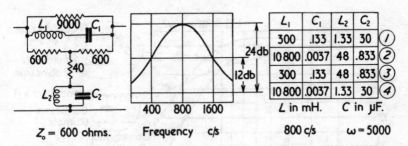

	L_1	C_1	L_2	C_2	
	300	.133	1.33	30	①
	10800	.0037	48	.833	②
	300	.133	48	.833	③
	10800	.0037	1.33	30	④

L in mH. C in μF.

$Z_o = 600$ ohms.   Frequency c/s   800 c/s $\omega = 5000$

This is really a double application of the simple peaking circuits, based on the prototype step-networks (see 71-B). The bridge elements in conjunction with the terminating load provide the desired response, while the internal 600-ohm resistor and the center leg of the T provide a duplicate response, using a configuration that is the dual of the first, so the combined input impedance is constant, and the outgoing arm of the T is across a null at all frequencies. Only the bridged-T can achieve this particular response, while providing constant resistance reflection both ways.

After using the relevant formulas, find which of the groups of values is the correct one for this purpose. If you select no. 1, turn to 86-C; if 2, turn to 92-A; if 3, turn to 94-A; if 4, turn to 90-A.

91-B. (From 75-B) *Wrong.* Were you uncertain between this answer and number 1? Try again.

92

92-A. (From 91-A) *Wrong.* One pair of values is right, but, for the other, you inverted the value of S. Try again.

RESPONSE SYNTHESIS

92-B. (From 100-A) Networks of this type and more complicated types can be used to synthesize a desired overall characteristic, for which proper calculations can save a lot of experimenting time. First let us suppose a two-reactance roll-off is to be combined with a single-reactance roll-off, to give maximal flatness response—that is, minimum deviation from flatness before the

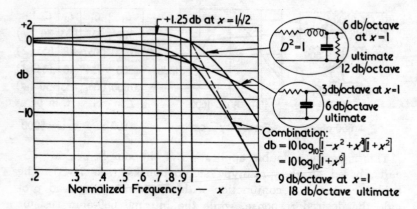

roll-off actually commences. The proper combination for that purpose is shown here. The two-reactance network gives a peak of 1.25 db one-half an octave below the ultimate roll-off and crosses the zero line at the ultimate roll-off frequency. The single-reactance roll-off has its 3-db point at the ultimate roll-off frequency. The combination, a product of $(1 - x^2 + x^4)$ for the two-reactance network and $(1 + x^2)$ for the single-reactance one, gives a response that is $10 \log_{10} (1 + x^6)$.

The 1-db point on a single-reactance network is an octave from cutoff. For a two-reactance maximal flatness, this distance is reduced to half an octave. This network reduces it to one-third. A combination of two two-reactance networks of different characteristics can make a maximal flatness response where this ratio is one-quarter octave. The responses needed are (1) with $+3$ db at the 90° point and -6 db at the 90° point (see 94-B), or (2) with a 3-db peak one-quarter octave below cutoff and 5.33-db loss at the 90° point of the other network (see 86-D).

COMPLEMENTARY FILTERS

93-A. (From 59-A) Consider now some properties of a pair of simple filters, one of which is an inductance feeding a resistance load, and the other is a capacitor. With each normalized to the frequency where its reactance is equal to the terminating load, we derive expressions for attenuation (k), amplitude (db), and transfer phase response. Note that when $x = 1$, the transfer phase angle has a tangent of 1, so the angle is 45 degrees—half the ultimate of 90 degrees. We also take the input impedance and admittance, normalized to the terminating impedance and admittance respectively. Adding the two admittances together, we find that they add up to unity, independent of frequency (x).

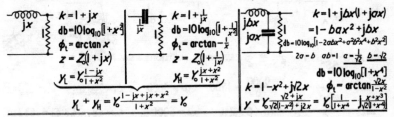

Now we turn to a network consisting of an inductance in series combined with a capacitor in shunt. Using factors a and b for the susceptance and reactance at the normalizing frequency, we derive an attenuation expression. In the db response, by substituting special relationships, we can simplify it to $10 \log_{10} (1 + x^4)$—that is, the x^2 term vanishes. Using these values of a and b, we also get the phase transfer response expression (for $x = 1$, the tangent is infinite, so the angle is 90°) and the admittance expression. In the final form of this, notice the effect of interchanging the position of L and C in the network: x becomes its reciprocal, $1/x$. The real part of y will have the same denominator, with x^4 for numerator. The imaginary part will be identical except for the sign ($+j$ instead of $-j$). So the total admittance of the two networks will always be unity.

Now look at the three-element network: by making the db response expression of the form $10 \log_{10} (1 + x^6)$, the phase and admittance exhibit similar properties (see 60-B) or do not exhibit similar properties (see 81-A).

94

94-A. (From 91-A) *Correct.* In case you had difficulty, here is the calculation. First, note that 24 db is almost exactly 16:1 attenuation ratio. So k is 16, $\sqrt{k}$ is 4, and a, or r/R, is 15. This gives the bridging resistor as 9,000 ohms and the middle-leg resistor as 40 ohms, verifying the values given on 91-A. Now the condition stated gives the values of f_2 and f_5, normalized to middle frequency, as one octave each side. Substituting the known values of k and $\sqrt{k}$ into the formula (88-A) gives S as 1/6. Don't make the mistake of taking this value as its reciprocal, 6. Again using the formula from 88-A, we find the correct set of values for this network.

$$24\,\text{db} = 16{:}1 \qquad k = 16 \qquad \sqrt{k} = 4 \qquad a = 15 \qquad\qquad 600 \times 15 = 9000 \checkmark \quad 600 \div 15 = 40\checkmark$$

$$\text{At } f_5 \ \sqrt{\tfrac{1}{4S^2 k} + 1} + \tfrac{1}{2S\sqrt{k}} = 2 \qquad \sqrt{\tfrac{1}{64S^2} + 1} + \tfrac{1}{8S} = 2 \qquad \sqrt{\tfrac{1}{64S^2} + 1} = 2 - \tfrac{1}{8S}$$

$$\tfrac{1}{64S^2} + 1 = 4 - \tfrac{1}{2S} + \tfrac{1}{64S^2}$$

$$\text{At } f_2 \ \sqrt{\tfrac{1}{64S^2} + 1} - \tfrac{1}{8S} = \tfrac{1}{2} \quad\text{same solution}\Longrightarrow\quad S = \tfrac{1}{6}$$

$$\omega L_1 = \tfrac{1}{\omega C_1} = Sr = \tfrac{9000}{6} = 1500 \qquad \omega = 5000 \qquad L_1 = \underline{300\,\text{mH}} \quad C_1 = \underline{.133\,\mu\text{F}}$$

$$\omega L_2 = \tfrac{1}{\omega C_2} = \tfrac{R}{S} = 40 \times 6 = 240 \qquad \omega = 5000 \qquad L_2 = \underline{48\,\text{mH}} \quad C_2 = \underline{.833\,\mu\text{F}}$$

An interesting check is to follow through on the symmetry of values to the operating impedance, 600 ohms. The reactances with subscripts of 1 each have a value that is 1,500 ohms, or 2.5 times 600. The reactances with subscripts of 2 each have a value that is 240 ohms, or 600 divided by 2.5. Now turn to 75-B.

94-B. (From 92-B) This is close but not strictly correct. But because of its closeness, it has some useful possibilities. The expressions for these two networks are, for peaking, $10 \log_{10} (1 - 1.5x^2 + x^4)$, and for the other, $10 \log_{10} (1 + 2x^2 + x^4)$. The log of the product of the two arguments is $10 \log_{10} (1 + 0.5x^2 - x^4 + 0.5x^6 + x^8)$. Notice that at the cutoff frequency, $x = 1$, the middle three terms cancel, which they almost do for quite a stretch on either side of this frequency. In fact the maximum error from maximal flatness is about 0.1 db. Because the network combination comes this close, and because the second expression also represents two identical noninteracting single-reactance roll-offs, this combination is sometimes simpler to use in practical circuits than the one that is strictly correct. See 200-A for an example where this method is used. However, for the strictly correct method, see 86-D.

95-A. (From 60-B) Here we summarize the constant-resistance filter types, also commonly known as *crossovers*. Each pair consists of a low-pass and high-pass output and, when correctly terminated by the normalizing impedance at both outputs, presents that value at the input at all frequencies. Values of reactance at the crossover frequency are given (low-pass and high-pass have the same cutoff frequency) normalized to the terminating impedance.

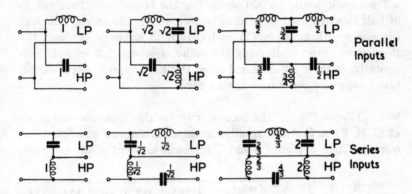

Response is 3 db down at crossover to each output (half-power to each) and total power delivered to the two outputs is constant. The more elements in the network, the sharper is the transition from one network to the other. The difference in phase transfer is also constant. For the single-element networks it is 90°, for the two-element networks it is 180°, and for the three-element networks it is 270°. It is a useful mathematical exercise to verify these statements from the formulas developed on pages 60-B and 93-A.

Now suppose you had to design filters to provide band-pass or band-stop characteristics, instead of low- or high-pass. To get correct performance you would:

1. Put low- and high-pass elements of the type shown here in cascade, instead of in series or parallel (see 72-B).
2. Combine individual series and shunt elements for each function, using the respective cutoff frequencies, in series and parallel resonant combinations (see 75-C).
3. Use a configuration identical to that described in answer 2, but with values differently derived (see 81-B).

96

96-A. (From 90-B) *No.* This is not the way to treat a mathematical solution. The result will be nothing like the original expression if you change signs. When a sign is changed, the coefficient is just as different—if not more so—than that obtained by substituting a different number.

96-B. (From 103-A) The correct answer is (4) 265 and 75.2 ohms. Using the formula for a in this network, the whole resistance for a T network would be 530 ohms. For the H network, four values of half this are used instead of two values at 530 ohms. This was the error with answers (1) and (3). With answers (1) and (2) there is an error in deriving the value of b, which does not, incidentally, have to be changed from the prototype T network because only one resistance is still used.

96-C. (From 104-A) The basic circuit for this example was given at 81-B. First find the relative reactances needed at center frequency. Then evaluate L and C for each element of the network,

$\frac{1}{3}$ octave $= 2^{\frac{1}{3}}$ which is
$2^{\pm\frac{1}{6}}$ from center frequency
$2^{\frac{1}{6}} - 2^{-\frac{1}{6}} = 1.1225 - .891$
$= .2315$

$\omega L_1 = \dfrac{1}{\omega C_1} = \dfrac{15000}{.2315} = 64800$

$\omega L_2 = \dfrac{1}{\omega C_2} = .2315 \times 7500 = 1737$

$\omega L_3 = \dfrac{1}{\omega C_3} = \dfrac{5000}{.2315} = 21600$

Center freq.	20	25.2	31.7	40	50.4	63.4
ω	125.8	158.2	199	251.6	316.4	398
L_1	515H	410H	325H	258H	205H	163H
C_1	.123µF	.0975µF	.0775µF	.0615µF	.0487µF	.0388µF
L_2	13.8H	10.97H	8.71H	6.9H	5.49H	5.36H
C_2	4.58µF	3.64µF	2.89µF	2.29µF	1.82µF	1.45µF
L_3	172H	136.7H	108.5H	86H	68.4H	54.3H
C_3	.368µF	.293µF	.232µF	.184µF	.146µF	.116µF
Continue by dividing both Ls and Cs by 2 every third column $\longrightarrow$						

for each frequency in turn. This is easier to do by tabulating in the manner we have shown here. As each reactance is between 4 and 5 times (reciprocal of .2315) the working impedance required at the center frequency (or, on the shunt elements, divided by this factor) the Q-factor on inductors should be several times this factor. For the lower frequencies a value of 20 might be accepted because of the difficulty in attaining higher values. For higher frequencies, at least 30 would be considered essential.

97-A. (From 75-B) *Wrong*. You were apparently trying to deduce it, instead of figuring it out. Try another answer.

97-B. (From 101-A) *Wrong*. The derivation of the formula on 101-A is more arduous than difficult. In it, the imaginary parts cancel, leaving only the part which we gave as the real part. This indicates that, because the numerator is not zero, any residual must be either in-phase or phase-reversed, according to whether the sign of the numerator is positive or negative.

97-C. (From 104-A) Dividing numerator and denominator of the expression on 61-B by c^3, to normalize values to c, and equating to $1/10$ (for the 20-db phase-reversed level), we solve for b/c

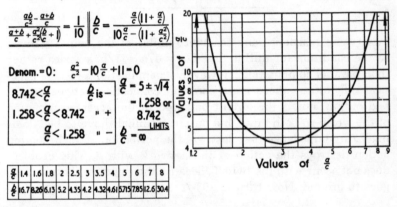

$$\frac{\frac{ab}{c^2}-\frac{a+b}{c}}{\frac{a+b}{c}+\frac{a^2}{c^2}\left(\frac{b}{c}+1\right)}=\frac{1}{10} \quad \middle\| \quad \frac{b}{c}=\frac{\frac{a}{c}\left(11+\frac{a}{c}\right)}{10\frac{a}{c}-\left(11+\frac{a^2}{c^2}\right)}$$

Denom.$=0$: $\quad \frac{a^2}{c^2}-10\frac{a}{c}+11=0$

$$8.742<\frac{a}{c} \qquad \frac{b}{c}\text{ is }-$$
$$1.258<\frac{a}{c}<8.742 \qquad \text{" }+$$
$$\frac{a}{c}<1.258 \qquad \text{" }-$$

$$\frac{a}{c}=5\pm\sqrt{14}$$
$$=1.258 \text{ or}$$
$$8.742$$
$$\underline{\text{LIMITS}}$$
$$\frac{b}{c}=\infty$$

$\frac{a}{c}$	1.4	1.6	1.8	2	2.5	3	3.5	4	5	6	7	8
$\frac{b}{c}$	16.7	8.26	6.13	5.2	4.35	4.2	4.32	4.61	5.15	7.85	12.6	30.4

in terms of a/c. From the solution we deduce the variation of b/c as a/c varies. The denominator of the expression for b/c is a quadratic in a/c and thus has a value of zero for two values of a/c, which prove to be 1.258 and 8.742 (approximately). Between these values b/c is positive, while beyond them it is negative and thus has no real significance. So we can plot between a/c values of 1.4 and 8, with values of b/c (obtained from tabulating the range, as shown) between 4 and 20 (only the value for $a/c = 8$ goes beyond).

The curve may be plotted to linear, log, or hybrid scales (one way of each); we have used log-log. A minimum required value of b/c occurs at $a/c = 3$, which makes $b/c = 4.2$. Use of this pair has the advantage that the value of a/c is quite uncritical, while precise value of b/c will control precise amplitude of phase-reversed output, the value 4.2 giving precisely the 20-db level.

98-A. (From 66-B) *Wrong.* There are no special circumstances for this coincidence in this network.

98-B. (From 82-C) *Correct.* The twin-T, or parallel-T, has both inputs and outputs in parallel. So its dual form, the twin-π, has both inputs and outputs in series, as shown here. In one respect its design is simpler than the twin-T: the values are the recipro-

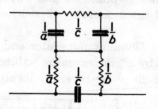

cals (using resistance and reactance units) of the twin-T values; so the condition for null is that $1/c = 1/a + 1/b$, a series rather than parallel combination. However, its application presents practical difficulties: there is no common connection between input and output, nor is the circuit balanced in the accepted meaning of the word; so both input and output terminals have to be "floating." Any impedance that destroys the perfection of such floating action destroys the action of the network with it. This problem does not occur with the twin-T, because the common "bottom leg" goes to ground. Now turn to 103-A.

98-C. (From 104-A) To give 6-db depth of "hole," both R_1 and R_2 need to be the same as the working impedance: 600 ohms.

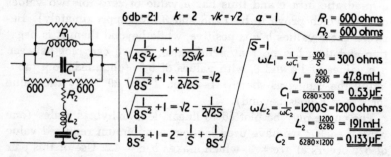

Next, from the formula on 88-A, we evaluate S, using $\sqrt{k} = \sqrt{2}$, or $k = 2$, and u also as $\sqrt{2}$. S comes out to be 1. Again using the formula for L_1, C_1 and L_2, C_2 from 88-A, we calculate the reactance-element values.

99

99-A. (From 103-A) Correct answer is (1) 31.4 cycles. Here errors hinged around the value assumed for source resistance. From Thevenin's Principle (see 48-A) it is the parallel combination of plate resistance and coupling resistor, which is found to be 37.5K. This is denoted by r on 57-A. So the total value, $r + R$, is 507.5K. Using the formula for reactance of a capacitor (see 35-A) and substituting to the form $\omega = 1/CX$, then dividing the result by 2π to get frequency, the answer is found to be 31.4 cycles.

99-B. (From 104-A) All-pass lattice networks are covered at 59-A and 75-B. To give the 90° point at 600 c/s, each reactance must be 600 ohms at this point, from which L evaluates to 159 mH, and C to 0.443 microfarad. Two of each of these values are required.

Substituting $x = \frac{1}{2}$ and $x = 2$ into the expression for ϕ_t gives actan 4/3 and $-4/3$ respectively. So the angles (to the nearest degree) are 53° and 127° at 300 and 1,200 c/s respectively.

99-C. (From 104-A) Here is the calculation. Note that the deviation from flat, below the compensated point ($x = 1$), is less than 0.1 db, with the maximum error one-half octave below.

$\underline{4.77\text{db}}$ Antilog $0.477 = 3$ $k^2 = 3$ db$= 10\log_{10}[1 + x^2 + x^4]$ coeff. of x^2 is 1

Required boost db$= 10\log_{10}[1 - ax^2 + bx^4]$ At $x=1$ $1 - a + b = \frac{1}{3}$

Slope $= \frac{2x^2(2bx^2-a)}{bx^4-ax^2+1}$ At $x=1$ $\frac{2(2b-a)}{b-a+1} = -2$ $\begin{bmatrix}\text{because slope of}\\\text{original is} +2\end{bmatrix}$ $a - b = \frac{2}{3}$

$4b-2a = -2b+2a-2$ $4a-6b=2$ $2a-3b=1$ $a=1$ $b=\frac{1}{3}$

Required compensation response db $= 10\log_{10}[1 - x^2 + \frac{1}{3}x^4]$ $\begin{cases}\text{peak} +6 \text{ db at } x^2 = \frac{3}{2}\\ 90° +5.7\text{db at } x^4 = 3\end{cases}$

Resultant db$=10\log_{10}[1 + x^2 + x^4][1 - x^2 + \frac{1}{3}x^4] = 10\log_{10}[1 + \frac{1}{3}x^4 - \frac{2}{3}x^6 + \frac{1}{3}x^8]$

maxima & minima:

$\frac{dk^2}{dx^2} = \frac{2}{3}x^2 - 2x^4 + \frac{4}{3}x^6$ Equate to 0: $x^2 = 0$ or $x^2 = \frac{3}{4} \pm \sqrt{\frac{9}{16} - \frac{1}{2}}$
$= \frac{3 \pm 1}{4} = \frac{1}{2}$ or 1

$x^2 = 1$ db$= 10\log_{10}[1 + \frac{1}{3} - \frac{2}{3} + \frac{1}{3}] = 0$ ✓
$x^2 = \frac{1}{2}$ db$= 10\log_{10}[1 + \frac{1}{12} - \frac{1}{12} + \frac{1}{48}] = 10\log_{10}\frac{49}{48} = 10\log_{10}1.0208 = \underline{0.089\text{ db}}$

100-A. (From 102-A) *Correct.* This should have been obvious from the expression $r = L/CR$ (102-A). If R is increased, the corresponding value of r is decreased. Now we'll summarize the possible variations of this network.

The quantity we have abbreviated into D^2 can have values from close above zero (positive) up to any positive finite value. The purely theoretical limit of $D^2 = 0$ results in an infinite peaking curve, where the amplitude reaches infinite "gain" at $x = 1$, for which the phase response is rectangular, suddenly changing

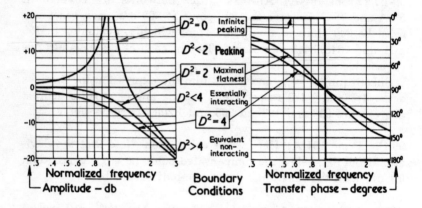

from 0° to 180° at this frequency. For all finite networks the change is gradual, and the peak is finite. If D^2 is less than 2, the response has a peak. If $D^2 = 2$, the response is the maximal-flatness one, with no terms in the db amplitude expression below x^4 in order. If D^2 is less than 4, the network is essentially interacting, by which we mean that it cannot be synthesized from equivalent single reactance-element networks, using real values. If $D^2 = 4$, the performance is identical with that of two identical noninteracting networks. If D^2 is greater than 4, it can be synthesized by equivalent nonidentical, noninteracting networks.

Notice that whatever contour the amplitude takes, the phase transfer is lagging. This changes the rule for simpler circuits (see 89-A) that upward slope is accompanied by phase advance. Conversely, the high-pass (low cutoff) version, achieved by interchanging places of L and C, always has a phase advance, even where the peaking produces a slope that goes down with increasing frequency. Now turn to 92-B.

TWIN-T NETWORKS

101-A. (From 89-B) A type of network which has many uses in advanced electronics is the twin-T (sometimes called the *parallel-T*), whose configuration is shown here. One particular combination of values is used much more than other possibilities, but to simplify the derivation even basic theory makes the assumption that at some frequency which we will designate as critical (because it is not always a null point, but always has some special feature), the pairs of values grouped together have identical resistance and reactance values (designated here by symbols a, b and c).

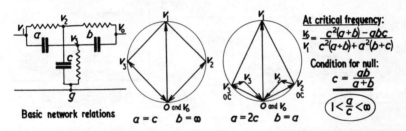

Basic network relations

At critical frequency:
$$\frac{V_o}{V_1} = \frac{c^2(a+b) - abc}{c^2(a+b) + a^2(b+c)}$$

Condition for null:
$$c = \frac{ab}{a+b}$$

$$1 < \frac{a}{c} < \infty$$

$a = c \quad b = \infty$

$a = 2c \quad b = a$

If a and c are made equal and b is made infinite (a purely theoretical concept), the left-hand vector diagram applies. Practical circuits produce loading by the b elements on the voltage division between the a and c elements. The classical circuit, where $a = b = 2c$, is represented in the right-hand vector diagram. This version is by far the most used.

It is most convenient to start performance calculations with critical frequency, taking first the voltage division between the a and c elements, then the voltage division between the b elements. Thevenin's Theorem (48-A) is used, taking into account the source impedance presented by the a and c elements. The result is given at the top right. Equating the numerator to zero gives the necessary condition for null at critical frequency. Note that it can be viewed as making c equivalent to a and b in parallel combination. Now if values other than critical occur, will the residual output due to imbalance be in quadrature (see 97-B) or either in-phase or phase-reversed (see 61-B)?

101-B. (From 82-C) *Wrong.* How do you parallel inputs of two networks, each of which has a shunt-input member, without causing interaction?

102-A. (From 87-C) *Correct.* To see the circumstances involved, we show a value (working toward the right) for this impedance, Z_1, and find the condition for it to be resistive (imaginary part zero). When this substitution is made the value proves to be simply L/CR.

Now we make substitutions into the value of x for peak frequency in the complete network (under the schematic). Con-

$$Z_1 = j\omega L + \frac{R}{1 + j\omega CR} = \frac{R(1 - \omega^2 LC) + j\omega L}{1 + j\omega CR}$$

$$= \frac{R + j\omega L - j\omega CR^2 + j\omega^3 LC^2 R^2}{1 + \omega^2 C^2 R^2}$$

$$x^2 = \frac{2 - D^2}{2} \qquad D^2 = \frac{(d + \frac{1}{d})^2}{1 + a} = \frac{\frac{L}{CRr} + \frac{CRr}{L} + 2}{\frac{R+r}{r}} = \frac{\frac{L}{CR} + \frac{CRr^2}{L} + 2r}{R + r}$$

$$= \frac{2(R+r) - \frac{L}{CR} - \frac{CRr^2}{L} - 2r}{2(R+r)} = \frac{2R - \frac{L}{CR} - \frac{CRr^2}{L}}{2(R+r)}$$

$$\omega^2 = \omega_\phi^2 x^2 = \frac{R+r}{RLC} x^2 = \frac{2R - \frac{L}{CR} - \frac{CRr^2}{L}}{2RLC} = \frac{1}{LC} - \frac{1}{2C^2R^2} - \frac{r^2}{2L^2}$$

Real when $\omega^2 = \frac{CR^2 - L}{LC^2 R^2}$
$$= \frac{1}{LC} - \frac{1}{C^2 R^2}$$

Then $Z_1 = \frac{R}{1 + \omega^2 C^2 R^2}$
$$= \frac{L}{CR}$$

same

Make $d = \frac{1}{d} = 1$ $\frac{L}{CRr} = \frac{CRr}{L} = 1$ $r = \frac{L}{CR}$ $\omega^2 = \frac{1}{LC} - \frac{1}{2C^2R^2} - \frac{1}{2C^2R^2} = \frac{1}{LC} - \frac{1}{C^2R^2}$ $Z_1 = \frac{L}{CR} = r$

verting this special value into terms of ω by substituting the value for ω_ϕ, we get an expression that gives peak frequency in its basic terms. The required condition is $d = 1/d = 1$, making which substitution gives $r = L/CR$. Substituting this into the expression for ω^2 at peak reduces the expression to the same form as that for Z_1, showing that the conditions coincide. Also, it is found that the impedance Z_1 is then equal to r.

What we have shown is that, for this special case (*i.e.*, $L/CRr = 1$, regardless of the relationship r/R), matching between R and r occurs at the peak frequency. For lower frequencies, where the reactance of L and the susceptance of C are negligible, the attenuation is the mismatch loss between r and R (due to their being unequal) while at peak-frequency the matching occurs, which can be regarded as the cause or explanation of the peak.

When L/CRr is not equal to 1, this does not occur. Peak does not coincide with resistive value of Z_1, nor does Z_1 match r at any frequency. Using the same values for L and C, does making the value of R larger make the matching value of r larger (see 81-C) or smaller (see 100-A)?

103-A. TEST QUESTIONS ON SECTION 2

1. Design an L-pad for 250 ohms impedance, 26-db attenuation, having shunt-input and series-output resistors. These are: (1) 238 and 13.2 ohms; (2) 263 and 4,750 ohms; (3) 249 and 0.626 ohms; (4) 251 and 99,750 ohms. After identifying your answer, turn to 89-C.

2. Design an H-pad for 600 ohms impedance, 24-db attenuation. Required are four series resistors and one central shunt resistor. Their values are, respectively: (1) 530 and 47.9 ohms; (2) 265 and 47.9 ohms; (3) 530 and 75.2 ohms; (4) 265 and 75.2 ohms. After working this out, turn to 96-B.

3. In an RC coupling circuit, the plate resistance of the preceding tube is 60K, the plate coupling resistor is 100K, the coupling capacitor is 0.01 microfarad, and the following stage grid resistor is 470K. Is the low-frequency cutoff (3 db, 45° point) at (1) 31.4, (2) 30.4, (3) 28, (4) 25.3 cycles? Turn to 99-A.

4. In the same RC coupling circuit (as in Question 3), the high-frequency turnover point (3 db, 45°) is at 30 Kc. From this deduce the total circuit shunt capacitance to be: (1) 44.5, (2) 64.5, (3) 100, (4) 153 micromicrofarads. Turn to 89-D.

5. In the circuit for this question, values for elements r and R need to be chosen so that total boost (ultimate step height) at

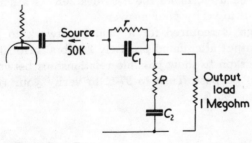

Question 5.

each end of the response range is 20 db, while the approximate 3-db lift points (from mid-range level) will be at 200 cycles and 2,000 cycles. Calculate values for r, R, C_1, and C_2. If you encounter difficulty, turn to 83-C.

6. Design a bridged-T network to produce a dip in response, 6 db deep at 1,000 c/s, with 3-db points at 707 and 1,414 c/s, for an impedance of 600 ohms. The formulas on 88-A will help. If you have difficulty, turn to 98-C.

7. Design a lattice all-pass network for 600 ohms impedance, to have the 90° phase-shift at 600 c/s. Turn to 99-B for solution.

8. Design a crossover network, with an ultimate cutoff rate of 18 db/octave, 3 db down and 135° phase-shift at crossover, for 16 ohms impedance, 1,000 c/s, and so the inputs connect in parallel. Turn to 88-B to verify your solution.

9. A series of bandpass filters, each one-third octave wide between 3-db points and with an ultimate slope in excess of 18 db/octave, is to be designed so combination of their outputs will produce a complementary flat response. Working impedance is to be 10,000 ohms and mid-band frequency of the first (lowest frequency) filter is to be 20 c/s. Tabulate values for the series. Turn to 96-C to verify your answer.

10. A response due to two interacting reactance-elements is 4.77 db down at its 90° phase-shift point. Derive the basic constants from which a two-reactance peaking circuit can be designed that will extend the response to this same frequency, with zero loss at this point. What will be the maximum deviation below this frequency, when the correct compensation is applied? The principle to be applied is given on 90-B. Turn to 99-C to verify your result.

11. Design a twin-T network to give a 6 db/octave roll-off with its 3-db point at 2,120 cycles and its null at 38 Kc. Since various values can be used, make the c values 20K as a starting point. Turn to 59-B to verify your answer.

12. A design is required for a twin-T network to give phase-reversed output attenuated precisely 20 db at critical frequency. Prepare a graph to show possible relationships between a/c and b/c for this purpose. Turn to 97-C to verify your result. After that, turn to 105-A.

Section 3

TRANSMISSION LINE PROPERTIES

105-A. A long transmission line (usually called just line, for short) consists of continuously distributed elements. Resistance of the conductor (s), their inductance, leakage between them as a conductance (very small), and capacitance between them can be expressed with units of impedance for series elements and admittance for shunt, the total quantity in a length being proportional to the length. Using R, L, G, and C to represent the quantity of these elements per unit length (the unit may be the foot, mile, kilometer or other—it is immaterial, so long as all use the same), we write Rdx, etc., to represent the resistance, etc., of an elemental length of line, dx.

$$-dv = i(R + j\omega L)dx \qquad\qquad -di = v(G + j\omega C)dx$$

$$\frac{dv}{dx} = -i(R + j\omega L) \qquad\qquad \frac{di}{dx} = -v(G + j\omega C)$$

$$\frac{d^2v}{dx^2} = -\frac{di}{dx}(R + j\omega L) = v(R + j\omega L)(G + j\omega C)$$

$$\frac{d^2i}{dx^2} = -\frac{dv}{dx}(G + j\omega C) = i(R + j\omega L)(G + j\omega C)$$

$$\frac{d^2v}{dx^2} = \gamma^2 v \qquad\qquad \frac{d^2i}{dx^2} = \gamma^2 i$$

Make
$$\gamma^2 = (R + j\omega L)(G + j\omega C) \qquad \begin{cases} \alpha = \sqrt{RG} \\ \beta = \omega\sqrt{LC} \end{cases} \quad \text{Condition}$$
$$\gamma = \alpha + j\beta \qquad\qquad\qquad\qquad\qquad\qquad ?$$

From this we can derive expressions relating voltage and current along the line. To aid solution, these may be simplified by making the substitution shown for γ^2. γ has a dimension per unit length, because it is the square root of a product of quantities, each of which has a dimension per unit length. Thus it is the propagation constant for the line in terms of the unit length adopted. It is a complex quantity and can be resolved into real and imaginary parts: α, the attenuation constant, and β, the phase constant. The attenuation depends primarily on R and G, and the phase primarily on L and C. We have written an equation for both α and β in terms of the basic elements. These equations are (1) universally true (see 110-A); (2) only true one at a time, provided the other two elements are zero (see 112-A); (3) both true, provided a certain proportionality exists (see 108-A).

LINE DERIVATION OF FILTERS

106-A. (From 108-A) Filters can be designed by regarding them as sections of line using lumped elements, instead of continuously distributed ones. Sections can consist of either two series elements (or half-elements) and one shunt, or vice versa. Here we consider the T or mid-series derived section. Assuming it to be terminated by Z_0, we refer back impedance, admittance and impedance again, and equate the input impedance to Z_0. Solving for Z_0, we get an expression for Z_0 passing through zero.

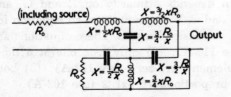

$$Z = Z_0 + j\frac{X}{2} = \frac{2Z_0 + jX}{2}$$

$$Y = \frac{2}{2Z_0 + jX} + jB = \frac{2 - XB + j2BZ_0}{2Z_0 + jX}$$

$$Z = \frac{2Z_0 + jX}{2 - XB + j2BZ_0} + j\frac{X}{2} = \frac{Z_0(2 - XB) + jX(2 - \frac{XB}{2})}{2 - XB + j2BZ_0} = Z_0 \text{ (required)}$$

$$Z_0(2 - XB + j2BZ_0) = Z(2 - XB) + jX(2 - \frac{XB}{2}) \quad \Rightarrow \quad Z_0^2 = \frac{X}{B} - \frac{X^2}{4} \quad Z_0 = \sqrt{\frac{X}{B} - \frac{X^2}{4}}$$

Dual: $\quad Y_0 = \sqrt{\dfrac{B}{X} - \dfrac{B^2}{4}} \quad$ **Condition for cutoff:** $BX = 4$

Doing the same thing with the π or mid-shunt derived section, we get a solution for Y_0 that is similar to the previous expression for Z_0. The condition for cut-off is where the product $BX = 4$ in either case. Which of the following statements is correct? When BX is less than 4, the image impedance is real (resistive), signifying a pass condition, whereas when BX is greater than 4, the image impedance is imaginary (reactive), signifying an attenuation condition (see 109-A); completely vice versa (see 113-A); or as first stated for the T network, but vice versa for the π type (see 114-A).

106-B. (From 151-A) Here we have the solution in terms of normalized values. Note that correct input termination is important for the effect to be achieved.

(including source)
R_0 $X = \frac{1}{2}xR_0$ $X = \frac{3}{2}xR_0$ Output

$X = \frac{3}{4} \cdot \frac{R_0}{x}$

$R_0 \lessgtr$ $X = \frac{1}{2}\frac{R_0}{x}$ $X = \frac{3}{2}\frac{R_0}{x}$

$X = \frac{3}{4}xR_0$

Constant resistance source at output, therefore response does not depend on termination.
Circuit is one from 95-A reversed.

107-A. (From 109-A) *No.* The clue should be in the second term under the radical in each case. For low-pass, it is ω^2 times something over 4. For high-pass, it is 1 over 4 ω^2 times something. They are not simple reciprocals, which this answer evidently assumed. Try another.

107-B. (From 113-B) *Correct.* The theory was based on terminating both ends by the image impedance. Here are plotted the consequences of various extremely incorrect terminations of the prototype filter, because this is much simpler to calculate than that for the derived types. We have assumed that the input some-

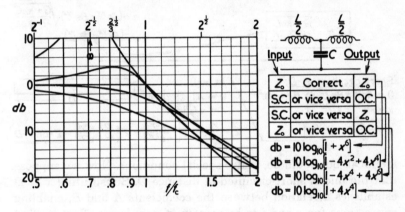

times is fed from a constant voltage source, or zero impedance, while the output is sometimes unterminated (open circuit). The response for the four possible combinations of correct and incorrect termination at input and output are shown. As an exercise you may wish to derive the formulas from which these were plotted and shown below without their derivation. The response would be precisely the same if the terminations are reversed between input and output—a condition that may be approached, if not completely met, in transistor work. Note that a short circuit of one end combined with open circuit of the other results in infinite peaking because there is then no resistance associated with the network at all. Note that termination with a short circuit, or low value, tends to cause peaking, while termination with an open circuit, or high value, causes increased loss in the vicinity of the cutoff point. Now turn to 119-A.

108-A. (From 105-A) In this case, two of the three answers were right. The other one is given in 112-A. The condition for both expressions to be true at once is that the real and imaginary parts of the two factors of γ^2 be in the same proportion, i.e., $R/G = L/C$. Here we take the solution for v from the differential equation on 105-A, and derive an expression for i from it, to get an expression for Z, the characteristic impedance of the line. Note that the active parts of the voltage and current expression are not

Solution of $\dfrac{d^2v}{dx^2} = \gamma^2 v$ of form

$$v = A\varepsilon^{\gamma x} + B\varepsilon^{-\gamma x}$$

$$\boxed{Z = \sqrt{\dfrac{R+j\omega L}{G+j\omega C}}}$$

$$i = -\dfrac{dv}{dx} \Big/ (R + j\omega L)$$

$$= -\left(A\varepsilon^{\gamma x} - B\varepsilon^{-\gamma x}\right)\left(\dfrac{\gamma}{R+j\omega L}\right)$$

$$= -\left(A\varepsilon^{\gamma x} - B\varepsilon^{-\gamma x}\right)\sqrt{\dfrac{G+j\omega C}{R+j\omega L}}$$

$$= \dfrac{-\left(A\varepsilon^{\gamma x} - B\varepsilon^{-\gamma x}\right)}{Z}$$

__Short circuit at $x = D$:__

$$0 = A\varepsilon^{\gamma D} + B\varepsilon^{-\gamma D} \text{ so } B = -A\varepsilon^{2\gamma D}$$

$$v = A\left[\varepsilon^{\gamma x} - \varepsilon^{\gamma(2D-x)}\right]$$

$$i = -\dfrac{A}{Z}\left[\varepsilon^{\gamma x} + \varepsilon^{\gamma(2D-x)}\right]$$

At $x = 0$:

$$v_i = A\left[1 - \varepsilon^{2\gamma D}\right]$$

$$i_i = -\dfrac{A}{Z}\left[1 + \varepsilon^{2\gamma D}\right]$$

$$Z_i = \dfrac{v_i}{i_i} = -Z\left[\dfrac{1 - \varepsilon^{2\gamma D}}{1 + \varepsilon^{2\gamma D}}\right] = Z\dfrac{\varepsilon^{\gamma D} - \varepsilon^{-\gamma D}}{\varepsilon^{\gamma D} + \varepsilon^{-\gamma D}} = \underline{Z\tanh\gamma D}$$

identical, but could be, under special conditions. Now we suppose that the line is short-circuited at distance D. Substituting $x = D$ establishes a relation between the coefficients A and B, enabling expressions for v and i to be written in new forms. Now we find the input impedance by substituting $x = 0$. The expression then simplifies to the characteristic impedance multiplied by tanh γD.

As an exercise, if you substitute zero into the expression for i at $x = D$, to represent open-circuit termination, and follow the same procedure, you should obtain an input impedance that is Z multiplied by the hyperbolic cotangent (i.e., the reciprocal of the short-circuit value, using Z as the normalizing value). This means that Z is the mean between the measured short-circuit and open-circuit impedances, measured at any distance.

Two special cases have particular practical value: the distortionless line and the loss-free line. The distortionless case is that where $R/G = L/C$, which enables Z to reduce to $\sqrt{L/C}$. The loss-free case makes R and G both zero, for which Z_i becomes Z tan γD (verify this for yourself), which makes the line impedance fluctuate between the short-circuit and open-circuit impedances. Now turn to 106-A.

109-A. (From 106-A) *Correct.* A substitution of values less and more than 4 for BX in the two expressions will quickly verify this. Now assume we make simple (called constant-K) low- or high-pass filters using this method. The characteristic impedance in the passband is $\sqrt{L/C}$, or the admittance is $\sqrt{C/L}$, the second term under the radical being small until cutoff is approached.

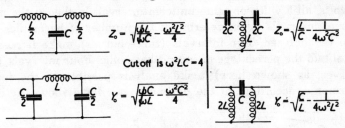

This fact enables us to form appropriate values for L and C that can conveniently form a basis for normalizing. For the low-pass case, cutoff is found by writing $\omega^2 LC$ equal to 4. For the high-pass case, (1) the expression is the same (see 107-A), (2) it is equal to 1 instead of 4 (115-A), (3) it is equal to $1/4$ (111-A).

109-B. (From 138-A) *Correct.* Here's the derivation, which is simple enough. Now we can put in some constants in the proportionalities established on 117-B, 128-A, and 138-A (where we had not before), so the formulas can be used. These apply to modern, grain-oriented, silicon-alloy iron, working at fairly high a.c. flux density (but still less than the d.c.H). As the curves showed, other materials do not result in substantial improvement of overall potential for this application, so there is little point in applying them.

$R \propto L^{\frac{3}{4}} I$ Constant dissipation: $I^2 R$ = constant $R \propto \frac{1}{I^2}$ $L^{\frac{3}{4}} I^3$ = constant
or LI^2 = constant

Formulas	Procedure
(1) $R = 1.75 \cdot L^{\frac{3}{4}} I \cdot \frac{L_m L_i^2}{A_w V_i^{\frac{2}{3}}}$	Use (1) to select core size, or choose L, I, R combination
(2) $T = 1.28 \times 10^3 \cdot L^{\frac{3}{4}} I^{\frac{1}{2}} \cdot \frac{L_i}{V_i^{\frac{1}{4}}}$	Use (2) to calculate turns, wire gage tables to verify.
(3) $\frac{L_G}{L_i} = 10^{-4} \left(\frac{IT}{L_i}\right)^{\frac{4}{3}}$ $L_G = 10^{-4} (IT)^{\frac{4}{3}} L_i^{\frac{1}{3}}$	Use (3) to calculate total air gap. No d.c. ?

Now we come to the design of inductors where no d.c. is present to polarize the core. This involves a different procedure. Presumably, as there is no d.c., the best design will use a closed core (see 118-C); or is there another reason for an air gap in this kind of design (see 145-A)?

110

110-A. (From 105-A) *Wrong.* Try one of the other answers.

DISTORTION IN TUBES AND TRANSISTORS

110-B. (From 147-B) Here we take typical pentode and triode plate-characteristics. It is important that the intervals between grid voltage curves are uniform, *e.g.*, all 1 volt, all 0.5 volt, all 2 volts, all 5 volts, or some uniform interval. In theory the number of intervals taken determines the number of harmonics that can be analyzed. Two intervals (three curves) make it possible to obtain the percentage of second harmonic. Four intervals (five curves, as shown here) make analysis possible to the fourth harmonic, according to the derivation we have shown here.

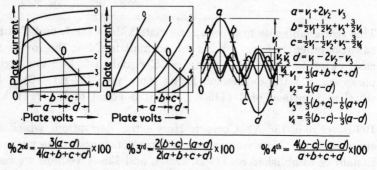

$$a = v_1 + 2v_2 - v_3$$
$$b = \tfrac{3}{2}v_1 + \tfrac{1}{2}v_2 + v_3 + \tfrac{3}{2}v_4$$
$$c = \tfrac{1}{2}v_1 - \tfrac{1}{2}v_2 + v_3 - \tfrac{3}{2}v_4$$
$$d = v_1 - 2v_2 - v_3$$

$$v_1 = \tfrac{1}{3}(a+b+c+d)$$
$$v_2 = \tfrac{1}{4}(a-d)$$
$$v_3 = \tfrac{1}{3}(b+c) - \tfrac{1}{6}(a+d)$$
$$v_4 = \tfrac{4}{3}(b-c) - \tfrac{1}{3}(a-d)$$

$$\% \, 2^{nd} = \frac{3(a-d)}{4(a+b+c+d)} \times 100 \qquad \% \, 3^{rd} = \frac{2(b+c)-(a+d)}{2(a+b+c+d)} \times 100 \qquad \% \, 4^{th} = \frac{4(b-c)-(a-d)}{a+b+c+d} \times 100$$

As an example, suppose the plate voltages, in order, are 60, 72, 86, 99, and 110. This makes $a = 26$, $b = 14$, $c = 13$, and $d = 24$. Substituting in the final formulas, we have: % $2^{nd} = 150/77$, or 1.95%; % $3^{rd} = 200/77$, or 2.6%; % $4^{th} = 200/77$, or 2.6%. Note how critical these results are for each exact reading. Results are likely to be more accurate with curvatures that result in more distortion. It is essential that accurate curves for the tubes be used in order to get results that are meaningful at all, and it is best to calculate distortion over a larger swing, if possible (but not into clipping, where an abrupt change occurs), and then interpolate the distortion for smaller swing (see 187-A). Obviously distortion can change as the value of load, represented by the load line, is changed.

Transistor characteristics are similar to those of pentode tubes, except that the curves represent values of input current, instead of input voltage. So can distortion in a transistor stage be calculated in the same way, merely using input current in place of input voltage (see 130-A); or, is there something else to take into account (see 134-B)?

111-A. (From 109-A) *Correct*. The factor is 1/4, which is evident from the form given in 106-A. So putting the frequency term into the denominator, instead of the numerator, as the high-pass does, changes the factor from 4 to 1/4.

Now we turn to m-derived filters. The main concept here is that sharpness of cutoff can be accentuated by reducing the basic values of L and C (in the low-pass configuration) by a factor m between zero and one. Then a piece of the opposite kind of element is added to the center limb of the network, so the image impedance requirements are still held within the passband. Mak-

$$\frac{1}{B} = \frac{1}{\omega m C} - \omega a L \;\Big\|\; Z_o = \sqrt{\frac{L}{C} - \omega^2 a m L^2 - \frac{\omega^2 m^2 L^2}{4}}$$

Z_o passband: $\longrightarrow \underbrace{\frac{X}{B}} \quad \underbrace{\frac{X^2}{4}}$

Cut off: $4am + m^2 = 1 \quad \boxed{a = \frac{1 - m^2}{4m}}$

Infinite attenuation at $\omega^2 amLC = 1$

$$\omega^2 LC = \frac{4}{1 - m^2}$$

Above cutoff by factor $\dfrac{f_\infty}{f_c} = \dfrac{1}{\sqrt{1 - m^2}}$

$m = 0.6$

$\dfrac{f_\infty}{f_c} = 1.25$

ing both L and C smaller by m means L/C does not change, which controls the passband value of Z_o. Cutoff has to be adjusted back (without the extra element, it would be extended) by the second half of the expression under the radical representing X/B, which adds to the third term, to make up an augmented value of $X^2/4$. The combined coefficient of these two terms is equated to that in the prototype and a value obtained for a in terms of m. This satisfies the cutoff requirements.

Now there will be infinite attenuation when the shunt-leg elements resonate, for which we can also find a frequency ratio in terms of m. Next we'll show how the response varies for different values of m, and the variations of this filter for π sections and high-pass response. See if you can figure these out for yourself first. Also, does the image impedance of an m-derived filter have an identical characteristic to its prototype within the passband (see 113-B) or not (see 116-A)?

111-B. (From 128-A) *No*. It is true the slope is the opposite way, represented by the negative sign. But this combination suggests that magnetic reluctance (total, which is the reciprocal of μ'_e) multiplied by air-gap length ratio yields the product IT/L_i. There is no reason to support this. Try another answer.

112-A. (From 105-A) Almost right. This statement is true, but it is not the only solution. Making L and C zero, quite obviously γ is equal to the square root of RG, and as it is wholly real, β is zero, and $\gamma = \alpha$. Making R and G zero, the reverse happens: γ squared is negative and therefore γ must be wholly imaginary, α is zero and γ is β. So each statement is true, provided each of the other two values is zero. But it is not necessarily true when all four values (or even three of them) are nonzero. This leaves 108-A as the alternative answer.

112-B. (From 144-A) *Correct.* The series element of the first attenuating action becomes $1 + jax$, instead of simply jax, which changes the expression for k to one different from that on 144-A. Note that this expression contains the constant 2, instead of 1, because the minimum attenuation is that between two identical

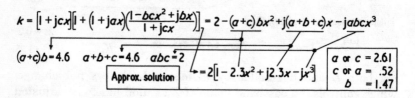

resistors when all reactances and susceptances are zero. This means the identity derived on 122-A must be multiplied through by 2; so the coefficients in this solution are 4.6, 4.6, and 2, in place of 2.3, 2.3, and 1.

The values obtained for a and c are interchangeable, the result of solving a quadratic in $(a + c)$, because the termination is symmetrical in this case, but the response does not require identical values in these positions. By following the same method a filter could be designed to work between asymmetrical impedance terminations. By the method adopted in writing the expression for k the values are in terms of a reactance equal to that of either termination at the half-phase frequency $(x = 1)$. If this is compared with the prototype low-pass network of 109-A, it will be found that both L and C in the latter have twice the value on which this calculation is based. In this case, $L/2$ of a series arm will be the same as L in this calculation, but the C of 109-A is still twice the value of C here. Now turn to 115-B.

113-A. (From 106-A) *No.* Just substitute values in these groups, and you'll see.

113-B. (From 111-A) *Correct.* The fact that the expression under the radical on 111-A is identical in form, *i.e.*, has an equivalence in its variation with frequency, with that on 109-A, means the image impedance in the pass range is identical. On the assumption that the network is terminated by its image impedance, there is zero attenuation right up to cutoff frequency, at which point the impedance becomes either zero (T type) or infinite (π type). Practical networks are not terminated by their image impedance,

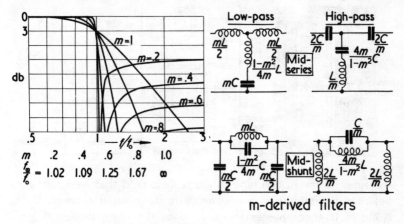

m-derived filters

but usually by its passband value, Z. Here we show typical responses, for *m*-values of 0.2, 0.4, 0.6, 0.8, and for 1, which is the prototype; also, to verify your own figuring, the configuration and values of *m*-derived filters of T and π type for low-pass and high-pass.

Now regarding practical terminations, use of the correct (design) value is important: only at the output end (see 117-A); only at the input end (see 118-A); at both ends (see 107-B).

113-C. (From 121-B) *No.* Your thinking is probably based on the fact that current in the secondary affects current in the primary, which in turn affects voltage induced in the secondary due to the primary. But the coupling factor does not change with this change in external circuit conditions—at least for air-core coils. As we shall see, it could be argued that coupling factor is subject to such change in coils using a common iron core (see 114-B), but this is due to a different effect. See the other answer.

114

114-A. (From 106-A) *No.* It's the same for both of them. Try one of the other answers.

114-B. (From 123-A) *Correct.* "Leakage *inductance*" is a better name, and the concept of "close to 100%" coupling can be misleading. Here we show the fields that give rise to the main inductance, totally in the core, and to leakage inductance, totally out of the core and in the gap between windings. The magnetic field in the core is related to the transformed *voltages*, whereas the leakage field is dependent on transformed *currents*. Primary and

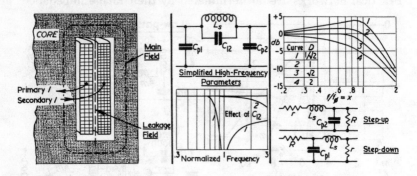

secondary current combine to generate a field that basically goes *between* the windings, but is actually distributed *through* them. None of it encompasses them, as does the main field.

In the middle diagram we show a simplified form of the equivalent circuit for high-frequency response. The effect of interwinding capacitance (C_{12}) may take the form shown at curve 1 (bottom middle). If the windings are simple (as shown at left), reversing both windings so that the grounded points are at opposite ends of each, fixed by the external circuit, results in curve 2 with no other change in performance.

Assuming that interwinding capacitance is avoided, either by design of the transformer or by careful connection, response due to leakage inductance and capacitance of the higher-impedance winding (of a step-up or step-down) varies as shown at the right, where the significance of the quantities is exactly the same as on 137-C for low-frequency response. In either case, r and R are the terminating impedances, but their effective position is reversed according to which way the step is. Now, how about distortion: can leakage inductance contribute to it? Answer: yes; see 143-A. Answer: no; see 147-B.

115-A. (From 109-A) *No.* This time you're guessing. You may have seen formulas for these filters in terms of f and π, instead of using ω. In these, you will find 4π's in one group and just π's in the other. But this is a different presentation of similar information.

THE COMPLEX *P*-PLANE

115-B. (From 112-B) On pages 13-B and 27-B we treated the solution of a capacitor discharging through a resistor by means of a differential equation, which is repeated here. On pages 25-B and 30-A a similar expression is given for an inductive time-constant network. On page 51-A the solution of a differential

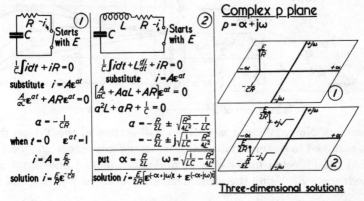

Three-dimensional solutions

equation for a decaying oscillation in a resonant circuit is deduced, which we also repeat here in substance. Note the similarity: there are two coefficients which (in this case) happen to be different by a factor of 2 for both exponential functions, and one or more exponential functions (which may not always share the same coefficient), the exponents of which may be wholly real (as in the discharge case) or partly real and partly imaginary. By writing p as the exponent of ϵ, (in complex form, consisting of $\alpha + j\omega$) we can place each exponent in a complex plane (called the *complex p-plane*) and represent the coefficient by a magnitude in the third dimension, as shown here. This is a mathematical device to aid in the understanding of circuit behavior.

A steady sinusoidal current or voltage in a network would be represented by (1) a point on the $j\omega$ axis, just as the time constant is represented by a point on the α axis; (2) a pair of such points, symmetrically positive and negative, on the $j\omega$ axis. Answer: (1); see 144-B. Answer: (2); see 118-B.

116

116-A. (From 111-A) No, the answer is 'yes.' You were probably thinking of reflected impedance, which is that seen at one end of a network when the other end is terminated by a specific impedance, not necessarily identical with that reflected. Calculation of the reflected impedance with constant termination is very involved. The concept shown here is indicative of a similar thing but is simpler. Viewing the filter as part of a continuous line, T type and π type can be obtained by taking different pairs of half-

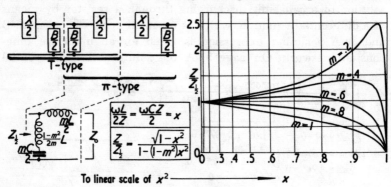

To linear scale of x^2 ——————→ x

sections. Now, taking a m-derived half-section of the T type that is assumed to be terminated with its image impedance, Z_o, we can find the reflected impedance at mid-point (called mid-shunt impedance), $Z_{\frac{1}{2}}$. Using the same derivation of x for f/f_c, we find an expression for $Z/Z_{\frac{1}{2}}$ (for the π filter, the equivalent will be the reciprocal, $Z_{\frac{1}{2}}/Z$, using the same expression). Plotting this for various values of m, using a scale of x^2 for convenience and to expand the critical area, we can see that the reflected impedance changes considerably. Now turn to 113-B.

116-B. (From 119-A) *No.* The fact that the maximal flatness curve does not coincide with best approach to phase linearity in this case leaves the matter to trial and error as to which way does give the best approach. It is not this way. So turn to the other answer.

116-C. (From 126-A) *No.* This is never completely true. In tightly coupled coils it sometimes comes very close to being true, but it is never quite correct. In loosely coupled coils it is a long way from true. See the other answer.

117-A. (From 113-B) *No.* This was true with the type of filters which in groups reflected constant resistance at their inputs (see 60-B, 81-B, 93-A and 95-A), because correct termination at the outputs of the group caused an overall constant resistance to be reflected, which means that the source resistance will not affect characteristics, any more than would feeding any other constant resistance. But this type of filter does not reflect a constant resistance under any circumstances, so the input impedance is important. Try another answer.

117-B. (From 128-A) *Correct.* Because the optimum we seek occurs where slopes of reluctance due to air gap (which is linear with gap dimension) and reluctance due to a.c. permeability of the iron path match one another, the overall effective permeability at optimum, as d.c.H is changed, will vary at twice the *rate* of change of the air-gap ratio. This means that the exponent will be approximately the square of the other one (4/5). The fraction 4/5 squared is 16/25, which is near to 2/3—as close as an empirical method such as this is likely to be. Experimental plotting of the values of μ'_e (or optimum inductance obtainable with so many turns at varying d.c.H, which is the practical equivalent) yields curves whose slopes are close to an exponent of $-2/3$. Units of μ'_e are not shown, because they are based on experimental tests with a coil of so many turns, and thus have no direct significance at this stage. The curves for the three materials lie closer together here (128-A) than they did on 127-A.

$$L \propto \frac{T^2 \mu'_e A_i}{L_i} \qquad \mu'_e \propto \left(\frac{IT}{L_i}\right)^{-\frac{2}{3}} \qquad \text{So } L \propto T^{\frac{4}{3}} \cdot I^{-\frac{2}{3}} \cdot \frac{A_i}{L_i^{\frac{1}{3}}}$$

$$T = 1.28 \times 10^3 L^{\frac{3}{4}} I^{\frac{1}{2}} \frac{L_i^{\frac{1}{4}}}{A_i^{\frac{3}{4}}} \qquad T \propto L^{\frac{3}{4}} \cdot I^{\frac{1}{2}} \cdot \frac{L_i^{\frac{1}{4}}}{A_i^{\frac{3}{4}}}$$

L in henry's I in amps L_i in inches A_i in square inches

Best core shape has large A_i small L_i **?** YES NO

When the expression for μ'_e is substituted into the expression for L (inductance) and exponents in T and L_i are collected, the approach begins to look more direct. We can transpose to obtain an expression for T in terms of L, I, L_i and A_i, which has been underscored. The formula in the box uses constants pertaining to silicon iron alloy. Now, does the expression show that a core shape with a fat, stocky core path is best (see 149-A), or has something been overlooked (see 138-A)?

118

118-A. (From 113-B) *Wrong*. Why is correct termination not important at the output end? See another answer.

118-B. (From 115-B) *Correct*. Notice that any solution for frequency, based on simple algebra, invariably yields a value of x^2, f^2, or ω^2. To verify this, see pages 31-B, 39-C, 44-A, 46-A, 50-A, 51-A, 59-A, 60-B, 70-B, 73-B, 86-D, 87-C, 90-B, 92-B, 93-A, 102-A, and 107-B. This may be explained with reference to vectors (see page 20-A): if positive frequency is represented by a vector rotating in the conventional counterclockwise direction, negative frequency would be represented by the same vector rotating the opposite way—clockwise. For many purposes, both rotations give the same result. Only where phase angles are involved does the dirction of rotation become important. Consequently, you will notice, solutions for ϕ_t invariably have odd powers of x or ω.

Pairs of points on the $j\omega$ axis represent steady frequency (unchanging in amplitude). Pairs of points above and below the α axis and to the right (α positive) represent a growing sine wave. Pairs of points above and below the α axis and to the left of the $j\omega$ axis (α negative) represent a decaying sine wave.

Points in the complex p-plane are found by solving differential equations in which *time* is the independent variable. Solutions for frequency response, of the kind introduced at page 92-B, use *frequency* as the independent (reference) variable. Work on transmission lines (see page 105-A) uses linear measure along the line as the reference variable (and sometimes time or frequency as well). It is important to clearly delineate which is your reference variable in a specific application. Now turn to 125-A.

118-C. (From 109-B) Maybe this question did not give enough information about the purpose for which the required design would be best. For transformers without d.c. polarization, or those in which any d.c. is balanced or neutralized, this may be true. But the statement referred to an inductor, by which we will assume that its inductance is its most important property—free from resistance losses. In this case an air gap is usually required for a different reason. See the other answer.

LINEAR PHASE NETWORKS

119-A. (From 107-B) So far we have been more concerned with the db, or amplitude aspect of frequency response, than with the phase response. For some applications, however, phase may be more important than db or amplitude, at least in certain parts of the system. This may occur when the time relationship between signals taking different paths has to be considered. A constant time delay is equivalent to a phase delay which is proportional to frequency.

The phase response normally presented (see 100-A) does not look as if any value-combination would make it linear. It curves one way up to the half-phase point and the opposite way beyond

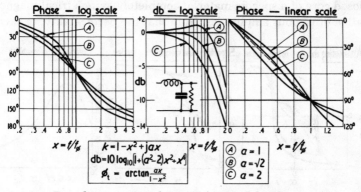

$$k = 1 - x^2 + jax$$
$$db = 10\log_{10}[1 + (a^2 - 2)x^2 + x^4]$$
$$\phi_t = \arctan\frac{ax}{1-x^2}$$

(A) $a = 1$
(B) $a = \sqrt{2}$
(C) $a = 2$

that point. But this is using the conventional log-frequency scale. On a linear scale the shape is different. Here a comparison is made between three responses using the same basic two-element network (it is shown with no input resistance, but the same characteristics may be achieved with terminations at both ends, using appropriately changed values). We can relate the responses to a constant a in the expression for k. The constant a happens to coincide with the quantity we wrote D for on page 66-B. At the left, phase is plotted to log-frequency scale; at the right the same responses are plotted to linear frequency scale. In the center the db response for the same group is given. Note that the closest approach to linear phase coincides with the maximal flatness curve. In a 3-reactance network, does the closest approach to linear phase, up to half-phase frequency, coincide with maximal flatness (see 120-A), need a slightly peaked combination (see 116-B), or need a combination giving greater loss at the cutoff point (see 122-A)?

120-A. (From 119-A) *Wrong.* This may have been a natural conclusion deduced from the simpler network, but it does not apply to the more complicated ones.

IRON-CORE INDUCTORS

120-B. (From 146-A) For low-frequency work, simple coils with nothing but air for the core are very low in efficiency, or Q-factor: their resistance is not appreciably less than their reactance. Use of a core, usually of an iron alloy, increases the inductance or reduces the losses—according to viewpoint—tremendously. To utilize the properties of such a core, the first step is to investigate its magnetization characteristic.

At the left are shown typical magnetization cycles using on a closed core of a specific material completely symmetrical magnetization of various amplitudes. Note that the permeability, or factor

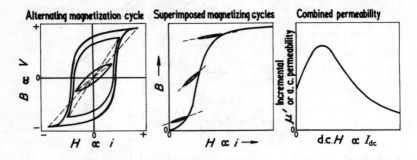

by which the core increases magnetization, changes with level of magnetization, as represented by the dashed lines joining the peaks of cycles of different amplitudes. When the magnetization is asymmetrical, as happens when both d.c. and a.c. are present, matters are complicated, as shown in the middle graph. Here the core without any gap (still closed) magnetizes according to the long curve of d.c. magnetization, and then follows one of the smaller incremental loops with the a.c. component. Note that the slope of the latter is always much less than that of the d.c. curve, or of a symmetrical a.c. curve, and that it too varies with position on the d.c. curve. The third curve shows the effective (incremental or a.c.) permeability, against d.c. magnetization, derived from loops taken at many points on the middle curve. In practical use the method is to include an air gap in the magnetic path, to reduce the d.c.H to (1) the point of maximum μ' (see 134-A) or (2) to some other point (see 127-A).

121-A. (From 122-A) No, it was the other way around—the larger inductance at the input end.

MUTUAL INDUCTANCE

121-B. (From 126-A) If you selected the second answer on 126-A, you were right. The inductance we discussed, beginning at 125-A, was that pertaining to a single coil, usually called self-inductance in basic treatments, because it is a measure of the voltage induced by a change in current in itself. When there are two coil windings, making a basic transformer, each coil, because of changing current, induces a voltage in the other coil. Each inductance will be proportional to the square of the turns in its winding, multi-

$$v_1 = L_1 \frac{di_1}{dt} - M \frac{di_2}{dt} \qquad v_2 = L_2 \frac{di_2}{dt} - M \frac{di_1}{dt}$$

$$L_1 = p_1 T_1^2$$
$$L_2 = p_2 T_2^2$$
$$M = p_m T_1 T_2$$
$$k = \frac{M}{\sqrt{L_1 L_2}}$$

where

p_1 is shape and size factor for L_1

p_2 is shape and size factor for L_2

p_m is shape and disposition factor for M

plied by the shape and size factor for that winding, and the mutual inductance will be proportional to the product of the turns in the windings, multiplied by a factor determined by the shape, size, and disposition of the two windings. The mutual inductance, M, is always less than the square root of the product of the individual inductances by a factor, k, called the *coupling factor*. It is a measure of the fraction of self-inducing field due to either winding that induces voltage in the other. Because mutual inductance is proportional to the product of the turns (field being caused by current in one winding, voltage being that induced by this field in the other), it is a measure of the voltage a given rate of change of current will produce, *either way*: current change in (1) producing voltage in (2), or vice versa.

Now this coupling factor, k, depends on the current flowing in the windings (see 113-C), or is only dependent on the physical disposition of the windings (see 146-A).

121-C. (From 138-A) *No.* Putting the I on the other side of the equation (or proportionality) inverts the exponent (gives it a negative sign), but it does not transfer the same exponent from one variable (L) to another (I) with merely a sign change. Try another answer.

122-A. (From 119-A) *Correct.* There are more variables with this network, so maximal flatness can be departed from in a variety of ways. The simplest analysis takes the family of cases where the asymptote of the 18 db/octave ultimate (when the coefficient of x^6 is 1) coincides with the half-phase point (which is not uniquely related in this network). By taking the general form and writing the coefficients of x^2 and jx from the expression for k into the expression for ϕ_t to make the latter arctan -1 for

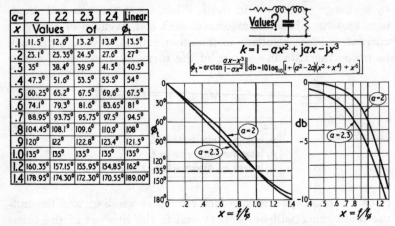

$a=$	2	2.2	2.3	2.4	Linear
x	Values	of		ϕ_t	
.1	11.5°	12.6°	13.2°	13.8°	13.5°
.2	23.1°	25.35°	24.5°	27.6°	27°
.3	35°	38.4°	39.9°	41.5°	40.5°
.4	47.3°	51.6°	53.5°	55.5°	54°
.5	60.25°	65.2°	67.5°	69.6°	67.5°
.6	74.1°	79.3°	81.6°	83.65°	81°
.7	88.95°	93.75°	95.75°	97.5°	94.5°
.8	104.45°	108.1°	109.6°	110.9°	108°
.9	120°	122°	122.8°	123.4°	121.5°
1.0	135°	135°	135°	135°	135°
1.2	160.35°	157.15°	155.95°	154.85°	162°
1.4	178.95°	174.30°	172.30°	170.55°	189.00°

Values?

$$k = 1 - ax^2 + jax - jx^3$$
$$\phi_t = \arctan \frac{ax - x^3}{1 - ax^2} \quad\Big\| \quad db = 10\log_{10}\left[1 + (a^2 - 2a)(x^2 + x^4) + x^6\right]$$

$x = 1$, the condition is that the coefficients of x^2 and jx are the same. In turn, this makes the coefficients of x^2 and x^4 in the db-attenuation expression identical ($a^2 - 2a$). From this point it is easy to run down, point by point, the phase response for a series of values for a, which we have tabulated here for $a = 2$ (maximal flatness), $a = 2.2$, $a = 2.3$, and $a = 2.4$. The middle one of these comes closest to linear phase response, up to the point $x = 1$. We have plotted the responses for $a = 2$ and $a = 2.3$ in both phase and db.

Now this gives us realizable responses, but not the values to achieve them. First we'll assume that the circuit works from zero impedance (constant voltage source) into a specific termination load. The correct values, normalizing to the values of L and C that have reactance equal to termination at reference frequency ($x = 1$), are: (1) $(1/2.3)L$, $(5.29/4.29)C$, $(4.29/2.3)L$ (see 121-A); or vice versa (2), reading from left to right toward termination (see 144-A).

HIGH-FREQUENCY RESPONSE

123-A. (From 132-B, 137-C, or 150-B) This depends on leakage reactance and winding capacitances. Leakage reactance results because the primary and secondary windings are not coupled 100% (coupling factor k is never quite unity). Winding capacitance is due to stray capacitance between individual turns of one winding, or between turns of one winding and those of an adjacent winding or screen. Which of these statements is wrong?

(1) Leakage reactance may be regarded as constant.

(2) Winding capacitance has the greater effect on high-impedance windings and little effect on low-impedance windings.

Answer: both wrong; see 131-C. Answer: both right; see 148-C. Answer: (1) wrong, (2) right; see 114-B. Answer: (1) right, (2) wrong; see 150-C.

123-B. (From 152-A) First deduce the physical parameters of the core. L_i figures out to be 8 inches and A_i is 2 square inches. V_i is their product, or 16 cubic inches. As a check you can figure volume directly. A_w is 1.875 inches by 13/16 inches, or 1.523 square inches. You can figure L_{mt} at 10 inches (this is based on a rectangular turn through the mean window-space, which is close to the right value; the corners actually curve, shortening it a little, but the coil always bulges a little more on the open sides than in the core window; so the rectangular estimate is usually very close). Now, using the turns formula, $L_i/V_i^{3/4}$ is equal to 1 (very conveniently); so the turns are $L^{3/4}$ times $I^{1/2}$ times 1,280. $L^{3/4}$ times $I^{1/2}$ conveniently reduces to 5; thus the number of turns should be 6,400. Dividing this by A_w, we require 4,200 turns per square inch, and the square root of this is 64.8 turns per inch. Gage 27 comes close at 64.2 turns per inch. In a 1.875-inch layer it will give 120 turns. Thus 13/16 inch will accommodate 52 layers (there is a fractional part, but you can't wind a fraction of a layer thickness: it's either there or it isn't), making a total of 6,240 winding turns. Allowing for a slight loss, 6,200 is a reasonable figure. With a mean turn of 10 inches this is 5,165 feet of wire, with a resistance of 266 ohms. Formula (1) on 109-B gives 287 ohms, but we had to cut turns, which means inductance will be slightly low (gage 27 is a whisker too large). If we go to gage 28, then 6,400 turns are feasible, with a resistance of 347 ohms. That's our choice. Based on 6,400 turns the total gap, by formula (3), works out to be .047 inch, or .0235 inch actual spacing.

124-A. (From 144-A) *Wrong.* Although the external connection is similar to the image-impedance derived type of filter, the method of deriving its values follows the same derivation as the one on 144-A. See 112-B.

124-B. (From 129-A) *Correct.* Using a sinusoidal voltage (the current will be quite different in waveform) proportional to frequency, the magnetization cycle can be kept the same, and only the frequency will be changed. At the left a typical V/I trace (A) is analyzed. First, because of the nonlinear magnetization characteristic of the material, the curve exhibits harmonic content (B), which can be isolated by a suitable bridge circuit.

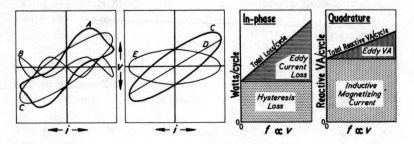

If the harmonic is removed, the remainder is an ellipse (C), which can be subdivided into in-phase (voltage in phase with current) and quadrature components $(D$ and $E)$. The pure quadrature component is identified by having its major and minor axes vertical and horizontal (or vice versa) respectively, never at an angle. When a plot of in-phase and quadrature components is made, and each reading is divided by frequency so that the ordinates are units *per cycle* (either watts or reactive VA), the result for each is a straight line at a slant. Because the hysteresis and magnetizing components will each follow the same course for every cycle of the same flux density, their graph will be constant when plotted in this way. Eddy current effects, on the other hand, will be proportional to frequency. If the curve is started at zero frequency and a linear scale is used, the separation is easy. The solid rectangle is hysteresis or magnetizing effect; the triangular wedge represents eddy current effect. As reflected in the electrical circuit to which the inductor is connected, eddy current effect is (1) equivalent to a constant resistance, slightly reactive (see 131-B), or (2) equivalent to a resistance whose value changes with frequency (see 149-B).

INDUCTANCE-COIL DESIGN

125-A. (From 118-B) We now turn from the design of networks and circuits employing inductances and capacitances to the design of those elements, particularly inductances. Capacitance design is largely a matter of solving the simple formula relating plate area, thickness of dielectric, and dielectric constant to give capacitance. Inductance design utilizes a few more variables.

First we shall consider the relatively simple, long solenoid, which exhibits the basic relationship between inductance and the physical dimensions of a coil. This relationship is derived from first principles of electromagnetism and a coil assumed to

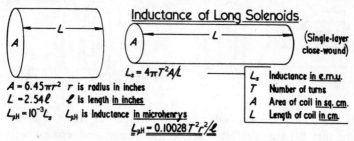

Inductance of Long Solenoids.

(Single-layer close-wound)

$$L_s = 4\pi T^2 A/L$$

$A = 6.45\pi r^2$ r is radius in inches
$L = 2.54\ell$ ℓ is length in inches
$L_{\mu H} = 10^{-3} L_s$ $L_{\mu H}$ is inductance in microhenrys

$$L_{\mu H} = 0.10028\, T^2 r^2/\ell$$

L_s Inductance in e.m.u.
T Number of turns
A Area of coil in sq. cm.
L Length of coil in cm.

be indefinitely long. Basically the result is a value of inductance per unit length, which is related to the turns per unit length. The total inductance is proportional to turns squared; the final inductance becomes inversely proportional to the length over which turns are spread.

Using dimensions in metric units (centimeters), the formula thus derived gives inductance in electromagnetic absolute units (e.m.u.). So we make conversions from centimeters to inches for both length and cross-section, conversion from cross-sectional area to radius (or it could be to diameter), and from e.m.u. to practical units (in this case, microhenrys). This results in a formula that is (1) true for coils whose length is greater than their diameter (see 148-A); (2) approximately true for coils whose length is much greater than diameter (see 132-A); (3) true for coils of any proportions (see 150-A).

125-B. (From 131-B) *No.* You were probably thinking of hysteresis *loss* as being inversely proportional to frequency—which it is. But as a shunt resistance, a value inversely proportional to frequency (on constant applied voltage) will take a current proportional to frequency, which is wrong. Try another answer.

126-A. (From 132-A) Multilayer coils can come in such a variety of shapes that there is no single, relatively simple approach to their design. If the winding turns are uniformly distributed through a given cross-section, the inductance is a complicated function of the ratios t/d and l/d, which completely describe its shape. From a factor thus derived, inductance is proportional to turns squared and also to linear dimensions of the coil (represented by d, because in the complete formula it starts as d^2 divided by length). Here we have shown the variety of coils that can occur in practice: (1) t/d and l/d both small; (2) t/d small, l/d large; (3) t/d large, l/d small; (4) t/d and l/d both large.

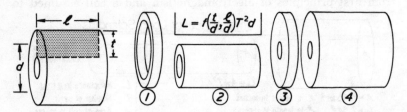

If the shape is specified, and the number of turns changed so as to just fill the available space uniformly, inductance will always change in strict proportion to turns squared. If the space is not filled, inductance will be changed, according to what part of the space is not occupied. For single-layer coils (see 125-A), inductance will be modified slightly if turns are uniformly spaced to occupy a certain length, instead of being wound with a wire diameter that will fill that space with the same number of turns. In all this work the best calculations serve to achieve results close to the required values, and correct values are obtained empirically.

Now, in a coil with two sets of turns, mutually coupled, the induction is identical in each set, so the voltage induced is always proportional to the respective numbers of turns (see 116-C), or this is not true (see 121-B).

126-B. (From 152-A) Answer (1) is correct. The impedance with which the hysteresis component compares for distortion generation is the parallel combination of 1.25K and 6K, which is 1.035K. The other answers use incorrect "source" impedances across which to "load" the magnetizing component. See 147-B.

127-A. (From 120-B) *Correct.* Here we show the situation as the length of the air gap is changed for one particular value of d.c. magnetization. Air-gap reluctance (which is what reduces the d.c.H in the core) increases linearly with the length of the gap. The d.c. field in the core drops in something like reciprocal fashion. The a.c. reluctance of the core, dependent on the d.c.H and the reciprocal of a.c. permeability (and also dependent on dimensions of the core) follows yet another curve. We have marked minimum a.c. reluctance of the core, which coincides

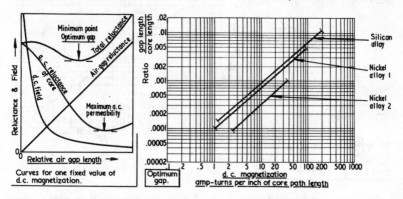

with the condition on 120-B of maximum a.c. permeability. Total reluctance to a.c. magnetization is the sum of that in the air gap and that in the core material. Its minimum corresponds with the optimum gap for this value of d.c.H, which we have also marked.

Making a plot (on the right, with log-log scales) of optimum gaps for various values of d.c.H, forms the basis for using cores under optimum conditions. To make the "curves"—which are very close to straight lines—universally applicable for each magnetic material represented (we have shown three typical ones), d.c.H is given in ampere-turns (current in amps multiplied by turns) per inch length of core path, and air gap is given likewise as a fraction of total path length. Now, to design an inductor, first assume (1) a number of turns (see 128-A); (2) a value of d.c.H (see 131-A); (3) an air-gap length (see 137-A).

127-B. (From 135-B) *No.* The air gap is in series with the main part of the magnetic core, but this does not mean its magnetization appears as a series element in the electrical circuit supplying the needed current. See the other answer.

128

128-A. (From 127-A) *Correct.* This may not seem like a very direct approach—it isn't. But at the outset T is the only reasonably independent variable with which to start. Polarized magnetization, d.c.H, depends directly on IT/L_i, where I (d.c. magnetizing current) is fixed by external circuit considerations, and L_i (length of magnetic path in core) is fixed by choice of core size, leaving only T variable. Also inductance L varies as T^2, as

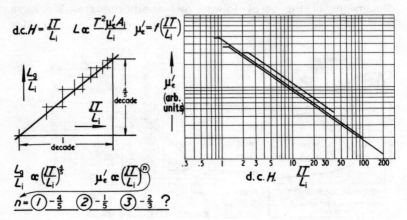

a quantity we have designated μ_e' (effective overall permeability to a.c. with air gap, at optimum point), and as the core path proportions A_i (cross-section area), over L_i. The quantity μ_e' must be some kind of function of IT/L_i. The question is: what kind?

Note that the curves on 127-A are almost straight lines. This means that the air gap expressed as a fraction of path length (L_g/L_i) can be deduced to vary as nearly a constant exponent of (IT/L_i); we find it to be close to the 4/5 power, by the method shown here. Now the appropriate exponent for variation of μ_e' with IT/L_i is the answer we have marked (1): see 133-A; (2): see 111-B; or (3): see 117-B?

128-B. (From 151-A) Assuming that the coils have identical dimensions, one will have twice the turns in the other. The last requirement hinges on the coupling factor for mutual inductance (see 146-A). There we find that short-circuiting one coil effectively reduces inductance of the other by the factor $(1 - k^2)$. This means the required value of k is 0.707. If the coils are not identical, so that the first requirement is met by other than a 2:1 turns ratio, the required coupling factor is unchanged and will achieve the required effect just the same.

CORE MAGNETIZATION LOSSES

129-A. (From 145-A) Here we examine a hysteresis loop, or magnetization cycle, of the kind introduced at 120-B, to see what it means. On the same square is shown a B/H cycle and a V/I cycle, as it would be reflected into the electrical circuit of the inductor. On the B/H cycle, the fact that it is a loop is due to hysteresis, which is a delay of magnetization (B) behind the applied magnetizing force (H). The area of the loop represents a loss of energy. The other curve displaces the vertical deflection

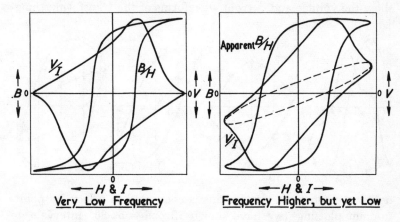

Very Low Frequency   Frequency Higher, but yet Low

(viewing this as you would a 'scope trace) by 90° relative to the horizontal, on the frequency of the cycle. The patterns in the left square represent a very low frequency, so low that eddy currents in the core material are negligible. The right-hand patterns show what happens when eddy currents begin to add their losses. The dashed ellipse represents the component of magnetizing current e.m.f. that supplies eddy currents in the core, which when added to the V/I curve at the left produces the V/I curve shown here. The corresponding B/H curve has its ends "blunted" and turned in, as shown. At higher frequencies, where eddy currents cause the biggest component of magnetizing current, both V/I and B/H curves approach an elliptical shape. To analyze what happens at different frequencies and amplitudes we need some way of separating these components of the losses. Is this achieved by: (1) making measurements where current is kept constant as frequency is changed (see 135-A); (2) making voltage proportional to frequency (see 124-B); (3) making current proportional to frequency (see 137-B)?

130

130-A. (From 110-B) *Wrong*. A tube's input can be simple grid voltage, with virtually no current, but a transistor's input is never this simple.

130-B. (From 141-B) This is sometimes the best method. One example is the case where part of the load is the magnetizing current of a choke or transformer (usually at low frequencies). Here the tube or transistor is operating under sensibly linear conditions, but nonlinear loading produced by transformer magnetizing current (for example) may cause trouble. At (1) we show the voltage and current waveforms of the transformer mag-

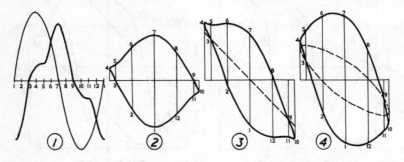

netizing component. At (2) this is converted to a loop by point-to-point plotting (we have shown 12 points at 30° intervals, to keep the diagram simple to read, but more are needed for an accurate job). Current is vertical, voltage horizontal. At (3) we add this, point by point, to a line representing a paralleled resistance load. Here, although the current amplitude (vertical height of (2)) is close to that in the resistance load (vertical height of dashed straight line (3)), the overall current amplitude is very little more than that for the resistance load alone. At (4) the same magnetizing current is combined with an ellipse representing an inductive reactive load with peak current slightly less than that of the resistance (3), but the current excursion increases considerably.

Loops of this kind are satisfactory, applied to the linear part of tube or transistor characteristics, or to determine whether they may be contained within the linear part or not. In this way possibility of distortion due to interaction between iron and tube characteristics may be predicted but not closely analyzed. Complete analysis would become very involved. Now see what other answers have to say.

131-A. (From 127-A) *Wrong.* Try one of the others.

131-B. (From 124-B) Correct, although a mistake is often made here. On page 124-B, eddy current effects were shown as being proportional to frequency, as plotted in loss or VA *per cycle.* Multiplying this by frequency, the effect would be proportional to frequency squared. But note that this series of measurements was made with voltage proportional to frequency, to obtain constant magnetic flux density. With voltage proportional to frequency and current also proportional to frequency, you have the properties of a linear resistance. It is important to see this clearly, to understand design problems involving core losses.

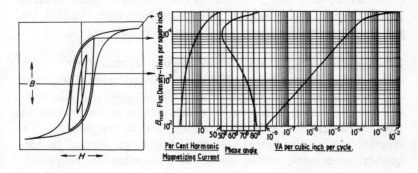

Once the eddy current component can be separated, the hysteresis and magnetizing component can be analyzed, as we have shown here. These are typical results for a nickel-iron alloy. The minimum phase angle occurs just as the material begins to go into saturation. Below that the loop is narrower, and above it the loop does not get any wider; it just "bends over," producing a rapid rise in current and distortion content. The complete core loss and magnetizing current at any frequency is obtained by adding the eddy current and hysteresis–cum–magnetizing components (also any due to an air gap) at that level and frequency. Next, we turn back to the question of inductor design for a.c. magnetization only. For this purpose, hysteresis loss may be approximated as (1) a constant resistance (see 141-A); (2) a resistance proportional to frequency (see 135-B); (3) a resistance inversely proportional to frequency (see 125-B).

131-C. (From 123-A) *No.* At least one of them was right.

132-A. (From 125-A) *Correct*. This should have been deduced from the statement about how the formula was derived. Except when length is *much* greater than diameter, end effects considerably modify the result.

Wheeler's Formula

Accurate to 1% $\frac{2r}{\ell} < 3$

Approx. 4% low when $\frac{2r}{\ell} = 5$

$$L_{\mu H} = \frac{r^2 T^2}{9r + 10\ell}$$

Example $\ell = 2r$ $L_{\mu H} = \frac{r^2 T^2}{14.5\ell}$

$$= \frac{r T^2}{29}$$

For shorter, more practical solenoids or coils, of single-layer construction, adaptations have to be made. A good approximation is *Wheeler's formula*, which is given here. Now turn to 126-A for the basic information about the design of multilayer coils.

132-B. (From 148-B) Most often correct for transformers designed to handle power at relatively low frequencies. The graph on log-log scales shows why. For a specific magnetizing flux density, corresponding to a level at which serious distortion sets in (due to saturation), voltage is proportional to frequency. At a specific design impedance, voltage rising in proportion to frequency represents power rising in proportion to frequency

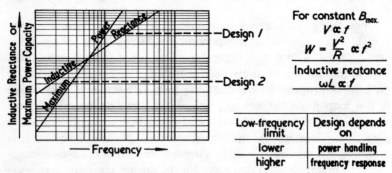

For constant B_{max}.

$V \propto f$

$$W = \frac{V^2}{R} \propto f^2$$

Inductive reatance

$\omega L \propto f$

Low-frequency limit	Design depends on
lower	power handling
higher	frequency response

squared. As compared with this, low-frequency response depends on an approximately linear relationship between inductive reactance (directly proportional to frequency) and working impedance, even though inductance may not be quite constant. Therefore, as the low-frequency limit is raised in frequency, inductive reactance causing cutoff in response is more likely to be the controlling factor (see 137-C). If you have already studied 137-C and 150-B, turn to 123-A.

133-A. (From 128-A) *No.* You correctly deduced that the slope is the opposite way, represented by the negative sign, but it is not the same numerically. Optimum air gap occurs (see 127-A) where increasing reluctance of the air gap is at the same rate as decreasing reluctance of the iron path. If this function had the same exponent as the air gap function, but of opposite sign, it would mean that the decreasing reluctance of the iron path is linear—which it cannot be. Try another answer.

133-B. (From 141-B) This is only true when the characteristics on which the load line has to be laid happen to be linear enough over the entire area covered by the ellipse so that nonlinearity need not be considered. As we were concerned with using load lines to evaluate distortion on 110-B, this method cannot be used

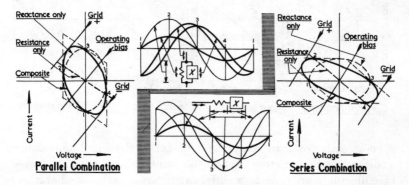

Parallel Combination   **Series Combination**

as an extension for that purpose. However, it is often useful to see whether an elliptical load line does fall within reasonably linear limits. To this end the constructions for an ellipse have been shown to represent both parallel and series combinations of reactance and resistance. As shown by the waveforms alongside, in the parallel combination voltage across the two elements is the same, so points 2 and 4 represent voltage maxima across both elements. At voltage zeros the resistance component current is zero (at the operating point on the tube characteristics), while the reactance current is a maximum (combination ellipse parallel to resistance component line at this point on voltage). In the series case, both elements carry the same current, represented by maxima at 2 and 4, while zero current corresponds with zero voltage in resistance, but with voltage maxima in reactance (points 1 and 3). As this only applies where conditions are relatively linear, try one of the other answers.

134

134-A. (From 120-B) *No.* This would only make the part of the magnetic path in the iron of maximum permeability; but a considerable part of the total *reluctance*, or magnetic resistance, would be in the air gap, so that a smaller gap will result in lower total reluctance, or higher effective permeability (based on the total magnetic circuit, including the gap), than when the iron by itself is working at its maximum.

134-B. (From 110-B) Yes, we have to take input impedance into account, and use the right value of source resistance or impedance to feed the input. Here at (1) is the current transfer characteristic as it might be derived from the collector characteristics (similar to the pentode plate characteristics on 110-B) for a

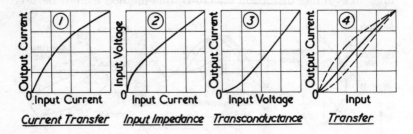

specific collector load resistance. At (2) is the input impedance (voltage against current) using the same collector load (change of collector load reflects a different input-impedance characteristic). At (3) is the transfer characteristic using voltage input (zero source resistance or impedance) instead of current input (infinite source resistance or impedance). At (4), with curves (1) and (3) repeated in dashed lines, is a transfer characteristic with a specific value of input resistance or impedance.

Although it may be possible to calculate a suitable value in some instances, usually the data given are insufficient to permit this, and the best method is to find the most nearly linear combination of values empirically, and then try an adequate number of samples to ensure a representative choice.

So far, we have assumed a plate or collector load-value (by the slope of the load line) without relating this to the actual circuit values. In practice the a.c. load may be (1) greater than the d.c. resistance in circuit (see 148-D); (2) less than the d.c. resistance in circuit (see 150-D); (3) either greater or less, in different circumstances (see 141-B).

135-A. (From 129-A) *Wrong*. Using current as a reference, this comes closest to being correct, but the object is to make measurements at different frequencies, but at the same magnetic flux density, as indicated by the voltage. Try another answer.

HIGH-Q IRON-CORE INDUCTOR DESIGN

135-B. (From 131-B) First, in answer to the question on 131-B, hysteresis loss may be represented as a shunt resistance of value proportional to frequency: based on 124-B, voltage and watts are both proportional to frequency and watts per cycle are constant; therefore current is constant. These are the dimensions of resistance proportional to frequency.

Now, to apply what was started on 145-A, the pertinent formulas (for one frequency) are given at the left. An analysis of losses with changing level for two different materials (N, a nickel-iron

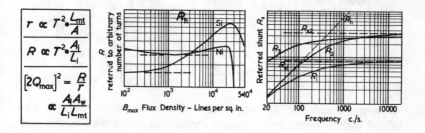

$$r \propto T^2 \cdot \frac{L_{mt}}{A}$$

$$R \propto T^2 \cdot \frac{A_i}{L_i}$$

$$[2Q_{max}]^2 = \frac{R}{r}$$

$$\propto \frac{A_i A_w}{L_i L_{mt}}$$

alloy; S, a silicon-iron alloy) shows how the effective value of R_h varies with level. Within saturation range a value can be taken which represents a minimum (dashed horizontal lines). At other levels R_h will vary above this, thus achieving a value higher than the calculated Q-factor for the inductor.

Now consider frequency dependence of the core losses, shown at the right. Curves R_1 and R_2 represent total core losses referred as a shunt resistance, for cores of the same material in two different lamination thicknesses; curve R_2 for laminations one-half the thickness of those for curve R_1. The dashed lines R_{e1} and R_{e2} represent the eddy current components, while R_h represents the hysteresis component. R_3 is for another core material. Now, can the current and voltage representing the main inductance property of the component, as controlled by the air gap, be regarded as an element (1) in series (see 127-B) or (2) in shunt (see 136-A) with the loss elements?

136

136-A. (From 135-B) *Correct.* The basis for this can be seen by considering the relationship between magnetic and electrical quantities. Voltage is caused by the rate of change of magnetic flux, which is proportional to flux density, being density times area. So for sinusoidal waveforms, voltage and magnetic flux are proportional with a 90° phase displacement between them. Magnetizing force (usually measured by unit length of path, and therefore multiplied by path length to get total force) depends on electric current directly. So if more reluctance is added in series with the magnetic circuit, as by an air gap, it requires more current in the electric circuit to provide the additional Hl.

The final stage of design of an inductor for a.c., once you have calculated the turns and wire gauge that will give the best r and R at the desired reference frequency, is to determine the

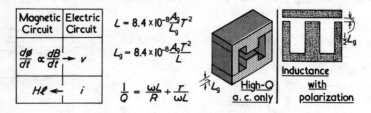

$$L = 8.4 \times 10^{-8} \frac{A_g}{L_g} T^2$$

$$L_g = 8.4 \times 10^{-8} \frac{A_g T^2}{L}$$

$$\frac{1}{Q} = \frac{\omega L}{R} + \frac{r}{\omega L}$$

air gap needed for the required inductance value. This is obtained by the empirical formula shown here (where lengths and areas are given in inches, and inductance is in henrys. Optimum air gap will be proportional to frequency in the range where eddy current effects dominate. When hysteresis effects dominate, the proportionality is nearer to the square root of frequency (and Q is deteriorating with lower frequency). Wider gaps may be too short, due to increased effective area by fringing. Very short gaps may be impractical physically because the core contribution to reluctance invalidates the formula and makes the inductance subject to nonlinearity. This can be overcome by using gaps larger or smaller than the theoretical optimum, with a slight degradation of Q. Turns can be changed so that the new gap still provides the correct inductance. For example, using double or half the optimum gap will degrade Q to ¾ of its maximum value. Here we also show the best form of core for this type of inductor, one using F laminations. It has only one gap, with practically no leakage field outside the component. The type most often used with polarized inductors (109-B) has a total gap of twice the physical spacing between lamination parts. Now turn to 148-B.

137-A. (From 127-A) *Wrong.* Try one of the others.

137-B. (From 129-A) *Wrong.* See one of the other answers.

137-C. (From 148-B) Sometimes correct, particularly for input and interstage types of transformers. There are two basic circuit networks in which such a transformer may control low-frequency response, according to whether or not a capacitor is used. Without the capacitor (left) we have simple R/L combination. It should be noted that L is not constant (unless the core is gapped, which deteriorates the response compared with an ungapped

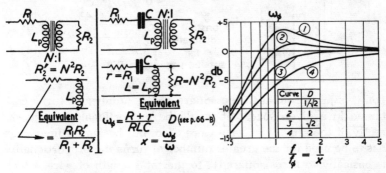

Low-Frequency Response

core). So response may not be the simple roll-off derived from 61-A. But it follows this general form and may change with level to some extent.

With the series capacitor (parallel-fed) a similar derivation of equivalent is followed. Again, the value of L_p may not be constant with either frequency or level, but, assuming that it is, the response uses the same formula developed in 66-B, merely by using $1/x$ instead of x, for ω/ω_ϕ. At the right, four responses for successive values of D are shown (see 66-B for the significance of this parameter). All are normalized to ω_ϕ, the phase reference-frequency, although this will invariably change according to how the elements are changed to produce the difference in D. This fact must not be overlooked. Now refer to one of the other answers from 148-D, or if you've already studied both of them, turn to 123-A.

138-A. (From 117-B) *Correct.* Efficiency of an inductor of this type depends not only on the core but also on the winding dimensions. The formula on 117-B merely shows the shape that would obtain a specific inductance with specified d.c. (*I*) and minimum turns. But these turns have to be squeezed into a space. Here we take all of these factors into account. Resistance of the winding, which is usually the important factor from this view-

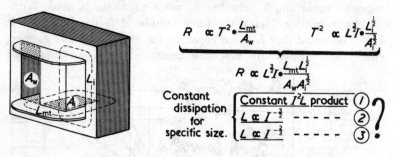

$$R \propto T^2 \cdot \frac{L_{mt}}{A_w} \qquad\qquad T^2 \propto L^{\frac{3}{2}} I \cdot \frac{L_i^{\frac{1}{2}}}{A_i^{\frac{3}{2}}}$$

$$R \propto L^{\frac{3}{2}} I \cdot \frac{L_{mt} L_i^{\frac{1}{2}}}{A_w A_i^{\frac{3}{2}}}$$

Constant
dissipation
for
specific size.

Constant $I^2 L$ product	①
$L \propto I^{-\frac{3}{2}}$ --------	②
$L \propto I^{-\frac{2}{3}}$ -------	③

point, is proportional to the square of the number of turns contained in a given space (it would be proportional to turns directly, if the same wire gage were used, but because a finer gage has to be used for the greater number of turns the proportionality is basically to turns squared); to the total length of wire, which is number of turns times length per turn, or, having taken number of turns into account, we take care of length by a factor L_{mt} for length of a mean (or average) turn; and, finally, resistance is inversely proportional to winding window area (the proportion of it actually occupied by wire), because the bigger the window, the bigger is the gage that can be used. Combining these facts with the proportionality established on 117-B, we find one that gives the overall picture in one statement.

Now, suppose we are designing a whole group of inductors on the same core size, to have the same dissipation at their rated d.c., what will be the relationship between *L* and *I* for different numbers in the product line? Answer (1): see 109-B; answer (2): see 121-C; answer (3): see 139-A.

138-B. (From 151-A) Applying the formula (and remembering that *r* is half the diameter) the number of turns is equal to the square root of 17,000, or 130 (well within 1%). If 130 turns occupy 1¼ inches, this is 104 turns per inch. From the table on 143-B the suitable wire gage is 30 Awg. So the answer is *130 turns of 30 Awg* enameled wire.

139-A. (From 138-A) *Wrong.* This would be the relationship for constant *resistance, i.e.,* using the same winding with different air gaps. But we specifically required constant dissipation, which means turns (and thereby resistance) must be changed so the dissipation is always the same, as current rating is changed. Try another answer.

139-B. (From 151-A) A question like this does not have a specific, correct answer, because it is open to interpretation as to what is the best approximation to linear phase-response. Also, the sharpness of the rejection may be important: it could be too sharp or too broad; this was not specified. First we can derive the attenuation factor k, normalizing to the rejection frequency. Then we try values that make the series element $\sqrt{2}$ times ter-

$k = 1 + j a x \left(1 + \dfrac{j b x}{1-x^2}\right) = 1 - \dfrac{a b x^2}{1-x^2} + j a x = \dfrac{1-(1+ab)x^2}{1-x^2} + j a x$

$\phi_t = \arctan \dfrac{a x (1-x^2)}{1-(1+ab)x^2}$ Write $B = 1 + ab$

$\phi_t = \arctan \dfrac{a x (1-x^2)}{1-Bx^2}$

$X - jax$
L_1
$B = \dfrac{jbx}{1-x^2}$ L_2 $G=1$ Impedance normalizing reference C

Plot for various combinations of a and B

$\sqrt{2}/.8 = 1.77$ Try $a = 1.75$ $b \approx 1/3$ Try $B = 1.6$

$a = 1.75$ $B = 1.6$

x	num.	den.	ϕ_t	
.1	.1732	.984	10°	numerator controls small angle change
.2	.336	.936	19.25°	
.3	.478	.856	29.2°	
.4	.588	.744	38.35°	
.5	.656	.600	47.5°	denominator controls large angle change
.6	.672	.424	57.7°	
.7	.625	.216	70.9°	
.8	.504	-.024	92.74°	

$a = 1$ $B = 1.1$

num.	den.	ϕ_t
.099	.989	5.7°
.192	.956	11.4°
.273	.901	16.85°
.336	.824	22.2°
.375	.728	27.4°
.384	.604	32.4°
.357	.461	37.85°
.288	.296	44.25°

Make output load = 10K
$f_\infty = 38$ Kc. so $\omega_\infty = 2.38 \times 10^5$
Using $a=1$ $B=1.1$ $1 + ab = 1.1$
$ab = .1$
$b = .1$

$L_1 = \dfrac{10^4}{2.38 \times 10^5} = 42\,mH$ $L_2 = 420\,mH$

$C = \dfrac{1}{2.38 \times 10^5 \times 10^5} = 42\,\mu\mu F$

mination at the 0.8 frequency and the shunt element correspond at this particular frequency; this gave best approximation in the simple network (see 119-A). Here, however, the approximation is not too good. But from it we can see that the numerator of the arctan expression controls the phase slope for small values of x, while the denominator controls it at larger values, approaching $x = 0.8$. Using this fact, and juggling values of a and B (the latter is used in place of b, because it has more direct significance in terms of response, both phase and amplitude), a satisfactory compromise can be found. The one we chose was $a = 1$ and $B = 1.1$, from which we find $b = 0.1$. Assuming the output load to be 10K (an arbitrary figure), we can obtain values for the two L's and the C. Note that these are not the only values that would be acceptable to this question. The test is to determine whether the phase linearity is good enough.

140-A. (From 141-B) This answer is probably correct in most cases. The nonlinearity of tube (or transistor) characteristics is very involved, having different curvatures in different directions in the two-dimensional plane of the voltage-current curves. As current is plotted vertically and voltage horizontally, both are distorted in a different way, and the relationship between the two waveforms has to satisfy the "dimensions" of the load, as an impedance of greater or less complexity. Even the simplest variety will have some reactance, which is a function of frequency. Since distortion is present, the reactance for different components of the waveforms will differ. Assuming that a satisfactory calculation could be evolved, to be meaningful it should be valid for different frequencies, which would involve a prohibitive amount of work. The empirical approach is the best.

But there are some cases in which sufficient information can be achieved by one of the other methods. So try another answer. When you have tried all the answers, turn to 151-A.

140-B. (From 151-A) We make four calculations of attenuation factor k for values of r equal to 0, 1, ½, and 2. Then substitute the condition that fixes roll-off frequency at $x = 1$ (by the x^4

Case ① $r=0$: $k=1+jax(1+jbx)=1-abx^2+jax$
Amp. $k^2=1+(a^2-2ab)x^2+a^2b^2x^4$
$ab=1$
$a^2-2ab=0$
$a=\sqrt{2}$
$b=1/\sqrt{2}$

Case ② $r=1$: $k=1+(1+jax)(1+jbx)=2-abx^2+j(a+b)x$
Amp. $k^2=4+(a-b)^2x^2+a^2b^2x^4$
$ab=2$
$a-b=0$
$a=b=\sqrt{2}$

Case ③ $r=\tfrac{1}{2}$: $k=1+(\tfrac{1}{2}+jax)(1+jbx)=\tfrac{3}{2}-abx^2+j(a+\tfrac{1}{2}b)x$
Amp. $k^2=\tfrac{9}{4}+(a^2-2ab+\tfrac{1}{4}b^2)x^2+a^2b^2x^4$
$ab=\tfrac{3}{2}$ $a^2-2ab+\tfrac{1}{4}b^2=0$
$a=\frac{3\pm\sqrt{3}}{2\sqrt{2}}$ / $b=\frac{3\mp\sqrt{3}}{\sqrt{2}}$
≈ 1.67 or $.45$ / $\approx .965$ or 3.33

Case ④ $r=2$: $k=1+(2+jax)(1+jbx)=3-abx^2+j(a+2b)x$
Amp. $k^2=9+(a^2-2ab+4b^2)x^2+a^2b^2x^4$
$ab=3$ | $a^2-2ab+4b^2=0$ | $a+2b=3\sqrt{2}$ $a-2b=j\sqrt{6}$ Both a and b complex

asymptote) and amplitude coefficient of x^2 is zero. Solving, we find the values used in the crossover (see 95-A) for $r = 0$. Making $r = 1$, the series element is the same, but the shunt element is changed. Does this mean the output termination affects the series element, and the input termination affects the shunt element? Case 3 settles this; making $r = \frac{1}{2}$, we get alternative solutions—two pairs of values that will work. Case 4, making $r = 2$, finishes the picture. Only for values of r between zero and R is there a real solution. At the limits, $r = 0$ and $r = R$, there is only one solution. In between, there are two.

141-A. (From 131-B) Are you basing this answer on the solid rectangle representing hysteresis loss on 124-B? If so, you're wrong. That plot used constant magnetic flux density, not constant applied voltage, as a basis. As this was taken with voltage proportional to frequency, any R to represent it in the electrical circuit must have some dependence on frequency. Try another answer.

141-B. (From 134-B) Correct, and here are typical examples of each. When d.c. is supplied to the plate (or to the collector of a transistor) through an inductive element (a transformer is shown here, but inductance-capacitance coupling is similar), the d.c. resistance of the inductive element (in this case the transformer

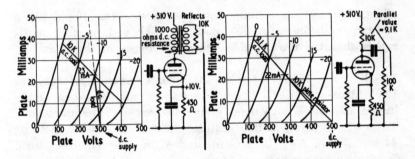

primary) determines the d.c. operating point. The a.c. load line is determined by the impedance reflected back through the transformer or that is capacitance coupled to the plate in the case of inductance-capacitance coupling. Bias resistance is calculated from the plate current and grid voltage needed at the operating point, in this case, 23 mA and 10V.

With resistance-capacitance coupling, the d.c. line, fixing the operating point, is determined by the actual plate (or collector) resistor. The additional resistance coupled in parallel combines to produce the a.c. load-line value, which in this case is always less than the d.c. value.

The load lines we have been drawing are all straight and thus represent linear resistance values. What happens for loads that have reactance components? (1) Simply draw the appropriate elliptical load line (see 133-B); (2) the load ellipsoid has to be plotted, point by point (see 130-B); (3) it cannot easily be predicted, but has to be found empirically (see 140-A); (4) a different method has to be adopted (see 149-C).

142-A. (From 151-A) Here is the correct calculation. Note that series elements of adjacent filters are combined into single elements of the composite network. As was shown (see 116-A), sections with $m = 0.6$ are used at the ends to minimize mismatch

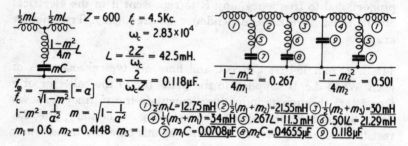

$$\tfrac{1}{2}mL \quad \tfrac{1}{2}mL \quad Z = 600 \quad f_c = 4.5\text{Kc}.$$

$$\omega_c = 2.83 \times 10^4$$

$$\frac{1-m^2}{4m}L$$

$$L = \frac{2Z}{\omega_c} = 42.5\text{mH}.$$

$$mC$$

$$C = \frac{2}{\omega_c Z} = 0.118\mu\text{F}.$$

$$\frac{f_\infty}{f_c} = \frac{1}{\sqrt{1-m^2}}[=a]$$

$$\frac{1-m^2}{4m_1} = 0.267 \qquad \frac{1-m^2}{4m_2} = 0.501$$

$$1-m^2 = \frac{1}{a^2} \quad m = \sqrt{1-\frac{1}{a^2}}$$

$$m_1 = 0.6 \quad m_2 = 0.4148 \quad m_3 = 1$$

① $\tfrac{1}{2}m_1L = 12.75\text{mH}$ ② $\tfrac{1}{2}(m_1+m_2) = 21.55\text{mH}$ ③ $\tfrac{1}{2}(m_2+m_3) = 30\text{mH}$
④ $\tfrac{1}{2}(m_3+m_1) = \underline{34\text{mH}}$ ⑤ $.267L = \underline{11.3\text{mH}}$ ⑥ $.501L = 21.29\text{mH}$
⑦ $m_1C = \underline{0.0708\mu\text{F}}$ ⑧ $m_2C = \underline{.04655\mu\text{F}}$ ⑨ $0.118\mu\text{F}$

effects, because the terminating impedance is (or should be) a constant resistance (of 600 ohms, at each end, in this case), rather than the unrealizable image impedance of the filter.

142-B. (From 152-A) First we shall find a complete reference to 1,000 turns at 100 c/s. The winding space may be taken as 1⅜ inches long by ⅜ inch deep, giving an area of .515 square inch. To get 1,000 turns in this requires 1,940 turns/square inch, or 44 turns/inch. Awg. 24 will fill this. With a 6-inch mean turn, 500 feet give a resistance of 13 ohms. Shunt loss is 100K eddy and 100K/8, or 12.5K, hysteresis. The total parallel loss is 11.1K. Mean reactance between 13 ohms and 11.1K is 380 ohms. Optimum Q-factor is 380/26 or 11.1K/760 = 14.6. Approximately, Q-factor increases in direct proportion to linear dimension, because r reduces and R increases in that proportion. According to this a size using a unit dimension of 1⅜ inches should achieve a Q of 20. Winding space is 1.9 inches (active) by 0.5 inch, giving 0.95 square inch. This needs 1,055 turns/sq.in., or 32.5 turns/inch. Awg. 21 will do this, with 690 ft of wire (8¼-inch mean turn) and 8.8 ohms. Shunt resistance will be 11/8 times 11.1K, or 15.3K. Mean reactance is 367 ohms, with Q of 20.8. Reactance of 950 mH at 100 c/s is 600 ohms (almost exactly). So the turns needed will be root 600/367 times 1,000, or 1,280 turns. This requires 1,250 turns/square inch, or 36.7 turns/inch, which fits Awg. 22. 1,280 turns on mean turn 0.69 ft requires 880 ft of wire with 14.2 ohms resistance. Using the formula of 136-A, with A_G 1.9 sq. in., L_G is 0.275 inch. So we can use a core with unit dimension 1⅜ inches, 1,280 turns of 22 Awg. and an approximate gap of 0.275 inch.

143-A. (From 114-B) This is a disputable question. In the way the statement is usually made it is incorrect: there is nothing nonlinear about leakage inductance to cause distortion. But in some instances leakage inductance can be a contributing factor to quite serious distortion. Here are two examples. Consider a class-B output stage where leakage between half-primaries is

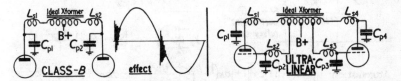

greater than that between secondary and each half-primary. Every time a primary current passes beyond cutoff, the leakage inductance with winding capacitance will "ring," causing the form of distortion known as "notch." The ultra-linear or screen-loaded circuit is another case where leakage inductance in the wrong places can cause distortion. Proper operation of this circuit depends on the voltage applied to the screens being of the correct relative amplitude (compared with the plate) and also on this amplitude being *in phase*. The equivalent filter networks shown here, which can be presented by leakage inductance and winding capacitances that have not been properly controlled in suitable distribution, can result in severe departure from the design requirements at certain high frequencies, with consequent severe distortion. Now turn to 147-B.

143-B. Wire Tables for Standard Enamelled Copper Wire

Awg.	Turns per inch	Ohms per 1,000 ft.	Awg.	Turns per inch	Ohms per 1,000 ft.	Awg.	Turns per inch	Ohms per 1,000 ft.
8	7.58	0.6281	21	32.7	12.8	34	138.8	261
9	8.48	0.7925	22	36.7	16.2	35	156.2	331
10	9.50	0.9988	23	41.0	20.3	36	172.6	415
11	10.63	1.26	24	45.8	25.7	37	192.5	512
12	11.90	1.59	25	51.3	32.4	38	213	648
13	13.33	2.00	26	57.6	41.0	39	244	847
14	14.95	2.52	27	64.2	51.4	40	270	1,080
15	16.70	3.18	28	71.9	65.3	41	303	1,320
16	18.77	4.02	29	79.3	81.2	42	333	1,660
17	20.92	5.05	30	89.3	104	43	385	2,140
18	23.48	6.39	31	100.0	131	44	416	2,590
19	26.22	8.05	32	110.0	162	45	476	3,200
20	29.35	10.1	33	123.5	206	46	525	4,050

144

144-A. (From 122-A) *Correct.* Here is the complete solution, with approximate values substituted in. Now, consider the type terminated at both ends with its characteristic impedance. The values for the two L's are (approximately) 2.61 and 0.52, while the C is 1.47. Are these relative to a L and C respectively whose re-

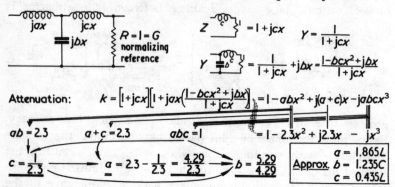

Attenuation: $k = \left[1+jcx\right]\left[1+jax\left(\dfrac{1-bcx^2+jbx}{1+jcx}\right)\right] = 1-abx^2 + j(a+c)x - jabcx^3$

$ab = 2.3 \qquad a+c = 2.3 \qquad abc = 1 \qquad = 1 - 2.3x^2 + j2.3x - jx^3$

$c = \dfrac{1}{2.3} \qquad a = 2.3 - \dfrac{1}{2.3} = \dfrac{4.29}{2.3} \qquad b = \dfrac{5.29}{4.29}$

Approx.
$a = 1.865L$
$b = 1.235C$
$c = 0.435L$

actance equals the characteristic impedance at the half-phase frequency (see 112-B), or are they relative to the prototype low-pass filter, based on line theory (see 124-A)?

144-B. (From 115-B) *Wrong.* See the other answer.

144-C. (From 152-A) First we assume the simple circuit, normalized to a source resistance and the roll-off when critical condition is reached (see 145-B). This is with the 900-micromicrofarad capacitance connected. Then we assume that removing the capacitance divides the output capacitance by a factor e. Solving this for the peak condition, the value of $e = 10$ proves to satisfy both the location and height of the peak, which confirms our assumption of the circuit. Now we proceed by assuming a value of output shunt conductance, c, and solving for maximal flatness condition (elimination of x^2 term in amplitude-squared expression). This yields a value of $c = .312$. As 900 micromicrofarads was 9/10 of the residual or internal capacitance, the reference R must be equivalent to a reactance that is $\sqrt{2}$ times that of 1,000 micromicrofarads at 6 Kc. This reference R (taken as 1 in the normalizing) is 37.6K. Dividing this by 0.312 (which is a conductance factor) gives the required load resistor as 120K. Now the roll-off can be found by the assymptote for the x^4 term, or from the 90° point (real part zero). This leads to $x = 3.6$, from which the 3-db point will be 21.6 Kc.

145-A. (From 109-B) Correct for most purposes. On page 47-A, there was shown an equivalent circuit of a capacitor in series with a parallel combination of inductance and resistance. In a "wrong answer" to that page, on 41-B, we noted that an iron-core reactor is equivalent to a shunt resistance as well as a series resistance and that the shunt resistance seldom approximates a constant value. Here we take a different view.

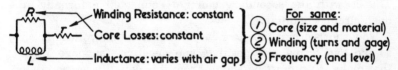

We assume that the component is fixed in every way except for the air gap in the core, and that frequency and level are fixed (the latter is not so important, but effective shunt loss does change with level to some extent). Under these circumstances, the quantities we have indicated by r and R remain constant, while L varies as the air gap is changed. As larger values of r, with L fixed, or smaller values of R, both degrade the component's Q-factor (see 47-A); correspondingly, with r and R fixed (and R many times the value of r in any practical component), if L's reactance gets too close in value to either r or R (low or high respectively) its Q will be degraded. Before considering this further, turn to 129-A.

145-B.

$$k = 1 + (1 + j\alpha x)j\delta x = 1 - \alpha\delta x^2 + j\delta x \qquad \text{Amp.}\, k^2 = 1 + (\delta^2 - 2\alpha\delta)x^2 + \alpha^2\delta^2 x^4$$

$$\alpha\delta = 1 \; [\text{for 6Kc. point}] \quad \delta^2 = 2 \quad \delta = \sqrt{2} \quad \alpha = \tfrac{1}{\sqrt{2}}$$

$$k = 1 + (1 + j\tfrac{1}{\sqrt{2}}x)j\sqrt{2}x$$

Removing 900 μμF: $\quad k = 1 + (1 + \tfrac{1}{\sqrt{2}}x)j\tfrac{\sqrt{2}}{e}x = 1 - \tfrac{1}{e}x^2 + j\tfrac{\sqrt{2}}{e}x \qquad \text{Amp.}\, k^2 = 1 + (\tfrac{2}{e^2} - \tfrac{2}{e})x^2 + \tfrac{1}{e^2}x^4$

$$\frac{dk^2}{dx^2} = \frac{2}{e^2}x^2 - \left(\frac{2}{e} - \frac{2}{e^2}\right) \quad \text{Equate to zero for peak: } x^2 = e - 1$$

Given, peak is at $x = 3$ so $e = 10$ and $k^2 = 1 - 1.62 + .81 = .19 \longrightarrow +7.2\,\text{db}$

$\boxed{\text{Checks} \checkmark}$

Add output termination resistance:

$$k = 1 + (1 + j\tfrac{1}{\sqrt{2}}x)(c + j\tfrac{\sqrt{2}}{10}x) = 1 + c - \tfrac{1}{10}x^2 + j\left(\tfrac{10c+2}{10\sqrt{2}}\right)x$$

$$\text{Amp.}\, k^2 = (1 + c)^2 - \frac{2(1 + c)}{10}x^2 + \frac{1}{100}x^4 + \frac{(10c+2)^2}{200}x^2$$

Required $(10c + 2)^2 = 20(1 + c)$
so $c = -\tfrac{1}{10} \pm \tfrac{\sqrt{17}}{10} = .312$

1000 μμF is ref. $R \div \sqrt{2}$ at Kc. so ref. $R = 3.76 \times 10^4$

Required value of resistor $37.6 \times 10^4 \div .312$ ohms = <u>120 K</u>

Cutoff at $x^2 = 10(1 + c) = 13.12$ $\quad x = 3.6$ $\quad$ **Frequency 21.6 Kc.**

146-A. (From 121-B) Correct (see figure on 147-A). Here we see how the interaction takes place. First we assume that a voltage is connected to one coil. This gives rise to a changing current in that coil, to sustain the applied voltage as an applied e.m.f. (assuming no resistance losses to complicate matters). The same changing current in the primary induces voltage in the secondary, proportional to the product of the turns ratio and k. This is with the secondary coil not connected externally—the open-circuit condition.

Now short-circuit the secondary. The secondary voltage is zero; so the two terms, one positive, one negative (on page 121-B), that make it up must be equal. From this equality we can determine a ratio between primary and secondary current: the reciprocal of the turns ratio, divided by k. Knowing the relationship between primary and secondary current under this condition, we can deduce each from the primary applied voltage. Note that primary current is increased over its open-circuit secondary value by the factor $1/(1 - k^2)$. So on short-circuit, a bigger primary current, with the same applied voltage, results in zero secondary voltage—an extreme refutation, if it is needed, of the notion that voltages are strictly proportional to turns. Now turn to 120-B.

146-B. (From 152-A) Starting with the same unit-dimension core (of 1 inch), the eddy component of shunt losses is 100K, and the hysteresis will be 125K at 1,000 c/s, totaling 55.5K. With the same value of r (see 142-B) of 13 ohms, mean reactance is 850 ohms, and Q is 32.6. On a strict scaling down, this means a unit dimension of 0.625 inch would do. But some winding space is lost on smaller sizes, so try 0.75 inch. Shunt will be 41.6K. The area is 1 inch layer length by 0.25 inch depth, needing 4,000 turns/ sq.in., or 63.2 turns/in., for which 27 Awg. will do. Length at 4½ inches per mean turn is 375 ft, giving 19.2 ohms. Mean reactance is 890 ohms, with Q of 23. Required reactance is 600 ohms (95 mH at 1,000 c/s), so turns need to be 820 (at 3,280/sq.in. or 57.1/in.) of 26 Awg. (57.6/in.). Completing for air gap, A_G is .56 square inch, and L_G figures to be 0.33 inch.

This is a much larger proportion of the unit dimension of 0.75 inch than 0.275 inch was of 1.375 inches, so fringing may be excessive, requiring a larger than practical gap before the desired result can be realized. It may be necessary to use a smaller number of turns with a workable air gap, which will reduce the value of (increase it as a loss) the shunt component.

147-A.

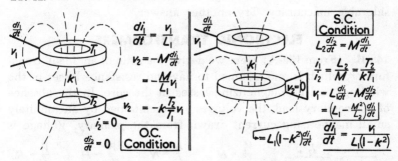

$$\frac{di_1}{dt} = \frac{v_1}{L_1}$$

$$v_2 = -M\frac{di_1}{dt}$$

$$= -\frac{M}{L_1}v_1$$

$$v_2 = -k\frac{T_2}{T_1}v_1$$

$$i_2 = 0$$

$$\frac{di_2}{dt} = 0$$ | **O.C. Condition**

S.C. Condition

$$L_2\frac{di_2}{dt} = M\frac{di_1}{dt}$$

$$\frac{i_1}{i_2} = \frac{L_2}{M} = \frac{T_2}{kT_1}$$

$$v_1 = L_1\frac{di_1}{dt} - M\frac{di_2}{dt}$$

$$= \left(L_1 - \frac{M^2}{L_2}\right)\frac{di_1}{dt}$$

$$= L_1(1 - k^2)\frac{di_1}{dt}$$

$$\frac{di_1}{dt} = \frac{v_1}{L_1(1 - k^2)}$$

147-B. (From 114-B) Strictly correct, but see what 143-A has to say, because there are distortion factors related to the presence of leakage inductance. However, the distortion caused *directly* by the transformer is due to nonlinear magnetizing current and occurs entirely at low frequencies. It should be noted that leakage field is caused by combined primary and secondary current and has essentially an air path, while the main field is caused (in practice by the voltages handled (see 114-B).

Distortion is caused solely by the nonlinear portion of the hysteresis component of magnetizing current, which we have represented in a circuit element, R_h. Taking the distortion percentage from 131-B as D, the formula here derives the distortion voltage

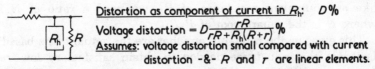

Distortion as component of current in R_h: $D\%$

Voltage distortion $= D\dfrac{rR}{rR + R_h(R+r)}\%$

<u>Assumes:</u> voltage distortion small compared with current distortion -&- R and r are linear elements.

produced by the transformer at the level and frequency corresponding to the magnetic field density used to obtain D. It is impossible to calculate distortion more closely than this, because the current measured as the basis for 131-B was taken with sinusoidal voltage. Presence of voltage distortion slightly invalidates this to an unpredictable extent, because of the complicated nonlinearity of core magnetization properties. This is not the only factor (nor even the most important, often) that can invalidate this calculation. If the source resistance r is a tube or transistor, it possesses nonlinearities which may normally be compensated to some extent by other factors, but which themselves combine with nonlinear magnetizing current to produce more distortion. Turn to 110-B for more on this.

148-A. (From 125-A) *Wrong.* This condition would allow considerable inaccuracy. Try another answer.

ELECTRONIC TRANSFORMERS

148-B. (From 136-A) Here we derive the ratio of an 'ideal' transformer, which is one assumed to have no resistance losses in the windings and no magnetizing losses in the core. In the absence of a secondary load, the voltages are maintained by an infinitely small magnetizing current drawn from the primary. Voltage is

$$\frac{V_1}{V_2} = N \qquad \frac{I_2}{I_1} = N \qquad \frac{V_2}{I_2} = R_2 \qquad \frac{V_1}{I_1} = R_1$$

$$\frac{R_1}{R_2} = \frac{V_1}{I_1} \cdot \frac{I_2}{V_2} = N^2$$

induced by the changing magnetic field and is thus proportional to turns, or to turns ratio, N. When the secondary has current drawn by its load, R_2, this will produce a magnetizing effect which has to be offset by an equal one in the primary. So secondary turns times current has to equal primary turns times current, which means current ratio is the inverse of turns ratio. From this we derive that the primary impedance, or resistance, R_1 is N^2 times the actual load connected to the secondary. Conversely, if we need a transformer to make an actual resistance of R_2 look like an equivalent resistance of R_1, we need a ratio of $N:1$, where N is the square root of R_1/R_2.

This gives us the ratio, but on what are the actual turns based? Is it (1) the inductance needed to obtain satisfactory low-frequency response (see 137-C); (2) equalizing series and shunt components of losses, as in the a.c. inductor design (see 150-B); or (3) achieving the required maximum power-transfer level at the lowest frequency to be handled (see 132-B)?

148-C. (From 123-A) *No.* At least one of them was wrong.

148-D. (From 134-B) *No.* Try one of the other answers.

149-A. (From 117-B) No, something has been omitted; turn to 138-A to see what it is.

149-B. (From 124-B) *Wrong.* There is a common error due to failure to correctly interpret the results obtained. Turn to 131-B for the explanation.

149-C. (From 141-B) Probably there are many different methods that can be adopted to analyze circuit behavior, only some of which have been fully explored. The objective of this book is to gain some insight into methods of attacking such problems, so that the individual can learn to devise for himself the best method

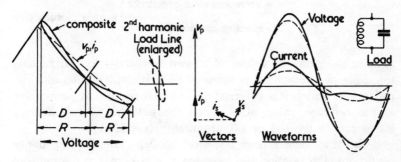

for the problem that faces him. Here we consider a dynamic load, consisting of a parallel-tuned circuit operating at resonant frequency, but in which the tube is operating with considerable nonlinearity, equivalent to about 10% harmonic in a resistance load (dashed straight line). The dynamic load has the same resistive impedance value as this resistance, but the distortion voltage is much lower (compare the relative equality of spaces DD with the inequality of spaces RR). To help explain the process, we use vector diagrams of voltage and current in the load at the fundamental (v_p, i_p) and the second harmonic (v_s, i_s), and also the voltage and current waveforms. The dashed-line waveforms are for the fundamental without the second-harmonic component added.

After studying this, turn to the other answers, which cover some other possibilities, or, if you've already examined them all, turn to 151-A.

150

150-A. (From 125-A) *Wrong.* The very method of derivation should have shown this. Try another answer.

150-B. (From 148-B) Correct for certain special cases, notably where response to really low frequencies is not required, and maximum efficiency for minimum size or weight is a prime consideration. Here the relevant parameters for this condition are shown. Don't forget that all elements must be referred to the impedance of one *or* the other winding. Where the transformer works between matched loads, highest efficiency is obtained by

r_1 = primary winding resistance

r_2 = secondary winding resistance

R = effective core-loss shunt

All referred to SAME winding impedance.

making the referred values of r_1 and r_2 equal—that is, each is the same percentage of its nominal impedance. The nominal impedance to which it is referred will be just twice that percentage of the referred value of R. Then the network of transformer losses can be treated as a T attenuator (see 72-A).

If the transformer does not work under matching-impedance conditions, the relationship between r_1 and r_2 may sometimes be varied advantageously. Making r_1 and r_2 equal, referred to the same reference point, means that the windings occupy equal proportions of winding space. Where matching in the usual sense is not required, a high winding with many more turns may occupy more of the space allocation without seriously reducing efficiency. Now refer to one of the other answers to 148-B, or if you've already studied both of them, turn to 123-A.

150-C. (From 123-A) This must have been a guess. Try again.

150-D. (From 134-B) *No.* Try one of the other answers.

151-A. TEST QUESTIONS ON SECTION 3

1. Find values of L and C in the simple half-section type filter shown, normalized to cutoff frequency and the output termination, for maximal response flatness: when the input termination is zero; when it is equal to the output termination; and when it is at an intermediate value. Can satisfactory values be found if r is greater than R? Show how the choice of values for L and C depends on termination at both ends. (If you have difficulty, turn to 140-B.)

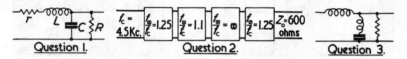

2. A four-stage, low-pass filter is required, using m-derivation and the points of infinite attenuation shown in the sketch. Cutoff frequency is to be 4,500 cycles, and impedance is to be 600 ohms. Calculate filter elements for the simplest network, using T-sections. Check your results at 142-A.

3. This configuration has to be used to produce a filter with the closest possible approximation to phase linearity up to a frequency 4/5 of the rejection frequency, which is 38 Kc. Find suitable values for the network elements. (If you have difficulty, turn to 139-B.)

4. Using a normalizing frequency and impedance, design a network that will have low-pass maximal flatness response, with an ultimate cutoff slope of 18 db/octave (9 db/octave at cutoff frequency), and which will give the correct response regardless of the load value with which it is terminated, without the use of a buffer stage or similar device (no active elements). If this one stumps you, turn to 106-B.

5. Using a former with outside diameter of 1 inch and a length of approximately 1¼ inches, design a coil with an inductance of 250 microhenrys (using Wheeler's formula: see 132-A). A suitable wire gage may be found from the wire tables on 143-B. Turn to 138-B to check your result.

6. For a certain laboratory application, a two-winding coil is required such that the inductance of one coil is four times that of the other and such that short-circuiting either coil reduces the inductance of the other to one half its value. Find the coupling factor needed. Check your answer on 128-B.

152

7. A choke is required with 25 henrys inductance with a d.c. of 200 milliamps, using a core of type *A* laminations, where the unit dimension is 1 inch (4 inches by 3 inches overall size) in a 2-inch stack. Complete the design, from the data on 109-B and wire tables on 143-B. Compare your answer with 123-B.

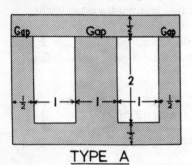

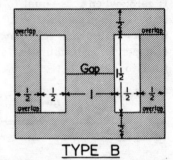

TYPE A   TYPE B

8. A core of high-grade alloy laminations 0.014 inch thick, type *B* shape, with unit dimension 1 inch and unit stack, produces an eddy-current core loss equivalent to a shunt resistance of 100K, referred to a 1,000-turn winding. Hysteresis loss may be taken as equal to eddy loss at 800 cycles. Design an inductor to have a *Q* of 20 at 100 cycles, with an *L* of 950 mH. Compare your results with 142-B.

9. Design a similar inductor with a *Q* of 20 at 1,000 cycles to have an *L* of 95 mH. Compare your result with 146-B.

10. An amplifier module has an output consisting of a step-up transformer, to give a high-impedance output. Unloaded, the response shows a peak of 7.2 db at 18 Kc. To find the nature of the output network, capacitance is added to load down this peak. When a 900-micromicrofarad capacitance is added, the peak is just eliminated, causing a roll-off with the 3-db point at 6 Kc. Deduce the value of loading resistor that will eliminate the peak, and find where the roll-off should then be. Check your result with 144-C.

11. The hysteresis component of transformer magnetizing-current at a certain frequency and level can be represented as a shunt resistance of 138K. The active source resistance is 1,250 ohms, and the reflected load impedance is 6,000 ohms. The magnetizing current has a harmonic content of 38% at this condition. The harmonic produced by this transformer in the circuit will be (1) .283%, (2) .34%, (3) 1.64%, or (4) 2%. Check your selection at 126-B.

Section 4

A.C. WAVEFORMS AND METERING

153-A. Measuring d.c. voltage and current is relatively simple; the meter may load the circuit, but what it reads is unambiguous. For a.c., however, different kinds of meters can give apparently conflicting readings, even when the meters themselves are accurate, and no appreciable loading effect is taking place. In power engineering the most important a.c. reading is the r.m.s. (root-mean-square) value, because this measures the heating effect of a current, the potential power obtainable at a voltage, etc.

Here we have derived the value for a sine wave in terms of the peak value, A. The r.m.s. value is equal to the peak (or

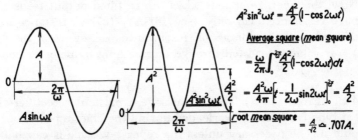

$$A^2 \sin^2 \omega t = \frac{A^2}{2}(1 - \cos 2\omega t)$$

Average square (mean square)

$$= \frac{\omega}{2\pi} \int_0^{\frac{2\pi}{\omega}} \frac{A^2}{2}(1 - \cos 2\omega t)\, dt$$

$$= \frac{A^2 \omega}{4\pi}\left[t - \frac{1}{2\omega}\sin 2\omega t\right]_0^{\frac{2\pi}{\omega}} = \frac{A^2}{2}$$

root mean square $= \frac{A}{\sqrt{2}} \simeq .707A.$

maximum) value divided by the square root of 2. This is the value read directly by any instrument in which the deflecting force at every instant depends on the square of the instantaneous value, *e.g.*, the deflection of a hot-wire ammeter, because the heating of the wire is proportional to current squared; the deflection of an electrostatic voltmeter, because the force of attraction or repulsion is proportional to the square of the instantaneous applied voltage. Normally, for this reason, such meters would tend to have a square-law scale. But the physical design offsets this, to give a scale that is more nearly linear, at least over the middle part of the range covered. Now, does the r.m.s. value of a waveform always have the same relationship to the peak value, provided the waveform is built up of sine waves (see 156-A)? This is not true (see 160-A).

154

154-A. (From 160-A) *Correct.* Here at the left we show the integration to prove it. Now, if the wave is only half-wave rectified, the average value is halved. This can be deduced in three ways: (a) the same half-wave is averaged over twice its time, the second part of which is constant at zero—so, the same average must be divided by two; (b) integrating and dividing by the full period confirms (a) mathematically; (c) the half-wave rectified form can be synthesized by a fundamental sine-wave of half-amplitude,

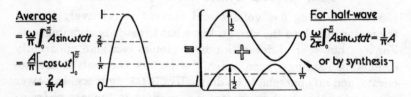

combined with a full-wave rectified wave also of half-amplitude. The average of the full sine-wave is zero (equally negative as positive), and the rectified wave is half the amplitude of the original full-wave.

Now, this average applies when the rectified output feeds (1) a pure resistance load only (see 161-A); (2) a resistance load combined with a storage or reservoir capacitor (see 164-A); (3) a resistance load fed through a smoothing inductor or choke (see 159-A).

154-B. (From 158-A) This might save a particular rectifier-element type from being overloaded during the charge pulse, but it should not be necessary unless the reverse voltage is capable of breaking down the element. Reducing the value of the reservoir capacitor would reduce peak current (more economically than using more elements in series) at some loss of output voltage. Try another answer.

154-C. (From 187-A) This answer could be correct. It is a matter of the reference point used on the signal waveform. In terms of vector analysis this would be correct. But if the input signal is taken as a *sine*, rather than a *cosine* wave, the reference point is where the signal starts from zero, rather than one of its maxima, and the resulting signs are different. If this factor bothers you, brush up on page 23-B. Here angles are all 0° or 180°, whereas there other angles were used, but the principle is the same. Turn to another answer.

155-A. (From 161-A) *Correct.* There are too many variables for the statement to be true. The only way to predict the performance of a rectifier with a reservoir capacitor input-filter is to use curves for that type of rectifier with the stated capacitor value and supply frequency.

The other kind of filter input is shown here—inductor input (also called *choke input*). Assuming, as we have here, that the inductor has constant inductance value (which is not true), the

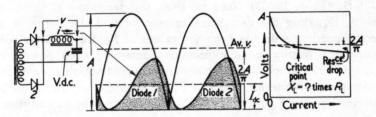

effect commences when the inductance is large enough to force current to flow throughout the cycle. As the positive-going voltage passes the output voltage (d.c. average), current is at its minimum, which critically is zero. Larger inductance values prevent the current from reaching zero or from rising so far above the mean I_{dc}.

Above this critical point the change in output voltage is due to d.c. drop in inductor and rectifier (including transformer) resistance only, which makes the inductor input filter capable of very good regulation over quite a range of current. The shading shows where current switches from one diode to the other.

The critical reactance of the inductor, measured at the supply frequency (assuming inductance to be constant over the cycle) is (1) equal to the load resistance (see 168-A); (2) ⅔ of the load resistance (see 165-A); (3) ⅓ of the load resistance (see 158-A); (4) ⅙ of the load resistance (see 175-A).

155-B. (From 200-A) This might be feasible if enough data were available about combined characteristics with varying applied voltages on both grids. But this is very difficult to present usefully, even if such data have been taken. It is possible to give the usual transfer curves for varying grid voltage when screen voltage is held constant. Many tubes also have similar transfer curves, taken with grid voltage constant (at zero, as a rule) for different screen voltages. But these are no basis for finding the combined effect. See another answer.

156-A. (From 153-A) *No*. This is only true for the single, simple sine-wave. As soon as another is added to it, the relationship may not be true. To appreciate this, consider a square wave, which can be theoretically synthesized from an infinite number of sine waves; its r.m.s. value is the same as its peak value because the instantaneous value is always equal to the peak value, either positive or negative. Turn to the other answer.

156-B. (From 196-D) Here we show the derivation of these results. Equating the derivative to zero to find the value of x_p corresponding with the peak for values of F_m (or F_x, after substitution) results in an expression containing even powers of x_p up to x_p^6, which is a cubic equation in that variable, involving only first-order terms in F_m or F_x. So a simple equation can be derived giving F_m in terms of x_p, from which (by substitution)

① or ② $n=1$	② $n \gg 1$
$D_1^2 = F_m^2 + (16-12F_m)x^2 + (2F_m+4)x^4 + 4x^6 + x^8$	$D_1^2 = F_m^2 + (n^2-6nF_m)x^2 + (3n^2+2nF_m)x^4 + 3n^2x^6 + n^2x^8$
$\frac{d}{dx^2}D_1^2 = 16-12F_m + 4(F_m+2)x^2 + 12x^4 + 4x^6$	$\frac{d}{dx^2}D_1^2 = n^2-6nF_m + 2(3n^2+2nF_m)x^2 + 9n^2x^4 + 4n^2x^6$
Equate to zero: $F_m = \dfrac{4+2x_p^2+3x_p^4+x_p^6}{3-x_p^2}$	Equate to zero: $F_m = \dfrac{n(1+6x_p^2+9x_p^4+4x_p^6)}{6-4x_p^2}$
$F_x = \dfrac{F_m}{F_{mp}}$ $\qquad F_x = \dfrac{3(4+2x_p^2+3x_p^4+x_p^6)}{4(3-x_p^2)}$	$F_x = \dfrac{F_m}{F_{mp}}$ $\qquad F_x = \dfrac{3(1+6x_p^2+9x_p^4+4x_p^6)}{3-2x_p^2}$
$db_{x_p} = -10\log_{10}\dfrac{16(1+x_p^2)(1-x_p^2)^2}{(4+2x_p^2+3x_p^4+x_p^6)^2}$ Between $x_p=0$ $x_p=1$	$db_{x_p} = -10\log_{10}\dfrac{(1-3x_p^2)(1+16x_p^2)}{(1+x_p^2)^2(1+4x_p^2)^2}$ Between $x_p=0$ $x_p=\frac{1}{3}$

an expression for F_x is obtained. Substituting this in the original db expression, the amount of peak is derived in terms of x_p. If you check these formulas, don't forget that peak is referred to the mid-band gain *with feedback*, so the formula at the top needs dividing through by F_m^2 in each case. Note that the first formulas are the same, whether derived from either the two-and-two or the one-and-three combination, because either way there are four identical cutoffs. If the two-and-two combination is treated for n much greater than 1, the result is complicated by functions of n, making it impractical (every value of n gives a different curve, unlike the case of the one-and-three combination).

To plot the curves, which to save space we have not done here, take values of x_p between the limits stated (which we know fall on the curve by being between the boundaries), and calculate corresponding values of F_x and db_{xp}. For each point start on the x_p scale (at the left; see 157-B for the kind of curve), and plot the corresponding point on the frequency curve horizontally (along the bottom). Now, using the same horizontal reference point, plot the point on the db curve. Now turn to 170-B.

157-A. (From 160-A) *No.* There is a π in the formula, but it is not in the numerator. Try another answer.

157-B. (From 184-B) We take the db expression, as given at the top of 184-B, and make the substitution $n = 1$ to find that peaking begins at $F_m = 1.5$. Making the same substitution into the D_t expression, we solve for x_s and F_{ms}. Because we are concerned

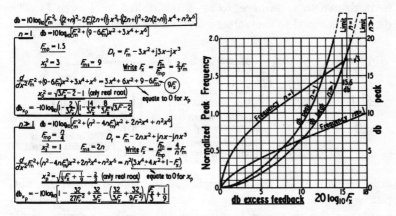

with db beyond the peaking point, we substitute F_x (for excess feedback) $= F_m/F_{mp}$. Differentiating with respect to x^2 (for convenience, rather than x), and equating to zero to find peak frequency, we obtain an expression for x_p in terms of F_x and, from it, an expression for db at peak (x_p).

This is repeated with the assumption that n is much greater than 1, which makes F_{mp} approximate $n/4$; the expression for D_t has n as a single factor for each exponent of x, and F_{ms} approximates $2n$. Making the same excess-feedback substitution, differentiating with respect to x^2, and equating to zero to find x_p, we find db at x_p, in just the same way. Note that because the spacing between the boundary curves on 184-B is asymptotic to 18 db (a ratio of 8:1) n disappears from both the x_p and the corresponding db expressions.

These four results are plotted. From $n = 1$ to $n = \infty$, spacing between peaking and oscillation changes only from 15.6 to 18 db. For small amounts of excess feedback, the curves for db peak are close. Frequency of peak can be predicted with good accuracy from the relevant curve. But to which cutoff is frequency normalized when n is very large: the single one, acting first (see 178-B), or the double pair, acting last (see 188-A)?

158

158-A. (From 155-A) *Correct.* In case you had difficulty finding the right answer, here is how it is calculated. The ripple across the choke is, of course, a complex waveform. But by far the biggest amplitude-component is the second harmonic of the supply frequency. With reference to the input amplitude, A, the d.c. output voltage (without losses) is A multiplied by $2/\pi$. Fourier analysis of the wave shows the second-harmonic component, drawn to scale here, to be A multiplied by 4 over 3π. The d.c. load is equal to the voltage divided by current. When critical

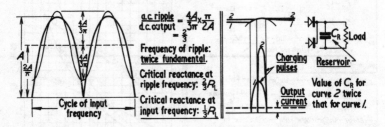

inductance is used, the a.c. ripple has its peak equal to d.c. output, while the ripple voltage consists mainly of this second harmonic; so the reactance is given by the relation between ripple voltage and current, which must be ⅔ of the load value at the second harmonic, or ⅓ of the load value at supply frequency.

Now, in a capacitor input filter using a high-efficiency rectifier (very small forward voltage drop) and larger reservoir capacitor the output voltage can get very close to the peak a.c. input. Because of the low forward-resistance the capacitor charges up in short, high-amplitude current pulses. The limitation on output current is the dissipation of the rectifier element. For maximum output efficiency (both voltage and current) in terms of rectifier cost it may be necessary to: put extra elements in series (see 154-B); put extra elements in parallel (see 166-A); use extra series resistance with the rectifiers (see 169-A).

158-B. (From 177-B) Good try, but you should have sensed the result was wrong. The output tube works along the same load line, with or without feedback, so you were right to take these figures, and right in dividing by five—the loaded feedback factor. But you omitted the presence of the load in considering the figure to be divided by five. It is true that the load is unchanged by feedback, but from the amplifier's viewpoint it is a gain-determining factor, with or without feedback. Try another answer.

159-A. (From 154-A) *No.* This statement comes close to being correct over a range of inductance values, relative to a specific load current and voltage (and frequency), but it is not unconditionally true. Try one of the other answers.

159-B. (From 178-A) *Correct.* To find the level we have here synthesized a transfer characteristic that could be represented to the general form of equation shown, using coefficients A, B, and D, with V for signal level. Making the appropriate substitutions we derive a condition for second harmonic to disappear, which gives V in terms of B and D. Note that for this to work,

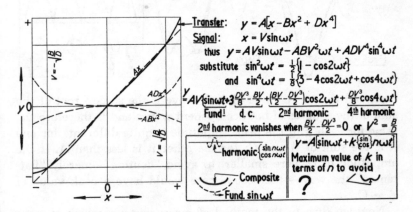

Transfer: $y = A[x - Bx^2 + Dx^4]$

Signal: $x = V\sin\omega t$

thus $y = AV\sin\omega t - ABV^2\omega t + ADV^4\sin^4\omega t$

substitute $\sin^2\omega t = \frac{1}{2}\{1 - \cos 2\omega t\}$

and $\sin^4\omega t = \frac{1}{8}\{3 - 4\cos 2\omega t + \cos 4\omega t\}$

$y = AV\{\sin\omega t + 3\frac{DV^3}{8} - \frac{BV}{2} + (\frac{BV}{2} - \frac{DV^3}{2})\cos 2\omega t + \frac{DV^3}{8}\cos 4\omega t\}$

Fund!   d.c.   2nd harmonic   4th harmonic

2nd harmonic vanishes when $\frac{BV}{2} - \frac{DV^3}{2} = 0$ or $V^2 = \frac{B}{D}$

harmonic $\binom{\sin n\omega t}{\cos n\omega t}$ Composite   Fund. $\sin\omega t$

$y = A[\sin\omega t + k\binom{\sin}{\cos}n\omega t]$

Maximum value of k in terms of n to avoid ?

B and D must have opposite signs, as assumed at the top. Also the d.c. term vanishes when V is slightly larger, at $V^2 = 4B/3D$. The second harmonic vanishes at the point where the curve crosses the straight (dashed) line representing the linear component. Below this it has one phase; above it the phase is reversed.

Now, take another look at the pair of waveforms on page 160-A; in the left one the harmonic (in this case, the third) makes the composite curve go through the zero-line horizontally, because the slope of the third harmonic at this point is equal and opposite to that of the fundamental. If the third harmonic were any bigger relative to the fundamental, the direction of the composite curve would reverse in this region. Fairly obviously the condition for this limit is that the coefficient of the harmonic is $1/n$ times the coefficient of the fundamental, where n is the number of the harmonic. But now at the peak of waveforms the condition to avoid peak-denting (or doubling) is: $k = 1/n$ (see 170-A); $k^2 = 1/n$ (see 196-C); $k = 1/n^2$ (see 160-B).

160

160-A. (From 153-A) *Correct.* To illustrate, here we have two combinations of fundamental with third harmonic: one to produce a peaked waveform, the other one with dents in. Amplitudes of fundamental and third harmonic components are identical in each

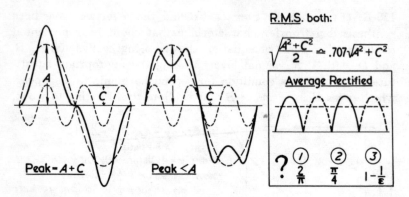

R.M.S. both:

$$\sqrt{\frac{A^2+C^2}{2}} \simeq .707\sqrt{A^2+C^2}$$

Average Rectified

Peak = A + C

Peak < A

? ① $\frac{2}{\pi}$ ② $\frac{\pi}{4}$ ③ $1-\frac{1}{\epsilon}$

case, and the r.m.s. value of each wave is the square root of the sum of the squares of both component waves and is therefore the same for each. But the peak amplitude is quite different: for one it is the sum of A and C; for the other it is less than A. If the amplitude of C were smaller, to avoid "denting"—merely "flattening" the wave—the second case would have a peak value of $A - C$.

Now we turn to the method of measuring a.c. which is more often used in electronic work and results in an average rectified value. When a sine wave is rectified and averaged, the result is which factor times the peak value? Answer: (1); see 154-A. Answer: (2); see 157-A. Answer: (3); see 162-A.

160-B. (From 159-B) *Correct.* This can be deduced from the fact that the limit occurs when the curvatures of the fundamental and harmonic curves are equal and opposite at this point. Since the curvature at this point depends only on the second derivative of each (the first derivatives being zero at this point), and as the relative magnitude of successive derivatives rises in proportion to n, to make the curvature of the fundamental and nth harmonic equal at this point requires that $k = 1/n^2$. Of course, the sign must be correct for odd values of n (even values giving flattening at only one extremity of the wave), and odd values will use a sine term, while even values will use a cosine term. Now turn to 168-B.

161-A. (From 154-A) *Correct.* Presence of either a storage or reservoir capacitor, which we consider here, or of a smoothing inductor involves time constants that can modify the effect. True, under a certain condition or conditions for each of the other cases, the d.c. output *may* be the same as the average rectified value, but this statement does not apply indiscriminately.

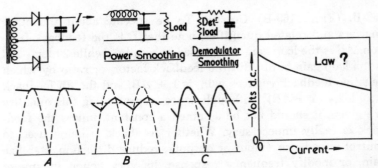

Now we consider full-wave rectification with a capacitor input filter for the d.c. output. With small current load the capacitor charges up to the full peak of the a.c. waveform and drops only a little before the next peak recharges it (*A*). As the load is increased, the forward resistance (due to rectifier, transformer, etc.) may prevent the charge from reaching peak voltage, while discharge between charges dips lower (*B*). If the forward resistance is virtually zero, a larger current can be taken, resulting in bigger drop between charges, with the same average d.c. output value (*C*).

These waveform analyses apply either to capacitor input power-rectifier filters (in which case smoothing may be completed by means of a choke and further capacitor) or to radio-frequency demodulation, in which case the load will more usually be directly across the rectifier capacitor, so that resistance-capacitance filtering can be used with equal efficiency because there is no d.c. flowing through the smoothing resistor.

Now, since (*B*) and (*C*) both give the same output, a rectifier resulting in the voltage drop of (*B*) can be regarded as an equivalent with zero resistance, as at (*C*), with the load-value multiplied by a factor, so that the voltage-current curve has a shape identical with a time-constant curve (see 163-A); this statement is not true (see 155-A).

161-B. (From 176-A) *No.* So turn to the other one.

162-A. (From 160-A) *Wrong.* Numerically, this answer is close —which is probably why the two expressions sometimes are confused. But an expression as this with *e* in it must relate to a time constant in some way. True, there would be a time constant if we included smoothing elements in the circuit, but here we are considering raw, rectified a.c., unsmoothed. Try another answer.

162-B. (From 168-B) *Correct.* To be specific about the other answers and related quantities, note that B is the feedback fraction, AB is the loop gain (expressed as a ratio), while $20 \log_{10} AB$ is the loop gain in db. But the feedback factor, or ratio by which negative feedback reduces gain, is $1 + AB$, and the db feedback is $20 \log_{10} (1 + AB)$. Although figures representing this quantity are given, it should *not* be assumed a constant, unless the feedback is really unnecessary. Whether feedback is being used to control impedance (input or output), reduce distortion, stabilize gain, or modify frequency response, its very action in any of these respects is indicative that the factor $1 + AB$ is variable with respect to the quantity being controlled: a change of impedance changes gain; distortion is a change of gain during the cycle; gain would not need stabilizing if it were already stable; if frequency response is changed, gain varies with frequency. So the quantities A and B must be specified adequately to identify the condition under which the factor $1 + AB$ applies and at which it may be used as a reference.

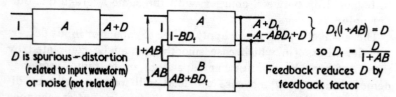

D is spurious — distortion (related to input waveform) or noise (not related)

$$D_f(1+AB) = D$$
$$\text{so } D_f = \frac{D}{1+AB}$$
Feedback reduces D by feedback factor

Now we consider the effect of feedback on distortion. First, we assume the amplifier without feedback has distortion represented by D (which with different significance could equally well stand for a noise generation). Then we move to the feedback case and write D_f for distortion with feedback. Following around the loop to inject reversed-phase distortion into the input and combine it with the original at the output, we equate the two expressions and solve for D_f; this shows that, in theory, feedback reduces distortion by the feedback factor. Is this universally true (see 171-A), or are there exceptions (see 183-B)?

163-A. (From 161-A) Take another look at (C), as well as (B); if the time interval during which discharge occurred did not change, the average voltage would be a direct function of the lowest voltage reached, which in turn would follow a time-constant relationship (function of e) to either discharge current or load resistance, used as a reference. But as the rate of discharge increases, the discharge time decreases until, when the initial discharge rate is equal to the fall rate of the half-wave output as it approaches zero, the discharge time approaches zero. Further drop in output voltage is then due solely to internal resistance.

In short, there are too many variables to be able to formulate any simple law relating output voltage to current for any specific values of frequency, internal resistance, and reservoir capacitance. The only direct reference possible is that, if frequency is doubled and reservoir capacitance is halved, the curve will remain the same. Turn to the other answer.

163-B. (From 169-B) *Correct.* Here we start with the expression for gain with feedback, A_f, in terms of gain without feedback, A, and the feedback fraction B. To find the reduction of variation of A_f as compared with variation of A we differentiate A_f

$$A_f = \frac{A}{1+AB} \qquad \frac{dA_f}{dA} = \frac{1+AB-AB}{(1+AB)^2} = \frac{1}{(1+AB)^2}$$

$$\frac{d\log A_f}{d\log A} = \frac{d\log A_f}{dA_f} \cdot \frac{dA_f}{dA} \cdot \frac{dA}{d\log A} = \frac{1}{A_f} \cdot \frac{1}{(1+AB)^2} \cdot A = \underline{\frac{1}{1+AB}}$$

with respect to A and find the result is the reciprocal of the feedback factor squared, thus disproving the first answer. Now we find the reduction in the logarithms of the quantity A_f with respect to A. It does not matter that db uses logs to the base 10, multiplied by 10 or 20 (power or voltage derivation), while the calculus uses natural logs—this only introduces an arbitrary constant that disappears from the answer. We find that $d \log A_f/d \log A$ is the reciprocal of the feedback factor $(1 + AB)$. So change in gain is reduced by the feedback factor when the gain, with and without feedback, is expressed in db.

Note that this applies only for small changes such that the feedback factor can be considered constant. As change in basic gain results in change in feedback factor, large changes in basic gain will not be accompanied by constant reduction due to feedback. Now turn to 181-B.

164-A. (From 154-A) *No.* The storage or reservoir capacitor fills up the voltage dip between half-waves to some extent, and produces a voltage that is nearer to a steady value throughout the cycle. Under only one loading condition for any particular circuit will it happen that the d.c. output voltage is the same as the average value of the a.c. input. See one of the other answers.

164-B. (From 191-C) Here we take a different feedback application that will show a variety of aspects. It's an adaptation from the output stage of 177-B. A pair of these tubes (only one is shown for simplicity) has a push-pull output transformer in both plate and screen connections and in the cathode circuit, handling equal parts of total output power. Screen signal-voltage is in the same phase as the cathode of each tube. Half the nominal plate load is between plate and B+, the other half between cathode and ground; so plate and cathode have equal signal swings, opposite in phase. The output transformers each deliver half the out-

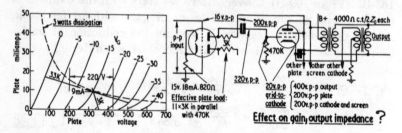

put load current, so they are each matched for double the nominal output impedance. Positive feedback is used to help get the grid drive (220 volts peak-to-peak) from the double-triode driver stage. The top end of the plate resistor is connected, not to B+, but to the corresponding output-tube screen. As this swings 200 volts, for the 220 volts at the plate, the *effective* plate load for the drive-stage tube is eleven times its actual value. The grid resistor (470K), being connected to ground return, appears as its actual value. The characteristics at the left show how this helps. With a 3K plate resistor, the B+ drop is less than 50 volts, but the a.c. load is 33K, making the needed 220 volts peak-to-peak well within the available swing. Other values are calculated as shown. Does this positive feedback (sometimes called "bootstrap") increase gain and reduce output impedance by the factor of 11? If you think so, see 192-A; if not, see 166-B; if one but not the other, see 192-B.

165-A. (From 155-A) If you calculated this based on voltage and current relationship in an inductor, you overlooked the fact that the effective frequency of ripple is twice that of the supply. Try another answer.

165-B. (From 190-A) We have treated the basic circuit of 177-B fairly completely. It would obviously be impossible to treat every possible type of feedback circuit in equal detail. So we must give the best leads possible in applying the principles to other circuits. The circuit of 177-B used voltage feedback. Here we show two ways of deriving current feedback from an output stage, either

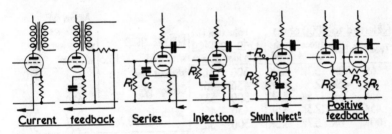

Current feedback   Series   Injection   Shunt Injectⁿ   Positive feedback

from the cathode resistor or a series resistor. With the cathode-resistor feedback, either the reflected primary impedance or the primary current can be used as the reference.

Now consider the input end. With series injection the resistor marked R_1 does not have its value changed by feedback, but the resistor R_2 and capacitance C_2 do. The resistance or reactance of the latter is increased by the feedback factor (with negative feedback). With shunt injection, resistor R_1 is unchanged by feedback, as part of the input resistance, while resistor R_2 is changed, being reduced by the feedback (negative feedback). Now, is it correct to say that the source resistance connected to the amplifier affects shunt injection (R_o) but not series injection, or are there qualifications? After making your own deductions about this, verify them on 180-A.

Finally, we show the simplest way of introducing positive feedback between stages. Stage gain of each stage is calculated in the normal way, with the combined effect of R_1, R_2 and R_3 affecting bias. These three resistors also affect the degeneration of each stage and the regeneration between them. Sometimes one of the resistors may be omitted, or a T-configuration used instead of a π type. Only individual requirements can determine this. Now turn to 191-B.

166-A. (From 158-A) Putting additional elements in parallel would share current between them, thus reducing the dissipation in each. But their forward resistance is so low and temperature-dependent that current would not divide uniformly. Also it is not the economical solution. Try another answer.

166-B. (From 164-B) *Correct.* But a complete analysis is quite involved and usually the necessary data are not available. Here we make some approximations. First, take the twin-coupled output stage, with an assumed constant grid drive. To be complete the load lines should be analyzed for the push-pull operation.

Referred to 8000 ohms				Gain reduction 11:1 Twin coupled		Driver gain		Approx.O/P impedance with driver.	
Tube1	Tube2	Tubes Comb'd	With Load	With load	Source	With load	13.5	With load	Source
6K	100K	5.7K	3.3K	300	312	Without load	16	354	370
17K	45K	12.3K	4.8K	436	461	Change $\frac{16}{13.5}$ = 1.18		515	550
35K	35K	17.5K	5.5K	500	533			630	685
45K	17K	12.3K	4.8K	436	461	which is		515	550
100K	6K	5.7K	3.3K	300	312		0.7db	354	370

Driver nonlinearity not accounted for

Because of nonlinearity the distribution of output load between the two tubes changes at different points on the load line. For class-AB, or class-B working, this must be taken into account. Here a good approximation is obtained by assuming that each tube is linear and regarding the source resistances as in parallel with a common load resistance of 8,000 ohms.

Taking the input as constant at the grid of the output stage and using the method of 177-B, the source resistance varies between 312, 533, and back to 312 ohms. With constant input to the driver we have to know how change in output load affects gain changes. The only simple reference for this is the unloaded condition, which raises the output-stage gain from 20 (10 from grid to cathode) to 141 (70.5 from grid to cathode). So the factor by which the plate resistor of the drive stage is mutliplied rises from 11 to 71.5. We can assume the gain would rise from 13.5 to 16 (not more than this). As a consequence, a slight *increase* in output source resistance occurs (output rises more with load removal, when input is to the drive stage than when it is to output stage directly). These calculations can only be approximate at best and do not take nonlinearity of the drive stage into account. As the circuit is push-pull, and drive-stage nonlinearity is mainly second order, this almost completely cancels. Now turn to 199-A.

167-A. (From 176-A) *Correct.* The typical scales here show the effect. On the 100-volt scale, linearity is good, except for a very slight contraction close to the zero point. This is due to reverse current and, for modern instrument rectifier types, is exaggerated slightly. Reverse current may (on first-class meters) call for slight modification of the 0.9 factor in the multiplier resistance calculations (downward, to say 0.89), but otherwise it has very little effect. Forward voltage drop is what affects scale linearity on lower voltage scales, as shown on the 5-volt scale. At the lower end of the scale the resistance of the bridge (a.c.) input is higher than it is as it approaches full scale.

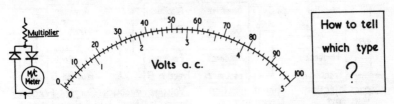

Some rectifier instruments use only two rectifier elements, as shown at the left. The shunt rectifier is needed to ensure that the series one does not have its reverse voltage broken down in the direction opposite from the one measured. Such a meter uses a multiplier of approximately half the value (for a.c.) required for the full-wave circuit. For sinusoidal or symmetrical voltages the half-wave circuit is as accurate as the full-wave one. But on asymmetrical waveforms the half-wave circuit will give different readings if connected in opposite ways to the voltage measured.

Now assume that a "universal" meter with a switch to change from d.c. to a.c. on each scale is used to measure a tube heater-supply, but it is not known whether the voltage is d.c. or a.c. When the a.c./d.c. switch is thrown, the reading is 11% higher on a.c. This means the voltage is a.c. (see 177-A); it is d.c. (see 196-A); the test is not conclusive (see 189-A).

167-B. (From 177-B) This answer is correct as giving the effective source resistance with the amplifier operating open-circuit, for one level of measuring signal. For smaller signal levels, dividing the simple figure 35K by 29.6, giving 1,180 ohms, is correct. But there is yet another answer which has practical significance. If you have not already found the correct method for the effective source resistance (loaded), try one of the other three. If you have found it, then turn to 181-A.

168-A. (From 155-A) *No.* This was probably a guess. Try one or the other answers.

FEEDBACK CALCULATIONS

168-B. (From 160-B) Here we show the four basic feedback configurations. There are two ways of combining the feedback signal at the input: series and shunt injection and there are two ways of deriving it at the output: from output voltage and current. According to the combination used, feedback circuits can thus have four variations. Amplification A and feedback fraction B

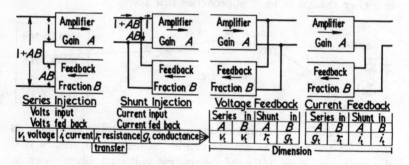

must in each case be in the dimensions indicated (see 55-A), so the product AB is always a numerical transfer ratio using either voltage or current as reference.

From the simple diagrams we can deduce that series injection (with negative feedback) increases input impedance, whereas shunt injection reduces it. Similarly, voltage feedback reduces output impedance (still with negative feedback), while current feedback increases it. Each of these statements will be reversed in case of positive feedback. Additionally, feedback can reduce distortion, stabilize gain, and modify frequency response, according to individual requirements. The primary measure of what feedback does is how much feedback there is; this is usually measured in db. In terms of the quantities shown on these simple diagrams "db feedback" may be defined as: $20 \log_{10} B$ (see 193-A); $20 \log_{10} AB$ (see 195-A); $20 \log_{10} (1 + AB)$ (see 162-B).

168-C. (From 181-B) *No.* This answer may seem more logical than answer (2), because D_f must be bigger than D; but the increase in value is not multiplication by a simple numerical factor, such as F_m. Note that D and its derivative D_f are complex quantities whose magnitude *and* phase differ. Try another answer.

169-A. (From 158-A) This is the most economical remedy. The form of the charging current pulse is similar to a half-wave, but it has shorter duration. To achieve a certain output current, the magnitude of the charge pulse must be inversely proportional to its duration. Instantaneous dissipation is proportional to current squared. So the dissipation of a whole pulse is directly proportional to the magnitude of the pulse (or inversely proportional to its duration). The larger capacitor value increases output voltage and rectifier efficiency, but with increased dissipation in the rectifier. To bring the dissipation down, a small series resistor will spread the pulse without dropping voltage too seriously. An extra element in series would do the same thing, but it would also increase total *rectifier* dissipation. Since resistors are cheaper than rectifier elements, this is the more economical method.

Two more facts need to be mentioned before we leave the subject of power rectification: (1) Relation of reservoir capacitance to current-pulse duration; the curvature at the top of a sinusoid approximates an inverted parabola, so the duration of the pulse will be inversely proportional to the square of the reservoir capacitance, assuming that circuit resistances remain unchanged. (2) A practical note about pulses: these represent frequency components much higher than the supply frequency, and they may cause trouble in signal circuits. The precautions are (a) to keep rectifier circuits physically compact and (if necessary) shielded, and (b) to change values to broaden pulse. Note that the switch from one diode to the other in choke filtering (see 155-A) can cause similar trouble. Now turn to 176-A.

GAIN STABILIZATION

169-B. (From 191-B) An important effect of feedback is its control of gain, to reduce changes due to any causes. In a sense its reduction of distortion can be regarded as gain stabilization: the gain varies at different points on a waveform or transfer characteristic, and feedback reduces this variation. But whatever the cause, gain stabilization can be expressed more generally than this so as to apply to effects due to changes in supply voltage or any other variable.

We have found that the important factor is $1 + AB$, and we would expect this to apply to gain stabilization as well as to gain itself. But does the factor apply to gain expressed as a ratio (see 195-B) or in db (see 163-B)?

170-A. (From 159-B) *Wrong*. This should be evident from the right-hand waveform on page 160-A, where reversal of the phase of the third harmonic produces a "dented" wave. So the third harmonic is too large at this value. Try another answer.

NYQUIST DIAGRAMS

170-B. (From 156-B) The presentation initiated by Nyquist is a help to understanding feedback-stability problems. As an aid to calculating, it is somewhat protracted, but it has visual advantages and for that reason is included here. At the top left here

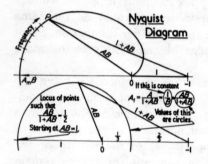

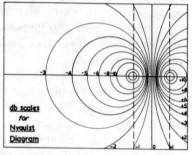

we illustrate the basic concept. The Nyquist curve is the locus of points, P, representing the value of the product AB in magnitude and phase. The part shown could represent the high-frequency cutoff characteristic; the low-frequency cutoff would be a similar curve below the horizontal reference for A_mB. Measuring off -1 in the same units as AB, to the right of origin O, the third side of the triangle, for each point on the curve, represents the feedback factor $(1 + AB)$ at that point.

To make the curves more meaningful, they can be drawn against a background of a family of circles, derived at the lower left and shown as a complete family at the right. Note that this is a valid aid only for systems in which B is a constant. When phase shift and/or magnitude discrimination occurs in B as well as A, it is not valid, although it may be used as a step. The way the Nyquist curve then crosses the family of curves tells more about response than the simple diagram does. Before turning to 198-A try to draw the Nyquist diagrams representing (1) two stages with 6-db feedback $(n = 1)$; (2) two stages with 12-db feedback $(n = 1)$; (3) four stages (one-and-three combination, $n = 20$) with 12-db feedback; (4) four stages (two-and-two combination, $n = 20$) with 6-db feedback. Then turn to 198-A.

171-A. (From 162-B) *Wrong*. As a matter of fact the treatment wasn't even rigorous as algebra, but apart from that discrepancy there are limitations to the application of this formula. See the other answer.

171-B. (From 195-C) As an exercise in applying some of the feedback principles, consider this high-pass feedback filter. It is to have zero insertion loss in the pass range and the characteristic shown at the right. As R_2 affects gain as well as feedback, it is usually simplest to choose this value first, then to pick R_3 and

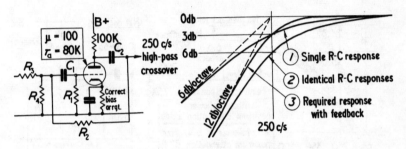

R_4 to give zero insertion loss, after gain with feedback has been fixed. Assume that gain without feedback is 50, which requires a plate load of 80K, or R_2 with 100K in parallel. This puts R_2 at 400K (a 390K resistor will serve, allowing for the series part of R_3, R_4 combination). This allows no extra output termination, which is suitable because R_2 provides a ground return. Now, to complete the design:

1. Feedback: 3 db, needs 0.414 of input fed back; gain: 50; attenuation must be 0.414/50; R_3, R_4 parallel must be 400K/121 = 3.3K. Gain with feedback 35; R_3 must be 34 times R_4. Values of 100K and 3.3K are close enough. R_1 and C_1 can be 330K and 0.002 μF, giving cutoff at 250 c/s. C_2 is cut off with 480K, needs to be 0.0013 μF for 250 c/s (see 194-D if you think this is correct).

2. Feedback: 6 db, needs signal equal to input fed back; gain: 50; attenuation must be 1/50; R_3, R_4 parallel must be 400K/50 = 8K. Gain with feedback 25; R_3 must be 24 times R_4. Values can be $R_3 = 200$K, $R_4 = 8.2$K. R_1 and C_1 can be 430K and 0.001 μF, giving cutoff at 350 c/s. C_2 is cut off with 445K, needs to be 0.001 μF for 350 c/s (see 172-B if you think this is correct).

3. Same as Answer 2, except for cutoff points, using 430K with 0.002 μF (twice) for 175 c/s cutoffs (see 179-A if you think this is correct).

172

172-A. (From 197-A) If you derived this from calculation, you made the mistake of relating the level to the mid-band level *without feedback*. Response is related to the level in operating condition, which in this case is with feedback. Try another answer.

172-B. (From 171-B) *Correct.* Enlarged here at the left is the explanation, which is a left-to-right reversal of the relevant part of 190-B. Note that 6-db feedback "slides" the tangent point 3 db and half an octave down the 6 db/octave tangent line, and achieves the maximal flatness condition.

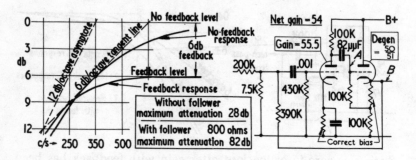

Now, there is a limitation to the attenuation this circuit can produce. Its shape may be excellent at crossover, but we have assumed that R_2 (171-B) is a *feedback* resistor. But the resistor does not know this. Signals can feed through it either way. When C_1 and C_2 reach reactance high enough to isolate the tube, the only attenuation to forward transmission is due to R_3 and R_4 (assuming the output unterminated), which is 28 db (ratio: 25). If a tube with lower gain were used, the maximum attenuation would be much less. For many purposes the 28-db maximum of this circuit would be enough: this reaches 25 db at slightly more than 2 octaves (12 db/octave) below 250 c/s. But a cathode follower can increase this maximum a long way. Here we've changed values to allow for (a) increased gain, because the plate is unloaded, and (b) the input impedance of the follower as termination for C_2, which now needs to be 82 $\mu\mu$F (reactance: 5.1 megohms at 350 c/s). The mutual conductance of the follower (same tube type) is 1.25 milliamps/volt, so the output source resistance is 800 ohms. This as termination for the 390K feedback resistor produces an additional 54-db (ratio: 500) attenuation, making a total maximum of 82 db. Now where should the output be taken from: *A* (see 195-D) or *B* (see 191-C)?

173-A. (From 196-D) If you know a simple procedure for solving cubic equations in which two coefficients are variable, then go ahead. The other answer explains a simpler approach.

173-B. (From 199-A) Here we show the important facts for this question. At the left the three curves clarify the problem. Curves *A* and *B* are for capacitor input filters, while curve *C* is for choke input filters (see 161-A and 155-A). In the middle the theoretical

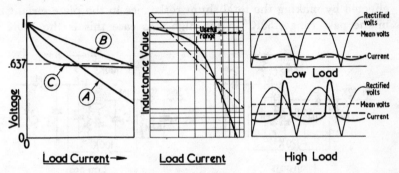

requirement for the choke is shown. The solid curve represents a typical variation of inductance with current, plotted on log-log paper. Using the simplified theory, the inductance needs to saturate at a rate faster than a reduction in value inversely proportional to current. If it only reduced in value in inverse proportion (dashed line), it would maintain critical value (see 158-A) or some fixed relation to it at all current values. Referring again to the left-hand diagram, the capacitor must be large enough for saturation to follow voltage to rise: curve *B* is for one with twice the capacitance of curve *A*. The larger capacitor would allow the voltage output to rise as the choke saturates—or at least to compensate for resistance losses. Critical values were given at 158-A, which would be for lowest current (where regulation begins to need control), whereas the capacitor value is best obtained from rectifier data, not simple RC time constants.

However, this simple theory does not apply completely. There is no sharp point at which the inductor or choke saturates, and its inductance is never constant throughout the rectifier cycle. This is illustrated at the right. The excursion above the current crossover line (short dashes, which divide the current cycle into equal *time* intervals) is always greater than that below it. Consequently the "saturation" effect starts to allow a rise, even below the critical value. Results must be derived empirically.

174-A. (From 197-A) Were you thinking the effect is similar to the single-stage case, where feedback merely extends range as it reduces gain, without changing response *shape*? Try again.

174-B. (From 200-A) For this kind of question, there may be several possible correct designs. Here we show one, with the method, as a check whether your solution meets the requirements. First, we decide that the gain, without feedback, will be 50, effected by making the total shunt resistance in the plate circuit, in the pass range, 50K. In the high-pass case this is the 100K

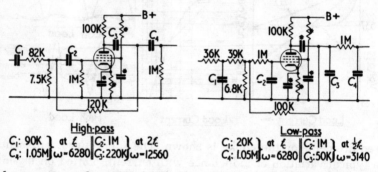

plate resistor, the 120K feedback resistor, and the 1-meg output resistor. In the low-pass case the feedback resistor is 100K to produce the same result. The required feedback is 12 db, using identical turnovers within the loop (C_2 and C_3 in each case). So the fed-back portion must be 3/50 ($AB = 3$, because $1 + AB = 4$). This determines the input resistance, in conjunction with the fact that zero insertion loss is required. Gain with feedback will now be 12.5, so the input resistors must divide by this: the series element (82K in high-pass and 36K + 39K in low-pass) must be about 11.5 times the shunt (7.5K in high-pass and 6.8K in low-pass). Now these turnovers (C_2 and C_3) each have their response extended by an octave by feedback, producing +3 db at 90° reference point. The remaining turnovers (C_1 and C_4) need to have their turnovers at the final point. Thus, in conjunction with the associated values, reactances of capacitors at designated frequencies are derived. The asterisked components are fixed by operating conditions, to maintain full gain over the range required, with negligible phase shift. As an example, if f_c is 1,000 cycles, the following values will serve: high-pass, $C_1 = .00175$ μF, $C_2 = 78$ $\mu\mu$F, $C_3 = 350$ $\mu\mu$F, $C_4 = 150$ $\mu\mu$F; low-pass, $C_1 = .008$ μF, $C_2 = 320$ $\mu\mu$F, $C_3 = .0063$ μF, $C_4 = 150$ $\mu\mu$F.

175-A. (From 155-A) To get this answer you made one of two mistakes: either you omitted to observe that ω (angular frequency or pulsatance) is 2π (not π) times frequency; or, you took ripple current at twice what it can actually be for this condition. Try another answer.

175-B. (From 199-A) We write the expression in the form here, for y, making the coefficient of x^3 positive and that for x^5 negative. Other combinations could be used, in which case a difference of signs would appear in the solution. This was selected as being

$$y = A(x + bx^3 - cx^5) \qquad x = V\sin\omega t$$

$$y = AV\{\sin\omega t + bV^2\sin^3\omega t - cV^4\sin^5\omega t\}$$

$$\sin^3\omega t = \tfrac{3}{4}\sin\omega t - \tfrac{1}{4}\sin 3\omega t$$

$$\sin^5\omega t = \tfrac{5}{8}\sin\omega t - \tfrac{5}{16}\sin 3\omega t + \tfrac{1}{16}\sin 5\omega t$$

$$y = AV\{(1 + \tfrac{3}{4}bV^2 - \tfrac{5}{8}cV^4)\sin\omega t + (\tfrac{5}{16}cV^4 - \tfrac{1}{4}bV^2)\sin 3\omega t - \tfrac{1}{16}cV^4\sin 5\omega t\}$$

Normalizing to $V=1$

$$y = A\{(1 + \tfrac{3}{4}b - \tfrac{5}{8}c)\sin\omega t + (\tfrac{5}{16}c - \tfrac{1}{4}b)\sin 3\omega t - \tfrac{1}{16}c\sin 5\omega t\}$$

Zero 3rd: $\tfrac{5}{16}c = \tfrac{1}{4}b$ or $b = \tfrac{5}{4}c$

4% 5th: $\tfrac{1}{16}c = \tfrac{1}{25}(1 + \tfrac{3}{4}b - \tfrac{5}{8}c) = \tfrac{1}{25}(1 + \tfrac{5}{16}c)$ and $\boxed{c = \tfrac{4}{5} \quad b = 1}$ so $y = A(x + x^3 - \tfrac{4}{5}x^5)$

Solutions

Fundamental: $AV\left(1 + \dfrac{3V^2 - 2V^4}{4}\right)$

3rd: $AV\left(\dfrac{V^4 - V^2}{4}\right)$ $\quad 5^{\text{th}}$: $AV\dfrac{V^4}{20}$

$\%3^{\text{rd}} = \dfrac{V^4 - V^2}{4 + 3V^2 - 2V^4}\times 100\% = \dfrac{100(V^4 - V^2)}{4 + 3V^2 - 2V^4}\%$

$\%5^{\text{th}} = \dfrac{4V^4}{20(4 + 3V^2 - 2V^4)}\times 100\% = \dfrac{20V^4}{4 + 3V^2 - 2V^4}\%$

the most probable practical combination: the x^3 term predominates at low levels (V much less than 1), while the x^5 term flattens the waveform as V approaches 1. We solve it as on 159-B, normalizing the coefficient of $\sin 3\omega t$ to zero for $V = 1$, and making the coefficient of $\sin 5\omega t$ $1/25$ that of $\sin \omega t$ (the 4% specified in the question). This gives the solution as $y = A(x + x^3 - 4/5x^5)$. From this expressions may be found for fundamental, third and fifth coefficients, in terms of V, and the percentage of each harmonic as a function of V^2.

Note that this curve for y reaches maximum and minimum values for $x = \pm 1$, beyond which the curve reverses (the transfer can be shown by differentiating the expression represented by y, and equating it to zero). Also note that the fundamental is not simply proportional to V. A further exercise, if you are interested, is to find the point where the third harmonic has the maximum value (or the maximum percentage) below the null.

INSTRUMENT RECTIFIERS

176-A. (From 169-A) The best-known type of instrument rectifier employs the bridge circuit; so the moving coil-movement passes current the same way for both directions of alternating current (or voltage) input. One direction of current flow is represented by the solid arrows, while the other is shown by broken-line

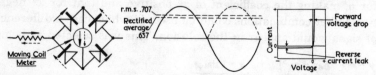

arrows. For any simple sine wave, the r.m.s. value is .707 times peak, while the rectified average is .637 times peak. Because r.m.s. is the conventional reference amplitude for alternating current and voltage, meters are usually calibrated in these values. So the voltage multiplier has to pass $.707/.637 = 1.11$ times the current needed for a corresponding scale reading on d.c. (The reading has to represent .707, although the driving voltage is only according to the .637 factor.) Alternatively expressed, the multiplier resistance is 0.9 times the value for a d.c. instrument (assuming 100% rectifier efficiency).

For d.c. meter multipliers the calculation is simple because the meter has a specific d.c. resistance which is subtracted from the calculated total resistance to find the multiplier value. On a.c. the resistance of the bridge circuit complete with meter varies with scale reading, due to the fact that the rectifier is not perfect: it has a forward-voltage drop and a reverse-current leakage. Does the forward-voltage drop modify the scale near zero, while the reverse-current leakage affects scale linearity more on low-voltage ranges than high-voltage ranges (see 161-B)? Or is it the other way around (see 167-A)?

176-B. (From 200-A) If you selected this answer, we suggest you try this for any tube for which curves are published for operation both as a pentode and as a triode. Invariably they are for different conditions from those practically applicable to ultra-linear: the maximum plate voltage, operating as a triode, is always lower than that operating as a pentode or ultra-linear; published curves as a pentode have fixed screen voltages, none of which is usually suitable for the ultra-linear condition. Try another answer.

177-A. (From 167-A) Presumably you concluded this instrument must use a full-wave rectifier. Then a.c. was the first possibility you tried, and it worked out right. But this is not the answer. Try another.

177-B. (From 183-B) Now we take a typical calculation of output impedance with voltage feedback. Here are the output tube characteristics with relevant load lines drawn and the plate resistance determined from the slope of curves where the load line crosses (inverting the method for finding load lines). The gain of the

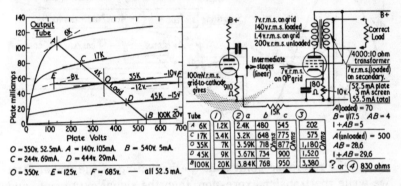

O = 350v. 52.5mA. *A* = 140v.105mA. *B* = 540v. 5mA.
C = 244v. 69mA. *D* = 444v. 29mA.

O = 350v. *E* = 125v. *F* = 685v. — all 52.5 mA.

Tube	(1)	(2) a	b	15K c	(3)	
A 6K	1.2K	2.4K	480	545	202	
C 17K	3.4K	3.2K	648	775	575	
O 35K	7K	3.59K	718	877	1,180	
D 45K	9K	3.67K	734	900	1,520	
B 100K	20K	3.84K	768	950	3,380	

A(loaded) = 70
B = 1/17.5 AB = 4
1 + AB = 5
A(unloaded) = 500
AB = 28.6
1 + AB = 29.6
? or (4) 830 ohms

amplifier (excluding the output stage) has been calculated by use of a.c. load lines (see 141-B), and voltages at operating level are filled in. Loaded, the output stage is close to being linear, but its a.c. resistance swings widely. The feedback factor is calculated, as shown, at 5 (loaded) and 29.6 (unloaded).

We also show the results of four methods of calculating output source resistance. Method 1 merely divides the a.c. resistance at each point by the factor 5. Method 2 first finds the parallel combination of load and source without feedback (at the plate, column *a*), divides this by 5 (column *b*), then removes the load (same value, 4K, as a parallel element) to give effective source resistance from the load's "viewpoint" (column *c*). Method 3 divides the a.c. resistance at each point by the factor 29.6. Each of these results gives a series of five values for representative points along the load line or around the signal waveform. Method 4 is obtained by finding the source resistance without feedback from the change of gain by removing the load (70 to 500), which gives 24.5K; dividing this by 29.6 gives the result shown. Which answer is right? Answer (1): see 158-B; answer (2): see 194-B; answer (3): see 191-A; answer (4): see 167-B.

178-A. (From 187-A) *Correct.* The first answer was wrong because it omitted the second-harmonic term. The power-series analysis introduces terms *up to* the harmonic bearing the same number (in this case, 4). Here we can see the condition in which answer (2) would be correct—all the elements are in phase at the 90° point. But using a function of sin ωt to represent the

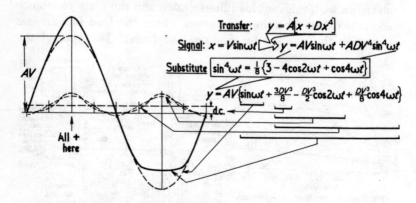

Transfer: $\quad y = A(x + Dx^4)$

Signal: $x = V\sin\omega t \implies y = AV\sin\omega t + ADV^4\sin^4\omega t$

Substitute $\quad \sin^4\omega t = \frac{1}{8}\{3 - 4\cos2\omega t + \cos4\omega t\}$

$y = AV\{\sin\omega t + \frac{3DV^3}{8} - \frac{DV^3}{2}\cos2\omega t + \frac{DV^3}{8}\cos4\omega t\}$

signal, the reference point is at the *beginning* of the wave. First we write the transfer expression, then the signal expression, and then substitute the second into the first. We have used A to signify gain or amplification (from input to output, or output/input). D is the coefficient of the x^4 term referred to the x coefficient as unity. V is signal magnitude, which we will in a moment consider as variable. Now we substitute the trigonometrical expression for the power term $\sin^4\omega t$ in terms of multiple-angle ratios and bring the overall amplitude expression, AV, outside the parenthesis. We have identified the trigonometrical analysis with a graphical representation of the component build of the waveform.

Now, since both second- and fourth-order terms produce second-harmonic components, is it possible to have a transfer characteristic in which the second harmonic vanishes, and only the fourth harmonic remains? Answer: yes; see 196-B. Answer: no; see 194-A. Answer: yes, at one signal level only; see 159-B.

178-B. (From 157-B) *No.* See the other answer.

179-A. (From 171-B) Almost correct, but you have the wrong direction in which feedback modifies the turnover. It extends frequency response (see 190-B) but does not move frequency *up*. Extension is up for high-frequency cutoff, but it is down for low-frequency cutoff (high-pass). Try one of the other answers.

179-B. (From 199-A, 200-A) This is the kind of problem that presents difficulty in knowing where to begin, because everything affects something else. We suggest the starting point to be a determination of the approximate operating point for the pentode, to provide a proper grid voltage for the triode. This is worked from

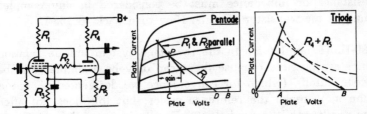

the dashed-line triangle under the triode dissipation curve. The minimum workable drop at peak signal across R_4 and R_5 is AB, of which the working drop will be about half—a quarter across each. The tube drop will be OA plus the other half. In this way a voltage OC is determined that should be suitable to drive the triode grid, whatever the values R_4 and R_5 turn out to be (within a reasonable range). A point P is chosen on curves where the screen voltage is lower than OC (because this has to be fed through R_2), and screen current is determined either from curves, tabulated data, or set-up measurement. This enables R_2 to be fixed, and the screen-current value drop in R_1 can be set off as DB, with the slope R_1 representing the drop due to plate current. To find the stage gain a load line is drawn for R_1, R_2 in parallel. R_3 is found from grid voltage (the curve or interpolation for point P) and total current (plate current at P plus screen current). This enables a value of R_5 to be calculated to make the feedback fraction the reciprocal of stage gain, modified by the slight degeneration from grid to cathode in the triode. R_4 is equal to R_5 (the voltage across R_3 being very small compared to that across R_4 and R_5). If this value for R_4, R_5 series invalidates the operating point P chosen as a starting point, start over. Finally, set the circuit up and check voltages against the calculated values, making any practical adjustments necessary.

180

180-A. (From 165-B) The first statement is substantially correct, especially for tube circuits. The operative feedback factor depends very considerably on R_o in shunt injection. A constant voltage input virtually short-circuits the feedback. In the series circuit the only requirement is continuity of grid circuit, to ensure that the injected feedback reaches the grid. Since tubes are not normally operated open-grid but need a circuit with finite impedance (or zero impedance) to introduce the input, there is no problem here.

In transistors the situation is different. We are not concerned with input voltage but with input current. Consequently, source resistance or impedance must be considered in any complete analysis for transistor circuits. Now turn back to 165-B.

180-B. (From 190-B) In the two-stage system unique relationships are possible because there can only be a simple ratio between cutoffs (which for convenience we designated n^2, rather than n, to make the reference easier; but this does not affect the result, only the symbology). For three stages the cutoffs can vary their relationships in a virtually infinite variety of ways. Obviously, however, an advantage is gained, as regards the amount of feedback that can be applied before peaking or instability is encountered, by using cutoffs at deviate points. The problem is to determine what kind of deviation is most useful.

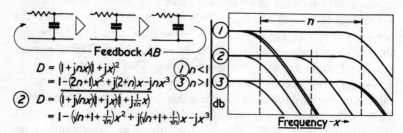

$$D = (1+jnx)(1+jx)^2$$
$$= 1-(2n+1)x^2 + j(2+n)x - jnx^3 \quad \text{①} \; n<1 \quad \text{③} \; n>1$$

$$\text{②} \quad D = (1+j\sqrt{n}x)(1+jx)(1+j\tfrac{1}{\sqrt{n}}x)$$
$$= 1-(\sqrt{n}+1+\tfrac{1}{\sqrt{n}})x^2 + j(\sqrt{n}+1+\tfrac{1}{\sqrt{n}})x - jx^3$$

Here we consider three cases that represent limiting possibilities: (1) with two cutoffs acting at the same point and also before the third by a ratio, n; (2) uniform staggering of the three so that the extremes have a ratio of n; (3) with one cutoff acting at a ratio n before the other two, which are identical. At the left we have deduced formulas for D to represent these three cases (the first calculation serves cases 1 and 3 by taking n and its reciprocal). If your choice for best scheme is (1), turn to 189-C; if (2), turn to 194-C; if (3), turn to 184-B.

181-A. (From 167-B, 194-B) The fifth answer is the value that would be computed from the change of gain when the load is disconnected *with* feedback. Gain (loaded) is 70 divided by 5, or 14. Gain (unloaded) is 500 divided by 29.6, or 16.85. The difference is $16.85 - 14 = 2.85$. Multiplying 4K (the load) by $2.85/14$ gives the result of this method, 812 ohms. It should be recognized that all of these measurements or calculations have a practical significance: the source impedance of an amplifier is by no means a simple number, even with feedback to help stabilize it. Now turn to 182-A.

PHASE-SHIFT EFFECTS

181-B. (From 163-B) Now we consider feedback with phase shifts. At both ends of the frequency range handled, there will be turnover points where phase shift occurs, before gain "disappears." At the high-frequency end, attenuation functions of the type $(1 + jax)$ will be introduced (see 73-B). At the low-frequency end the functions will contain reciprocal orders of x or ω (direct-coupled amplifiers avoid such low-frequency parameters). Here we have taken the general case for high-frequency turnover.

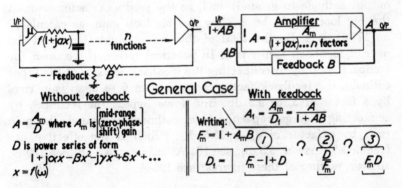

Amplifiers with a low-frequency cutoff as well may often be treated for both ends separately, but in some cases they must be considered on the interacting basis (see 203-A).

Here we assume that D represents the complex frequency function and proceed to see how feedback affects it. The subscript m denotes mid-band value—where phase shift has no effect. The subscript f distinguishes a parameter with feedback from the corresponding one without feedback. Which of the three values for D_f is correct? Answer, (1): see 193-B; answer, (2): see 183-C; answer, (3): see 168-C.

182

182-A. (From 181-A) The problem of 177-B figures the effect of feedback on output impedance, based on theoretical feedback. Now we run into a problem that may be encountered in checking the performance of the practical circuit, or it may arise during the calculations. It illustrates an important fact about feedback calculations in general: assume that the input stage has some

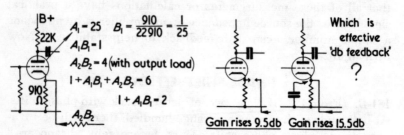

feedback of its own. Let's put in some figures. Suppose that, with a 22K plate resistor and a high-value grid resistor of the following stage, the stage gain is 25. This assumes that the cathode resistor is bypassed. Now we calculate the feedback for this stage (A_1B_1). The loop gain (from input grid to cathode, to output cathode to ground) is 1, so the feedback factor without the big loop would be 2. Now the big-loop gain, as calculated on 177-B, is 4. So the total of the AB products is 5, and the overall feedback factor is 6. In practical terms, if we open the feedback loop by disconnecting the feedback resistor at the input cathode, the feedback factor changes from 6 to 2, so gain rises by a factor of 3, or 9.5 db. But if we bypass the feedback by connecting a large capacitor from cathode to ground, the gain rises by a factor of 6, or 15.5 db. Which is the effective db-feedback? Answer, 9.5 db: see 184-A; answer, 15.5 db: see 189-B; answer, neither of these figures: see 190-A.

182-B. (From 188-A) *Wrong.* But the specific condition we added was really a catch. While the two-and-two combination does give slightly higher permissible feedback at the stability boundary, there is a big advantage to the one-and-three combination at the peaking boundary. Only if a very wide spacing between these boundaries is really required would the two-and-two combination be the better choice. Even then, the maximum feedback before peaking is less than 6 db, which means wide deviations in feedback are unlikely to occur, unless the circuit is deliberately designed to have them. See the other answer.

183-A. (From 187-A) *Wrong.* This is a mistake often made. Try another answer.

183-B. (From 162-B) There certainly are exceptions; here we show two of them. In the first place, the formula on 162-B omitted second-order (distortion of distortion) effects, under the assumption (not stated) that they are negligible. Under some circumstances they may be ignored, and sometimes they may even result in greater reduction of distortion than the simplified formula represents (by a very small fraction). But the product DD_t can also mean trouble, *i.e.*, distortion not appreciably reduced by feedback.

① Input is $1 - BD_t$ Gain and distortion are $A + D$

Output is $(1 - BD_t)(A + D) = A + D_t$

$A + D - ABD_t - \boxed{BDD_t} = A + D_t$

Usually —<u>but not always</u>—negligible

$D_t = \dfrac{D}{1 + AB + BD}$ <u>2$^{\underline{nd}}$ order distortion</u>

② Transfer Curve   *AB* zero   *AB* variable

The second approach may illustrate an example: a transfer curve with clipping. An alternate way to analyze distortion would be in terms of the way the product AB varies at different points on the characteristic. The result will be sensibly identical with the algebraic approach, all the while the curve represents a finite transfer. But when clipping occurs, the product AB almost suddenly drops to zero, so the feedback cannot "work" on this part at all. In practical circuits it may not be as bad as this; the feedback signal may be arranged so that it changes bias (d.c.) temporarily to reduce the degree of clipping. But in some practical circuits this action can result in a worse situation: over-biasing throwing the active range off the opposite end of the curve, with a time delay in its return. This must be analyzed with reference to time-constant effects. Now turn to 177-B.

183-C. (From 181-B) *No.* Your choice was probably intuitive, based on the fact that feedback divides most effects by the feedback factor, in this case $(1 + A_m B)$. But both D and D_t are complex expressions with frequency functions, so the change is not a simple numerical one, as this expression would suggest. Check your algebra and make another choice.

184-A. (From 182-A) Under their own circumstances both the given answers are correct. So the choice depends on what is meant by "effective feedback." This answer would be correct if it meant the effect of opening the loop. But that is all it would be correct for. It does not indicate the effect in controlling distortion, modifying output impedance, or anything else. Try another answer.

184-B. (From 180-B) For most purposes and for the strict wording of the question, this is best choice: it allows most feedback for a given n, for freedom from peaking and instability.

Here we show how all the results are obtained. For peaking to occur the coefficient of x^2 in the db expression must be nega-

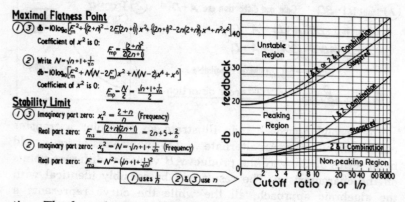

Maximal Flatness Point

①③ $db = 10 \log_{10}\left[F_m^2 + \left\{(2+n)^2 - 2F_m(2n+1)\right\}x^2 + \left\{2n+1)^2 - 2n(2+n)\right\}x^4 + n^2x^6\right]$

Coefficient of x^2 is 0: $F_{mp} = \dfrac{(2+n)^2}{2(2n+1)}$

② Write $N = \sqrt{n+1} + \dfrac{1}{\sqrt{n}}$

$db = 10 \log_{10}\left[F_m^2 + N(N - 2F_m)x^2 + N(N-2)x^4 + x^6\right]$

Coefficient of x^2 is 0: $F_{mp} = \dfrac{N}{2} = \dfrac{\sqrt{n+1} + \frac{1}{\sqrt{n}}}{2}$

Stability Limit

①③ Imaginary part zero: $x_s^2 = \dfrac{2+n}{n}$ (Frequency)

Real part zero: $F_{ms} = \dfrac{(2+n)(2n+1)}{n} = 2n + 5 + \dfrac{2}{n}$

② Imaginary part zero: $x_s^2 = N = \sqrt{n+1} + \dfrac{1}{\sqrt{n}}$ (Frequency)

Real part zero: $F_{ms} = N^2 = \left(\sqrt{n+1} + \frac{1}{\sqrt{n}}\right)^2$

① uses $\frac{1}{n}$ ② & ③ use n

tive. The boundary is when this coefficient is zero; making this substitution, we find the value F_{mp} where peaking commences. Instability commences when both imaginary and real parts of the expression for D_f are zero. The imaginary part fixes the frequency (in terms of x, given the symbol x_s) at which oscillation commences, while substituting this value into the real part determines the value of feedback needed, given the symbol F_{ms}. In working the staggered case we have used the simplification N for the duplicated expression in n in the equation for D (180-B).

Plotting the results of these solutions at the right gives a clear picture of the way these boundaries change, using these typical combinations. Now, assuming that we pick the best solution, the spacing between the boundaries does not change much, which gives us the opportunity to employ a further simplification in estimating the degree and frequency of peak for cases in the peaking region. To see how this is done, turn to 157-B.

185-A. (From 197-A) This answer was probably intuitive, but it is wrong. For this to be correct, the 6 db/octave 90° point would not change level, referred to the no-feedback gain, but it would merely move outward. In other words, at the peak (when feedback is enough to make one) the gain would not change as feedback is increased; merely the mid-band gain would be reduced. Although some presentations have pictured it this way, it is not correct. Try another answer.

185-B. (From 198-A) This is a possible answer, and the usual interpretation is explained here. A booster step might be applied in the feedback, as at D. Note at the lower left that a step may be analyzed as equivalent to an inverted cutoff (in this case, D_1) combined with a cutoff (in this case, D_2). This equivalence exists

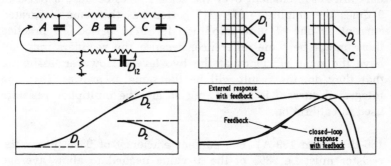

in both magnitude and phase, although we have not shown that of phase. Now, at the top right we show what can be done with it. Without D the arrangement is a two-and-one combination with an n of 10, which (see 184-B) allows 5.5 (say 6) db feedback for maximal flatness condition. With D the inverted cutoff (D_1) cancels the effect of A, leaving only B effective at the lower frequency, and adds another cutoff D_2 effective at the upper frequency. This alone would be good for 11-db feedback with maximal flatness. But, because the step is in the feedback it causes high-frequency loss in the external transmission (inversion of feedback response). So the closed-loop response can be allowed some 18-db peak, which means 14- or 15-db excess feedback, making a total of 25- or 26-db feedback possible. The responses shown at the lower right show how this combination builds up an external response with a dip before final cutoff that can be a reasonable approximation to flat. But this is only one way the steps can be used in feedback. Try one of the other answers.

186-A. (From 199-A) Answer (a) is that an r.m.s. reading has the same value as that which is the r.m.s. value of the wave.

Answer (b) is also irrespective of polarity because the meter is full-wave, and therefore reversal will merely use alternate elements for corresponding wave parts, but the overall effect will be unchanged. If the magnitude of the positive pulse is 9 units, and the negative one is 1 unit, the squares are 81 and 1 respectively. Taking the time into account, the 1 unit is multiplied by 9, and $81 + 9 = 90$. Dividing by 10 (total time units) and extracting the square root, the r.m.s. value is 3. The average reading will be $(9 + 9)/10 = 1.8$. On a sine wave used for calibration the average (actual) will be 0.9 of the r.m.s. (see 176-A), so the reading will be ⅔ of the true r.m.s. value.

Answer (c) would also be irrespective of polarity if the rectifiers are 100% efficient over the scale range, because a pulse of 9 times the amplitude for 1/10 period has the same integrated current as one of unit amplitude for 9/10 period. In practice there might be some difference, because the rectifiers may not have the same efficiency at the two levels. However, assuming that they do, the result will be the same as answer (b): the integrated current is halved, but so are the multiplier resistors used in calibration.

186-B. (From 199-A) The current efficiency of 98% means the resistor must be 98% of the .9 value needed to allow average rectified value to produce an r.m.s. reading. For 50 microamps full-scale the nominal resistance would be 20,000 ohms for every full-scale volt. So the actual total resistance needed for the various scales is 0.882 of 20,000, or 17,640 ohms per full-scale volt. From the total value the rectifier input impedance of 23,000 ohms must be subtracted. At center scale the total input resistance will be $38,000 - 23,000 = 15,000$ ohms higher than at full scale, so, with the same mid-scale current flowing, the required voltage must be half of 15,000/17,640, or 0.425 volt high. Now we can tabulate the results:

Range:	5	10	20	50	100
Multiplier, ohms:	65,200	153,400	329,800	859,000	1,741,000
Mid-scale reading:	2.925	5.425	10.425	25.425	50.425

Note how the mid-scale reading becomes relatively closer to an accurate half of full-scale reading.

POWER-SERIES ANALYSIS OF TRANSFER FUNCTIONS

187-A. (From 189-A) In the absence of phase shift a transfer characteristic is a line which is straight for linear transfer. Curvature shows that harmonics of the input signal will be generated. As we have shown here, the addition of a second-order

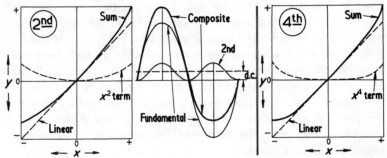

(x^2) term to the transfer function produces a d.c. component and a second harmonic in the output. What will a fourth-order term produce?

(1) d.c. and fourth harmonic (see 183-A);

(2) d.c. + second harmonic + fourth harmonic (see 154-C);

(3) d.c. − second harmonic + fourth harmonic (see 178-A).

187-B. (From 200-A) *Correct.* Here, at the left is shown the essential ultra-linear circuit. A possible problem for high-frequency response and distortion was covered at 143-A. In the

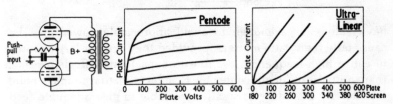

center are typical pentode curves. At the right are corresponding ultra-linear curves for a working voltage of 300. At this point, both plate and screen volts are the same. For every 100-volt change on the plate, screen volts are changed by 40 (this is for ultra-linear with a 40% screen tap). Note that, even with accurate data of this type, only one operating condition can be investigated. Bias, or plate load, can be changed on these same characteristics, but not the supply voltage or screen-tapping.

188-A. (From 157-B) *Correct.* This can be deduced from the derivation on 180-B. The combination consists of one cutoff with factor n and two without it. So the normalizing reference is the cutoff frequency of the two remote cutoffs.

Now we proceed to examine systems with four cutoffs or effective stages. Since the distributed or staggered arrangement was proved inferior to either of the others in the three-stage case, to simplify matters we can dismiss it here at the outset. This leaves a question how the four cutoffs should be distributed between two frequencies, spaced apart by a ratio of n. Is the best arrangement one where there are two cutoffs at each frequency (see 196-D), or where there is one at the first cutoff and three at the remote one (see 182-B)? After the last result with the three-stage case, you may expect that an unqualified choice is not possible, so let's be more specific: make the answer the arrangement that gives the most feedback (for a given value of n) before oscillation occurs.

188-B. (From 200-A) Here is the only practical circuit meeting these requirements. For feedback to stay constant the ratio of R_1 to R_2 must equal the ratio of the load to R_3. R_1 and R_2 may

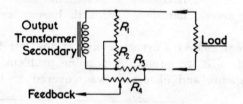

have values large enough to avoid appreciable power loss, because only their ratio matters, provided they are not large enough to cause high-frequency loss due to capacitance effects, or such that the position of the slider on R_4 affects virtual tapping point. Resistor R_3 should be as small as possible to give adequate feedback in the full "current" position (slider of R_4 at right-hand end). If other considerations make it convenient to dispense with the usual series resistor, using the above-mentioned ratio as the feedback ratio, so much the better; but this may not be feasible, and a compromise may have to be accepted. If the total feedback is constant at 20 db, for example, the output source resistance can be varied from one-tenth its value without feedback (full voltage, left end) to ten times the value (full current, right end).

189-A. (From 167-A) *Correct.* All this really proves is that the instrument uses a full-wave rectifier, with multipliers to suit. On either a.c. or d.c. there will be this 11% (or 9%, according to whether you measure it up or down) difference, and it will show the same reading in either position when the meter connections are reversed. So if the two readings are 5.8 and 6.45, for example, you have no way of knowing which of the two is correct, unless you already know the voltage is a.c. or d.c. For this case, the simplest thing is to insert a series capacitor. For d.c. the voltage reading will be zero. If it is rectified but unsmoothed, it will still read much less with the capacitor in series. If it is a.c., then the capacitor will make little if any difference to the reading.

Some instruments remove the rectifier altogether in the d.c. position of the switch, in which case the meter would not read (or the needle would vibrate near zero) when switched to d.c., if the voltage was a.c. Some meters switch in a capacitor on the a.c. position of the switch, or have an extra position that does, which will reverse the situation—zero reading on d.c., switched to a.c. With the half-wave circuit the change in the reading will be much greater, and in one direction d.c. will read, while in the opposite it won't. If the d.c. position removes the rectifier, only one way of d.c. connection will read *on scale*; but for the opposite direction the needle will be thrown back against the zero stop, which is slightly different from the half-wave, reverse-connected circuit, where the needle doesn't move. Now turn to 187-A.

189-B. (From 182-A) This answer would be correct if the significance of "effective feedback" is the change of gain when the input cathode is bypassed, but not for anything else, *e.g.*, distortion reduction or modification of output impedance. Try another answer.

189-C. (From 180-B) This would be correct for part of the question: it allows a maximum feedback for a given value of *n*, before instability is reached; but peaking is reached more quickly with this combination than with either of the others. However, if a maximum range of change in feedback from beginning of peaking to instability was required, this is the desired combination. But that was not the question. Try another answer.

190-A. (From 182-A) If you've tried the answers on both 184-A and 189-B, you've now turned to this page to find the correct answer. Or, you may already have deduced that the correct answer was the one we worked out originally on 177-B: 14 db, representing a factor of 5. Because of the interaction there is no direct way of measuring this. But the impedance change or the effect on distortion would substantiate this conclusion. Now turn to 165-B.

190-B. (From 197-A) *Correct.* Here we show the simplest derivation. To separate the gain-changing and frequency-response effects, we change the variable to normalize to the 6 db/octave,

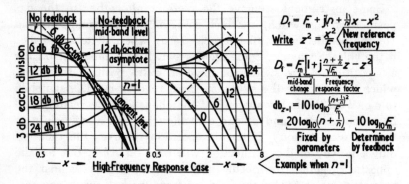

90° point *with feedback*, from x to z. Now we can divide out the effects of circuit parameters represented by n from the effect of feedback, represented by F_m.

To clarify, we have plotted a series of curves for the identical case, when $n = 1$. At the left we have normalized level to the no-feedback gain. Note the unique construction that results. Every curve touches the 6 db/octave tangent line and is asymptotic to the 12 db/octave line, both of which we have drawn as dashed. At the middle we have replotted normalized to mid-band gain *with* feedback in each case.

If n is other than 1, the 6 db/octave 90° point will be at greater attenuation than 6 db, given by the expression indicated at the right. Now turn to 180-B for three-stage cases.

190-C. (From 198-A) *Wrong.* To maintain stability the need in a feedback circuit is to produce not more phase shift, but less. There are applications where phase shift is needed without attenuation, but this is not one. Try one of the other answers.

191-A. (From 177-B) This answer is a contradiction. You assume that the tube is working along the 4K load-line (by taking the plate resistance at those points), and then you calculate effective plate resistances open-circuit, by dividing by the open-circuit gain. For the open circuit the load line would be a horizontal line, as we drew to find the open-circuit gain. Try another answer.

191-B. (From 165-B) Here, for convenience, we summarize the effect of feedback in various ways. Positive feedback can be divided into three classes. When AB is less than unity the effect is just opposite that of negative feedback. We have indicated quantities proportional to the relevant factor with an arrow

Property →		Gain	Output Impedance		Input Impedance		Relevant Factor
↓ Type of Feedback →			Voltage	Current	Series In	Shunt In	
Positive	$AB>1$	*	↓ −	↑ −	↑ −	↓ −	$AB-1$
	$AB=1$	∞	∞	0	0	∞	
	$AB<1$	↑	↑	↓	↓	↑	$1-AB$
Negative		↓	↓	↑	↑	↓	$1+AB$

pointing upwards, while quantities inversely proportional to the relevant factor have a downward-pointing arrow. When $AB = 1$ in positive feedback, gain reaches infinity, causing oscillation. Terminal impedances are either zero or infinite at this point. When AB is greater than unity in positive feedback, gain cannot be considered as an entity, because it is more than infinite; impedances become negative, which means the entire circuit can be used with external elements as an element of this dimension and sign. However much negative feedback is used, it never reaches instability (unless phase plays a hand: see 181-B). Gain continues to be reduced indefinitely, or until it reaches a fractional value where the feedback network itself becomes the transmission path in place of the amplifier path, and the effect of feedback on terminal impedances goes on indefinitely with an increase of the factor. Now turn to 169-B.

191-C. (From 172-B) This is the best choice. With a source impedance of 800 ohms any output termination will produce little effect. The only additional feature needed is an output d.c. blocking capacitor, which will not have any material effect on the feedback loop. Now turn to 164-B.

192-A. (From 164-B) Although the feedback is positive, or regenerative, it does not act directly on the gain of either stage. It can be viewed in two ways: (1) it increases the a.c. value of the plate resistor; (2) it changes the possible operating point to increase available *swing* or output, not *gain*. This is shown in more detail here. At *A* is a typical operating point with a 33K

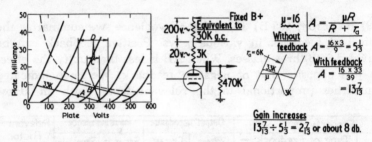

$$\mu = 16 \qquad A = \frac{\mu R}{R + r_a}$$

Without feedback $A = \frac{16 \times 3}{9} = 5\frac{1}{3}$

With feedback $A = \frac{16 \times 33}{39} = 13\frac{7}{13}$

Gain increases
$13\frac{7}{13} \div 5\frac{1}{3} = 2\frac{7}{13}$ or about 8 db.

plate resistor connected to B+ (350V). Using a resistor that is actually 3K enables the operating point to be shifted to *B*. Then feedback increases the gain from the length represented by *C* to that represented by *D*. Note that the change of slope extends the swing much more than it increases gain, which is only 8 db.

The 8-db increase of gain assumes that a plate load of 3K would be used without feedback, which is unlikely. If the 33K resistor were used without feedback, then feedback increases gain by a negligible amount. Turn to 166-B to see the effect on output impedance.

192-B. (From 164-B) Increasing gain would only coincide with reducing output impedance as a result of positive feedback, if the positive feedback is within the outer feedback loop (that's assuming negative-voltage feedback, which this is). However, in

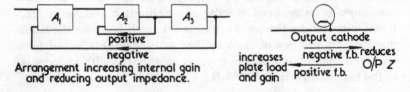

Arrangement increasing internal gain and reducing output impedance.

increases plate load and gain ←→ negative f.b. reduces positive f.b. O/P Z

this case the positive feedback is not within the negative loop. Note that the negative loop includes only part of the output stage. While the positive feedback is due to the same voltage (developed across the cathode of the output stage) as the negative feedback, its effect reflects back to the previous stage. Turn to 166-B.

193-A. (From 168-B) *No. B* is the feedback fraction, but does not alone determine the amount of feedback. Try another answer.

193-B. (From 181-B) *Correct.* Here we give the algebraic derivation of the expression. Note (below the line) the simple substitution procedure that this expression signifies. Into the

Substitute $A = \dfrac{A_m}{D}$ (into) $A_f = \dfrac{A}{1+AB} = \dfrac{A_m}{D+A_m B}$ Also $A_f = \dfrac{A_m}{D_f}$ ▷▷ $D_f = \dfrac{A_m}{A_f}$

$D_f = \dfrac{A_m}{A_f} = A_m \cdot \dfrac{D+A_m B}{A_m} = D+A_m B$ As $F_m = 1+A_m B$ ▷▷ $\underline{D_f = F_m - 1 + D}$

<u>Substitution becomes:</u>   Without feedback $A = \dfrac{A_m}{(1)+jax-bx^2-jcx^3+dx^4+\cdots}$
   Substitute F_m for 1 ◀——
   With feedback $A_f = \dfrac{A_m}{(F_m)+jax-bx^2-jcx^3+dx^4+\cdots}$

frequency/attenuation function, which starts with a figure 1, the mid-frequency feedback factor F_m is substituted. This describes completely the way this much feedback affects gain and frequency response in both amplitude and phase shift. Now turn to 197-A.

193-C. (From 198-A) This is a quite possible viewpoint, although to explore its possibilities requires extensive analysis with Nyquist-type diagrams. The essence of it is shown here. A straight

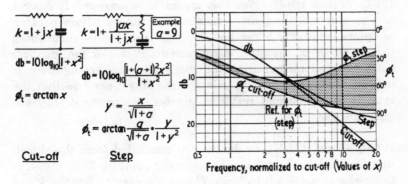

cutoff is compared in both db and phase response with a step that levels off 20 db below the cutoff point. The shaded area between phase curves shows the reduction in phase shift achieved, at practically no change in db response up to the mid-frequency point.

However, complete analysis of performance in a system requires much more than this. See one of the other answers for a more direct approach to complete system determination.

194-A. (From 178-A) *Wrong.* Try another answer.

194-B. (From 177-B) Presuming the source resistance required is that *with* the load connected, this is right. The fact that this is the only answer of (1), (2), and (3) which reduces the *ratio* deviation of effective plate resistance should have clued you that this was the correct one. In case you had difficulty about how those columns were obtained, observe that column a is the result of combining each of the figures in the "tube" column (taken from the curves) with 4K as a parallel resistance combination. Column b is column a divided by 5. (The product AB will deviate negligibly from 4 along this load line because the spacing is very nearly linear, although the plate resistance isn't). Finally, column c is found from $RZ/(R - Z)$, where Z is taken from column b and R is 4K; this gives the effective source resistance that will parallel with 4K to give the figures of column b.

If the source resistance without the load connected is required, another of the answers may be applicable, and there is yet a fifth answer which has a quite practical significance. Can you find it? If you have already studied 167-B and have difficulty finding that fifth answer, turn to 181-A; otherwise, try another of the remaining three answers.

194-C. (From 180-B) Was this an intuitive answer? It doesn't win on either of the scores—maximum feedback before peaking or before instability is reached. Perhaps it should be commented that in either of the other arrangements if one of the identical pair is moved farther from the single one, the arrangement is improved. But moving the pair (or the single one) so that the ratio is greater would result in greater improvement. Try another answer.

194-D. (From 171-B) Evidently you concluded from the sketch that feedback will push up the turnover point by 3 db if everything else is cut down by 3 db. This is not correct. Feedback not only changes shape, it also shifts turnover frequency—second error in this calculation. There was a third minor one: the reactance required for C_2 at its cutoff was incorrectly calculated. Try another answer.

195-A. (From 168-B) *No.* This is a measure of the signal fed back, as compared with the original input, but does not indicate the amount or effect of the feedback. Try another answer.

195-B. (From 169-B) *Wrong.* This was a creditable guess, but it is incorrect. See the other answer.

195-C. (From 198-A) This is a possible answer, an example of which we have illustrated here. We start with a two-and-one combination with $n = 10$, which allows from 6-db (for little above maximal flatness) to 28-db (for instability) feedback. Now apply the downward step, D. This can be regarded (see

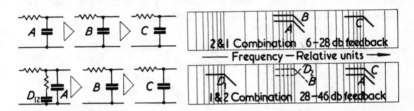

185-B) as a cutoff (in this case, D_1) combined with an inverted cutoff (in this case, D_2). The latter cancels one of the identical pair, in effect. A further effect of the step, evident from its physical combination with A, is the extension of the latter by a factor of 10, because the effective resistance that capacitor A shunts is divided by 10 at the acting frequencies. So we finish up with a one-and-two combination, in effect, with an n of 100, which (see 184-B) allows from 28-db (for maximal flatness) to 46-db (for instability) feedback. After you've compared this with other possible answers, turn to 171-B.

195-D. (From 172-B) This can be done, leaving the cathode follower virtually exclusively for the feedback path. However, a disadvantage of this connection is that any terminating load (the present termination is virtually 5.1 megohms at this point) will destroy the validity of the capacitor C_2 (82 $\mu\mu F$). A new value could be chosen to suit the actual termination used. Also d.c. blocking is needed. The advantages are to the other choice.

196-A. (From 167-A) Yes, the reading will be 11% higher when the switch is thrown, if the meter uses a full-wave rectifier, and the voltage is d.c. But does this prove that the voltage is d.c.? Try another answer.

196-B. (From 178-A) *Wrong.* Try another answer.

196-C. (From 159-B) *Wrong.* You apparently deduced that there was a power relationship, but this is not the correct one. Try another answer.

196-D. (From 188-A) Correct, but only by a small margin. Here we have the development of the relevant formulas for both combinations: (1) the two-and-two combination and (2) the one-

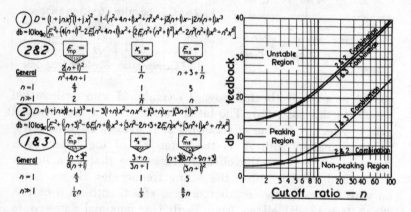

and-three combination. Plotting out the results, as before, the two-and-two combination, starting at $n = 1$, allows a small fraction more feedback before instability, but never more than 1 db. (If you take the ratio at $n = \infty$, it is 9/8, which is almost exactly 1 db.) On the other hand, the peaking boundary is asymptotic to 6 db for the two-and-two combination, but for the one-and-three combination it continues to rise almost parallel to the instability boundary.

Prediction of performance between these boundary conditions can be plotted out, as for the three-stage case. First solve for x_p in terms of F_x, then derive the db expression for this point (see 173-A); mathematically, there is a simpler approach in this case (see 156-B).

197-A. (From 193-B) Using this procedure it is easy to explore the performance of systems using different numbers of roll-off or cutoff responses progressively. Starting with the simplest case, in which there is only one high-pass (low-frequency cutoff) or low-pass (high-frequency cutoff) network, which we have shown here at the left, we make the substitutions into the formulas developed on 193-B; we find that gain is reduced and response extended, by the same ratio, F_m. We have drawn the high-frequency cutoff case here.

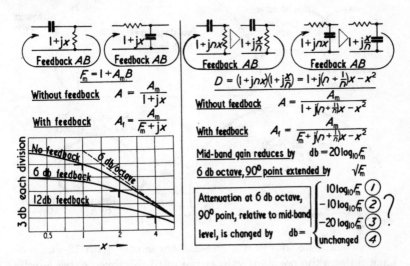

Now we turn to systems employing two cutoffs of the same kind, either low-frequency or high-frequency. To normalize the results to the 6 db/octave 90° point *without feedback* (for explanation of this point, see 66-B) we make one cutoff n times this frequency and the other this frequency divided by n. From the substitutions it is evident that mid-band gain is reduced by the factor F_m (as always). Because the denominator contains F_m with x^2 as terms, it is also evident that the 6 db/octave 90° phase-reference point is extended by $\sqrt{F_m}$. The magnitude of the imaginary term combined with these real terms determines what happens to the response shape, which for two-stage systems is uniquely related to the relative level of this point. Which is the correct expression? (Observe that positive answers mean increased attenuation, while negative answers mean reduced relative attenuation.) Answer, (1): see 172-A; answer, (2): see 190-B; answer, (3): see 185-A; answer, (4): see 174-A.

198-A. (From 170-B) Here they are. Note that with 6-db feedback the Nyquist curve stays within the constant-gain curve. With 12-db feedback, the same curve (expanded to three times the size, because AB is 3 instead of 1) crosses the constant-gain curve (and others if they were drawn), indicating a peak. But, however big this curve was made, it could never enclose the -1 point and hence represents inherent stability with any amount

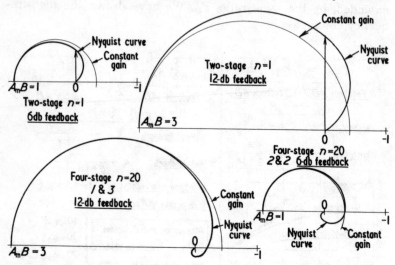

of feedback. The four-stage, one-and-three case with 12-db feedback follows the constant-gain curve until the three extra cutoffs start "bending it in." In the two-and-two case, less feedback is possible (in fact, 6 db produces a very slight peak) and the curve turns in more under the influence of the remaining two cutoffs. Any of these curves can produce instability if the size (represented by loop-gain product, AB) is increased to the value where the curve would enclose the -1 point, instead of going between it and the origin.

Now, for multistage amplifiers, step-networks (see 73-B) can be used to help allow more feedback to be used with stability. These are used (1) to hold response up farther into the cutoff region (see 185-B); (2) to shift phase more effectively than simple cutoff stages can (see 190-C); (3) to attenuate with less phase shift than simple cutoff stages (see 193-C); (4) to offset other cutoff stages in the system and delay their action (see 195-C).

199-A. TEST QUESTIONS ON SECTION 4

1. An asymmetrical wave has positive pulses of nine times the amplitude but one-ninth the duration of the negative part. Will reversing a meter make any difference to the reading, if the meter is (a) an r.m.s. type, (b) a full-wave rectifier type, (c) a half-wave rectifier type? Give your reasons and calculate the relative reading if each meter is calibrated in r.m.s. units. Check your conclusions at 186-A.

2. Under some circumstances, the output from a rectifier with a capacitor input filter is higher than that from one with a choke input filter. If the load current is arranged to progressively saturate the input choke, it is possible to offset other losses so as to achieve perfect or even negative regulation (voltage output rising with increasing load current). For this to happen, find (a) a condition in terms of dL/dI, and (b) in terms of C. Also state what approximation(s) may be included in the assumptions that are not strictly in conformance with practice. Check your answers at 173-B.

3. Find the correct multiplier values for a full-wave rectifier instrument requiring 50 microamps for full-scale reading, for 5-, 10-, 20-, 50-, and 100-volt full-scale ranges, assuming the rectifier has a full-scale current efficiency of 98%, and an input impedance of 23,000 ohms at full scale. If the rectifier has a half-scale input impedance of 38,000 ohms, find the center-scale reading on the lower ranges. Check your answers at 186-B.

4. Develop a power series, normalized to a level at which the only harmonic is the fifth, and from it show how harmonic magnitude will vary at other levels. Assume 4% fifth harmonic at reference level. Check your results at 175-B.

5. By appropriate adjustment of values in the positive-feedback circuit on 165-B, feedback can be made infinite. A choice of values such that the plate and cathode circuits of the second tube have equal effective resistance can produce the split-load type of phase inverter as part of the same arrangement, and by careful choice of first-stage biasing, the plate of the first stage can be direct coupled to the grid of the second. However, with infinite gain from positive feedback, the bias point becomes unstable. Stability can be achieved by using a.c. coupling between stages, with the grid resistor of the second stage returned to a cathode resistor tapping. Another way would be to use a triode-pentode, with pentode for the first stage, and employ screen de-

coupling to provide stability, retaining direct coupling between stages. Outline a design method for this. Compare your outline with that on 179-B.

6. A circuit designated "ultra-linear" or "distributed loading" uses pentode or beam tetrode tubes in push-pull, with extra tappings on the output transformer for the screens of the output tubes, which receive the same d.c. voltage as the plates, plus a signal voltage that is a specific percentage (somewhere between 16% and 50% in various designs) of the plate signal voltage. To design a circuit of this type we (a) start from pentode curves and regard the screen injection as negative feedback (see 155-B); (b) "split the difference" between triode and pentode curves for the same tube, based on the nominal percentage (see 176-B); (c) use specially derived curves, either as published by the manufacturer or obtained empirically by a method to be explained in answer to this question (check at 187-B).

7. The circuit on 177-B and the one second from the left on 165-B each show a way of taking feedback from an output transformer secondary. From these two ways develop a way to provide an adjustable source resistance, from more than normal to less than normal, utilizing a combination of voltage and current feedback so that with correct (nominal) output load the total negative feedback does not change with this adjustment. Check your method against that of 188-B.

8. Utilizing the theoretical response combination discussed on page 94-B, it is possible to build a 24 db/octave ultimate-slope crossover using R and C elements built around a single high-gain stage. Draw a suitable circuit for high-pass and low-pass networks, built around a tube (pentode), with a gain of 100 using a 100K plate load, with overall insertion loss of zero db. Compare your result with that of 174-B.

Section 5

201-A. The preceding sections have been organized into a study sequence, as well as being arranged for convenient use from the index for specific applications when needed. This section, being somewhat of a "catch-all," is not organized into a sequence and may be studied in any order, or not at all, until some part of it is needed. Use the index to find the part that you need.

EFFECTIVE CAPACITANCE IN TUBE CIRCUITS

201-B. (From 234-B) Compared with the possibilities for capacitance changes in transformers (according to connection), tubes seem relatively simple. The best-known effect is the increase of capacitance from plate to grid, viewed from the grid circuit (the increase in the plate circuit is not the same) called the *Miller effect*. Assuming that a tube is used as a straight amplifier with a resistive plate load, the voltage at the plate is antiphase to the grid signal voltage and of a magnitude determined by the working gain of the tube. Thus the voltage across any capacitance directly from grid to plate is $(1 + A)$ times the signal voltage on the grid. The current through the capacitance is increased by the factor $(1 + A)$ to correspond; so the grid circuit "sees" a capacitance of $(1 + A)$ times the actual plate-to-grid capacitance.

This only applies if the amplified signal voltage is developed at the plate. Almost the reverse happens in a cathode follower, except that the operative capacitance is from grid to cathode. Grid-to-plate capacitance is now effectively from grid to ground. In determining effects of this kind, only active capacitances must be considered. For example, in a pentode or other multielectrode tube the term grid-to-plate capacitance may be ambiguous. Each of these electrodes, grid and plate, will have capacitance to other electrodes. If those electrodes were "floating," *i.e.*, not tied to a specific potential, then they would enter into the total grid-to-plate capacitance. But if, as is more usual, they have fixed (d.c.) potentials, then capacitance to them from both grid and plate is effectively to ground and can be so counted. Only grid-to-plate capacitance direct, without ground intervention, counts in Miller-effect calculation. Now turn to 218-B.

INTERACTING NETWORKS

202-A. In the earlier part of this book (see 26-A, 30-A, 73-B, and the sequence beginning at 181-B), we have considered simple coupling configurations without interaction between them. Here we illustrate, with one possible form, the concept of interaction. The four elements R_1, R_2, C_1, and C_2 are a pair of low-pass R-C networks not isolated from one another. In the center grouping,

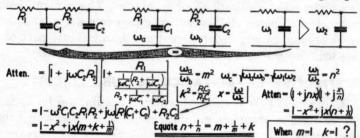

$$\text{Atten.} = \left[1 + j\omega C_2 R_2\right]\left[1 + \frac{R_1}{R_2 + \frac{1}{j\omega C_1} + \frac{1}{j\omega C_2}}\left(R_2 + \frac{1}{j\omega C_2}\right)\right]$$

$$= 1 - \omega^2 C_1 C_2 R_1 R_2 + j\omega\left[R_1(C_1 + C_2) + R_2 C_2\right]$$

$$= 1 - x^2 + jx\left(m + k + \frac{1}{m}\right)$$

$\frac{\omega_a}{\omega_b} = m^2 \quad \omega_c = \sqrt{\omega_a \omega_b} = \sqrt{\omega_1 \omega_2} \quad \frac{\omega_1}{\omega_2} = n^2$

$k^2 = \frac{R_1 C_2}{R_2 C_1} \quad x = \frac{\omega}{\omega_c} \quad \text{Atten} = \left(1 + jnx\right)\left(1 + j\frac{x}{n}\right)$

$= 1 - x^2 + jx\left(n + \frac{1}{n}\right)$

Equate $n + \frac{1}{n} = m + \frac{1}{m} + k$

$\boxed{\text{When } m = 1 \quad k = 1 \ ?}$

ω_a and ω_b represent the 3-db points of R_1, C_1 and R_2, C_2 respectively. But when the two networks are connected together, as at the left, their performance is equivalent to a different noninteracting pair, represented at the right, with 3-db frequencies ω_1 and ω_2.

The attenuation for the two arrangements is calculated, and factors m, k, and n inserted with the significance shown. Equating the real and imaginary parts of the two expressions, the fact that x, using the same derivation, makes the real parts identical proves that the mid-frequency, ω_c, which is the 90° phase reference and 6 db/octave slope point, is unchanged by the interaction. The difference between the coefficients of jx shows that a spreading takes place—that ω_a and ω_b are not separated as widely as ω_1 and ω_2. The factor k can be regarded as an interaction constant: the smaller it is, the nearer will m and n be to having the same values. If both R's and both C's have identical values, we have a case of particular interest. For this case, is $n = 2$ (see 212-A), $n = 2.5$ (see 210-A), or $n = 2.618$ (see 214-A)?

202-B. (From 204-A) You probably have in mind the maximal flatness curve as the limiting case. It is the limiting case before peaking begins, but it does not represent complete lack of interaction in identical time-constant networks, which is the limit here. This results in 6-db loss due to the combination of two networks. See the other answer.

203-A. (From 214-A) Here we consider one possible combination with the same kind of reactance element (capacitance here) in opposite positions (one series, one shunt). The treatment on 202-A would apply equally to series capacitors, but here we take one of each. Note that in this case the equivalent noninteracting networks have to include a loss section, the attenuation

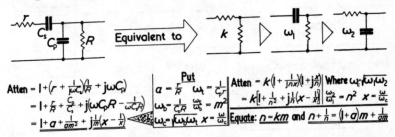

for which we write k. Here again, as the derivation shows, the effect of interaction is to spread the effective 3-db frequencies farther apart than without the interaction. The factor is k. For large values of a ($= r/R$), k is nearly the same as $1 + a$. For small values there is a greater deviation. Note the choice of pairs for low- and high-frequency cutoff that lead to this result: r with C_p and R with C_s. If the positions of the C's are interchanged (shunt before series) a different set of formulas must be derived. This one illustrates the method.

Now, both the combination on 202-A and the one here use the same kind of elements (capacitances with resistances; inductances with resistances would lead to similar results). What will happen if opposite kinds of reactance (inductance and capacitance) are combined in a network? Will the interaction still spread their separate effects (see 212-B), or will it concentrate them (see 206-A)?

203-B. (From 236-A) *Correct.* In other words, the economy is greatest when the common current flows through the few turns and the common voltage is across the many turns. In terms of the turns shown, the operative ratio can be considered as $N = (T + t)/T$, or $1 + t/T$. The total power transferred is $(T + t)/t$, or $1 + T/t$ times that transformed. So the economy of an auto-transformer, in terms of the external circuit ratio N, is $N/(N - 1)$. This obviously is greatest when N is not much greater than 1 and least when N has large values. Now turn to 237-A.

204-A. (From 206-A) *Correct*. In case you had not noticed it, there was some similarity between the treatment of the arrangement on 206-A, and the modified step-networks used for peak and absorption responses on 71-B. This arrangement, which is one of the types that were the basis of the question, has parallels

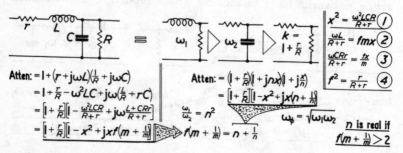

with the treatment on 66-B. In this case the attenuation needed in the noninteracting equivalent is exactly the same as that in the interacting prototype (left) when the reactance and susceptance of L and C respectively are zero (at zero frequency, but effectively until they start to take effect). Here, to make both real and imaginary parts identical (after extracting the constant factor, $1 + r/R$) two factors are needed to reconcile the prototype (f and m) with its equivalent (n). This is because the interaction has a shifting as well as a concentrating (fractional spreading) effect. A real value for n, and therefore for equivalent noninteracting parameters, is only possible if the product $f(m + 1/m)$, in the prototype analysis, is greater than 2.

What is the attenuation at the 6 db/octave and 90° phase-shift point (reference for x) when the product is exactly 2—(1) 3 db (see 202-B), or (2) 6 db (see 213-A)? For values smaller than 2, does peaking occur? The second question may help you answer the first.

204-B. (From 235-C) For some purposes this will be a sort of optimum, but for the basic network it does not result in maximum rate of phase shift away from zero and maximum rate of increased attenuation. However, it results in an attenuation of precisely 3 at zero phase-shift. Where this positive feedback is either balanced against negative feedback or the "bottom end" of the network (see 248-A) connected to a negative-feedback point, this choice will usually come close to optimizing overall performance. Now see another answer.

STABILITY MARGINS

205-A. On 170-B and 198-A we introduced Nyquist diagrams as a basic concept for visualizing feedback-loop behavior. Here we take this a little further. At (A) is the inner part (where the curve aproaches the origin or zero point) of a curve that is inherently stable with any amount of gain, such as that for a

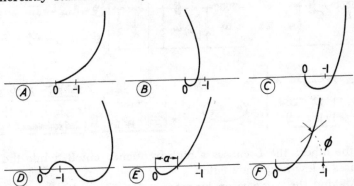

two-stage network. At (B) is the inner part of a curve that is stable and probably nonpeaking (how to discover this was treated on 198-A) *at the gain level shown.* But (C) shows the same curve magnified, by increasing loop gain, until it is unstable. At in-between gain levels, the same curve could be peaking, but not unstable. At (D) is one kind of curve, involving quite complicated circuitry, that has what is termed *conditional stability.* The curve avoids enclosing the −1 point, but crosses the zero-phase line (twice) at an amplitude greater than −1. Such a circuit can be stable because a fed-back signal will never be of the right magnitude to maintain an oscillation *unless* the circuit is excited to produce nonlinear action, in which case oscillation will be self-sustaining. For example, if gain temporarily drops so that the −1 point is between the crossing points on the zero-phase line, oscillation will build up and follow the gain back to normal. A variety of other "shock" effects could trigger instability in such a system.

Now we turn to two parameters related exclusively to the Nyquist curve: stability margins—at (E) is shown amplitude margin: the factor by which *a* falls short of −1; at (F) phase margin is shown: the angle, short of 180°, where gain (AB) is precisely unity. Are these parameters only referable to a plotted diagram (see 209-A), or can they be measured (see 218-A)?

206-A. (From 203-A) *Correct.* Here is the case of inductance and capacitance combined in series. Where R is small compared to the reactance of L and C at the frequency where these are equal, the arrangement is called *resonant*. The case where this approach is more useful is where reactances are small compared to R. Then each reactance may be considered *almost* independently

$$\frac{\omega_1}{\omega_2} = n^2 \qquad \omega_c = \sqrt{\omega_1\omega_2} \qquad x = \frac{\omega}{\omega_c}$$

$$\frac{\omega L}{R} = sx \qquad \frac{1}{\omega C R} = \frac{s}{x}$$

$$Atten = 1 + \frac{\omega L + \frac{1}{\omega C}}{R}$$
$$= 1 + j\left(\frac{\omega L}{R} - \frac{1}{\omega C R}\right)$$
$$= 1 + js\left(x - \frac{1}{x}\right)$$

$$k = \frac{n^2+1}{n^2}$$

$$Atten = \left(1 + j\frac{x}{n}\right)\left(1 + \frac{1}{jnx}\right)$$
$$= 1 + \frac{1}{n^2} + j\frac{1}{n}\left(x - \frac{1}{x}\right)$$
$$= \left[\frac{n^2+1}{n^2}\right]\left[1 + j\frac{n}{n^2+1}\left(x - \frac{1}{x}\right)\right]$$

$$s = \sqrt{\frac{L}{CR^2}} \qquad x^2 = \omega^2 LC$$
$$s = \frac{n}{n^2+1} \qquad n = \frac{1}{2s} \pm \sqrt{\frac{1}{4s^2} - 1}$$
Real equivalence if $s < \frac{1}{2}$

of the other: the L causes a high-frequency cutoff, while the C causes a low-frequency cutoff.

Making the comparison by means of the complex attenuation expressions, we find that the noninteracting networks with cutoffs at ω_1 and ω_2 introduce a loss not present in the interacting network, which we compensate for by putting an attenuation section in square brackets, with a reciprocal factor, $1/k$. If the attenuation k were added to the interacting network (at the left), its performance would completely simulate that of the equivalent noninteracting elements at the right, without attenuation.

The factors we use to solve are s for a spreading factor (or concentrating factor) and n for equivalent divergence of ω_1 and ω_2 from the central frequency, ω_c. The attenuation, k, of the equivalent noninteracting compared to the prototype interacting is a function of n^2. Then s is another function of n, from which we find n in terms of s, and from this expression the condition for real equivalence—that is, for it to be possible to synthesize response from noninteracting elements. It is that s is less than $\frac{1}{2}$. When s is greater than $\frac{1}{2}$, the circuit can be treated only as a resonant one, because there are no real noninteracting elements from which it can be synthesized.

Now, if the reactance elements are one in series and one in shunt, does a similar condition obtain (*i.e.*, beyond which there is no real equivalent noninteracting arrangement) (see 204-A), or does this have real equivalents for all cases (see 216-A)?

AMPLIFIER CLASSIFICATION

207-A. Here we illustrate the concept behind the customary amplifier classification as applied to tube amplifiers. The principle is not changed by application to transistors or other devices. In class-A amplification (left) each tube has an operating point (*C* and *C'*) such that their load lines (*AB* and *A'B'*) are wholly

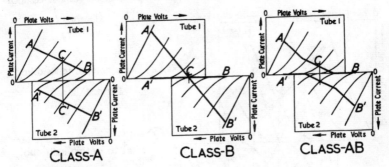

CLASS-A   CLASS-B   CLASS-AB

in the conducting region (finite, nonzero current-values). The combined load is usually provided by use of a push-pull output transformer.

In class-B amplification (center) each tube has an operating point at or very near zero current (*C*). Their common load line *AB'* is again provided by the output transformer, but only half of the active load line appears in each tube's plate circuit. The other half of the individual tube load-lines may be regarded as following the voltage axis (zero-current line). Thus tube 1's load line is *ACB*, while tube 2's is *A'CB'*.

Class-AB amplification "splits the difference," shown at the right. For small signals each tube has its individual share of the composite load, as in class-A, but beyond this swing range, one of the tubes cuts off in each direction, and the other supplies the full, active load-line.

Can the construction outlined here be used to find the correct operating conditions for each class? Answer: yes; see 217-A. Answer: no; see 208-A.

207-B. (From 224-A) The most likely reason for choosing an intermediate point would be that it compromised the advantages and disadvantages of the other two points. As the advantages really go to only one of the other points, there is no such compromise to make. Try another answer.

208

208-A. (From 207-A) *Correct.* Even the class-A condition will not correctly be predicted in this manner. Here, enlarged, we show the correct procedure. Even in class-A, the individual load-lines will be *curved*, a fact usually recognized by stating that push-pull operation cancels the second harmonic generation of

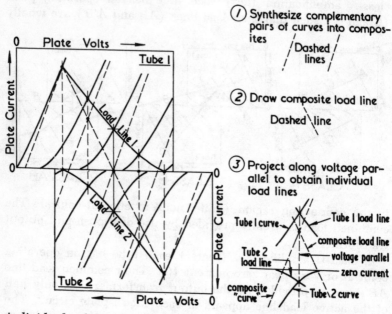

① Synthesize complementary pairs of curves into composites / Dashed / lines

② Draw composite load line — Dashed line

③ Project along voltage parallel to obtain individual load lines

individual tubes. It does this only by providing each tube with a curved load line so that each can have the same plate-voltage swing (but in opposite directions) at every instant.

Note that the operating point arrived at by this complete method will be at lower current per tube than the approximate method. Alternatively, it will allow greater power to be achieved from the pair of tubes with the same maximum plate voltage and maximum dissipation.

208-B. (From 216-D) Making the bypass capacitor larger than the grid input capacitance will not decrease operating time materially, because effective series capacitance will approach double and so will operative gain (in the same ratio, actually). What the increase will achieve is a slower recovery, to prevent a spurious signal close after the wanted one from triggering the circuit. (See the other answers.) A shorter recovery time can be achieved by reducing grid-circuit resistors.

209-A. (From 205-A) If only the external terminals of an amplifier or system are accessible, this is correct. But without access to the loop-return point, this is not a valid answer.

AMPLITUDE- AND FREQUENCY-MODULATION

209-B. On page 23-B, we showed how vectors can be used to represent more than one frequency. There the frequencies introduced were harmonically related. To analyze modulation methods by means of vectors, we regard the carrier as a fixed vector, while the side-band vectors rotate in opposite directions relative to the carrier. To complete the picture the whole assemblage of vectors can be regarded as rotating at the carrier frequency, while the much slower relative change of position is taking place. Here the carrier rotation is represented by the dashed-line arrow,

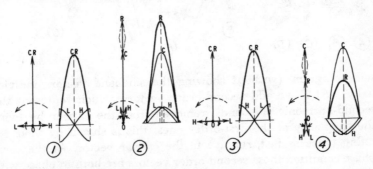

while the solid arrows crossing the sideband vectors (*L* for lower and *H* for higher) represent their movement relative to the carrier (*C*). At two points during the cycle of amplitude modulation the resultant vector (*R*) is identical with the carrier vector (*C*) (this is at positions (1) and (3) here). At position (2) the sideband vectors are approaching in-phase condition, adding to the carrier, while at position (4) they are approaching anti-phase condition, subtracting from the carrier. At each position a section of the three frequency-waves is shown from that point in the modulation cycle to illustrate how the carrier (*C*) and sideband (*L* and *H*) frequency-waves build up the resultant (*R*).

Now, how can frequency modulation be represented—by oppositely rotating vectors in a different phase relationship (see 221-A); by a succession of oppositely rotating vectors at different frequencies (representing multiple sidebands) and phase relationships (see 210-B); or can not they simply be represented by vectors at all (see 213-B)?

210

210-A. (From 202-A) *Wrong.* Try another answer.

210-B. (From 209-B) *Correct.* Here the successive approach is shown. Starting with the first-order sideband vectors (marked *L* and *H*, as for amplitude modulation on 209-B), we show how change in their phase relation to the carrier results in a phase swing, rather than an amplitude swing (*A* thru *D*). At *E* we show how the "motion" of the resultant can be superimposed on the

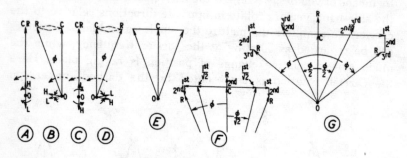

same diagram (without showing the sideband vectors individually). At *F* we add second-order vectors, which represent the second-harmonic sidebands, removed from the carrier by twice the frequency of the first-order ones; this is shown by their rotating twice as fast, relative to the carrier vector. At the zero-phase condition these second-order vectors are both in phase with the carrier. At the 90° phase condition, where there is a maximum phase swing of the resultant, the second-order vectors are precisely antiphase to the carrier. At a 45° phase, where the first-order resultant is its maximum magnitude divided by $\sqrt{2}$, the second-order resultant is zero.

With only first-order vectors (*A* thru *D*) the resultant length changes, unless the magnitude of the sidebands is very small, at twice the sideband difference frequency (maximum at both extremes, minimum at middles). Second-order vectors correct this to some extent, but as amplitude increases, more correction is necessary. At *G* we show the addition of third-order terms at 0°, 30°, and 90° positions of the first-order vectors. Now to pursue the analysis, if first- and second-orders produce a close approximation to true frequency (or phase) modulation, do the relative *magnitudes* of the two orders for maximum amplitude constancy coincide with those for linearity of modulation (see 222-A), or are they different (see 219-A)?

TRANSFORMER DESIGN AND UTILIZATION

211-A. In the section that began at 148-B the treatment aimed at utilizing electronic transformers. While their complete design is usually a specialist's job, there are aspects of it that help in understanding them.

First, we'll consider efficiency. The basic efficiency condition set forth on 150-B may seldom apply, but there is a further optimization that does: it is the relation between winding resistances of primary and secondary. The statement was made on 150-B that making r_1 and r_2 equal requires equal winding space for each winding, in the core window. Here is the derivation;

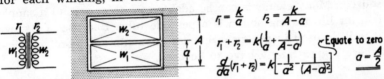

$$r_1 = \frac{k}{a} \qquad r_2 = \frac{k}{A-a}$$
$$r_1 + r_2 = k\left(\frac{1}{a} + \frac{1}{A-a}\right) \qquad \text{Equate to zero}$$
$$\frac{d}{da}(r_1 + r_2) = k\left[-\frac{1}{a^2} - \frac{1}{(A-a)^2}\right] \qquad a = \frac{A}{2}$$

w_1 and w_2 represent the windings in the core window; A is the total windings' space (less a fixed allowance for insulation, etc.) and a is the part of A occupied by w_1. Resistance of the winding is proportional to turns squared (assuming constant-space occupancy), to the length of the average turn (length, mean turn) and inversely to the cross-section area it occupies. Referred to a specific winding (turns for an impedance value) the constant k takes care of the first two of these proportionalities, while the denominators, a and $A - a$, take care of the last one. Writing the expression for total winding resistance, $r_1 + r_2$, differentiating and equating it to zero to find minimum, we arrive at the result $a = A/2$: each winding should occupy half the space.

This assumes both windings use the same mean-turn length. In many practical cases they don't. Does the rule still apply (see 221-B); should each winding use the same weight of wire (see 216-B); or should each winding have the same proportion, cross section to mean turn length (see 228-B)?

211-B. (From 235-C) A simple little check will show that making $k = 2$ (6-db attenuation) requires r/R and C/c to be ½. This value does not give such a sharp change of attenuation and phase shift away from the zero phase-shift frequency, but it may be more appropriate in some circuits (see 204-B). While one of these combinations may be practically appropriate, neither of them is the academic optimum. See one of the other answers.

212-A. (From 202-A) *Wrong.* This must have been a guess. Try another answer.

212-B. (From 203-A) *No.* See the other answer.

212-C. (From 219-A) *Wrong.* See the other answer.

GATING AND LOGIC CIRCUITS

212-D. In computers, both digital and analog, and other data processing and control equipment, there is need for what are termed *logic circuits.* These react in different ways, according to their design, with combinations of input pulses from different sources. Many elements can be adapted for this use, but a simple one for illustrating action is a pentode tube. Because of its size it is little used in practice. Smaller elements are more practical where a great many have to be used.

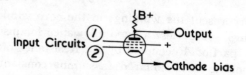

Suppose the combination of cathode bias and input signal bias is such that both input electrodes bias the tube to cutoff individually. That is, if either electrode receives a positive pulse by itself (with no signal on the other) the tube remains cut off. But when both electrodes receive a positive pulse simultaneously, a pulse appears at the plate (negative-going, but this can easily be reversed in phase). We have a basic AND circuit. Only when both inputs are present simultaneously, (1) *and* (2), does the circuit respond.

Now change the bias on the input circuits and reverse their polarity, so the tube is normally conducting. A negative pulse at either input will now cut off the tube, producing a positive pulse at the plate. This is a basic OR circuit. It responds to one *or* the other.

In the AND circuit, one input can be used as a gating control: only when that input is positive does the other input get transferred to the output. The first input gates the second. Reversing the polarity and bias of the second input makes the circuit represent: *and not* (see 240-B); *if* (see 250-B); *neither . . . nor* (see 249-F).

213-A. (From 204-A) *Correct*. Then the corresponding db expression is db = $10 \log_{10} (1 + 2x^2 + x^4)$. Substituting $x = 1$ into this gives db at phase reference frequency as 6. The boundary at which peaking commences is the maximal flatness case, for which the product $f(m + 1/m)$ needs to be $\sqrt{2}$ (approximately 1.414). Then the db expression becomes db = $10 \log_{10} (1 + x^4)$; substituting $x = 1$ into this gives db = 3. But this would involve complex values of n, although it can be achieved with real values of f and m.

213-B. (From 209-B) *Wrong*. See one of the other answers.

213-C. (From 220-A) Why not? See one of the other answers.

213-D. (From 237-A) *Correct*. If you tried the 1:3 or 3:1 ratio first, you probably assumed layer length was the same as flux path length in each case, because it's part of the formula we gave for the layer arrangement. But for end-to-end arrangement the quantities we designated by L_w and $a_1 + b + a_2$ exchanged places, resulting in change in magnitude by a factor of three in both numerator and denominator: an overall change of nine times. Note that we assumed that b is the same fraction of $a_1 + a_2$, whichever way this measured, vertically or horizontally. In practice this will not be far from true, but for precise calculations the actual dimensions should be used.

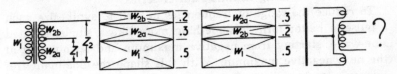

Now consider leakage inductance where tapped windings are used. Here, a common primary, w_1, may be used with either part, w_{2a} or the whole of the secondary, for different impedances, Z_1 or Z_2. Assuming the space distribution is that indicated on both the winding cross-section diagrams, find the effective leakage inductance to the part winding, w_{1a}, with reference to that for the whole winding, referred to primary turns in each case. Check your result at 228-D. Then, supposing the windings are sectionalized, how can the degradation of leakage inductance when the tapping is used be avoided? See if you can figure out a way, then turn to 221-C for more on sectionalizing.

214-A. (From 202-A) *Correct.* Substituting the values leads to a quadratic in n, the solution of which is $(3 \pm \sqrt{5})/2$, which gives 2.618 for one approximate value—the other is its reciprocal. Now turn to 203-A.

PULSE TECHNIQUES

214-B. Much modern work with computers, data transmission systems, etc., is concerned with the use of pulses, rather than steady frequencies. Ideal pulses are usually theorized as rectangular or triangular in form (as at the left) with variable spacing between them, determined by the time pattern of the pulses required for a particular piece of data or information. Analyzed in

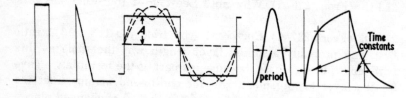

$$\text{Square wave} = \frac{4A}{\pi}\left\{\sin\omega t + \tfrac{1}{3}\sin 3\omega t + \tfrac{1}{5}\sin 5\omega t + \ldots\right\}$$

terms of frequency content, such a pulse produces a spectrum similar to a regular, periodic square-wave, which is given by a converging infinite series with a not very rapid convergence rate. The fundamental and third-harmonic components of a square wave are shown along with its Fourier series.

To reduce the range of frequencies needed to synthesize such a pulse, a better form is something more like a single, isolated sine-wave, starting from negative maximum and terminating at the next negative maximum. With this shape the dominant frequency present will be that corresponding to the period of the pulse, while a whole series of lower-frequency terms will be needed to "cancel" preceding and succeeding waves, according to the time interval between pulses. It may be more convenient to analyze the pulse in terms of a unit function, giving rise to a theoretical infinite frequency-series instead of discrete frequencies. As far as producing and handling the pulse form are concerned, the time constants in the associated circuits may be more important (shown at right). Shaping circuits can correct distortion of pulses and restore them to their correct form. Now which is the more correct analysis of pulses: in terms of frequency content (see 219-B) or by reference to a time axis (see 231-C)?

215-A. (From 219-A) *Correct.* This illustrates in a little more detail the addition of the third-order sideband pair. Up to the magnitude shown, the requirements for constant amplitude (nearest approximation) and linear phase-modulation are very

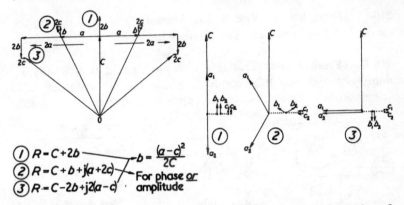

close. The expressions derived from the vectors for the 30° and 90° positions as well as the zero position are given. At the right are the sets of vectors for each of these positions. Equating positions (1) and (3) for magnitude yields an expression for b (the second-order magnitude) in terms of a and c (first- and third-order magnitudes) relative to carrier, C. Then the second position expression can be used, *either* to obtain a third equal-magnitude point *or* to obtain optimum phase-linearity (by making the larger angle exactly twice the smaller). Up to the magnitude shown, the conditions are very close but not identical. As the calculation is quite involved from this point, it is taken no further. Enough has been done to show the general approach and the principle on which the sidebands develop. Also, this shows that maintaining constancy of amplitude (unless an infinite series of sidebands is employed) cannot be achieved coincident with maintaining linearity of modulation in phase or frequency. The methods of optimizing from here depend more on empirical ingenuity than on mathematical precision.

One more form of modulation remains to be considered—suppressed carrier. From the treatment on 209-B and 210-B it is evident that phase of a reinserted carrier is vital to avoid distortion, because change of this phase can result in changing from one form of modulation to the other and also in introduction of nonlinearity. Now turn to 223-A.

216-A. (From 206-A) No, it doesn't. See the other answer.

216-B. (From 211-A) *No*. This answer is definitely not correct, and its application would lead to errors. See another answer.

216-C. (From 246-A) Yes, it does work on interwinding capacitance, but this is not all. Try another answer.

216-D. (From 245-B) This is a bistable circuit; it will stay indefinitely with one tube conducting and the other cut off until triggered, when it will flip to the opposite condition: the first tube

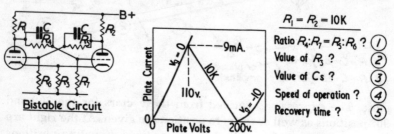

Bistable Circuit

$R_1 = R_2 = 10K$

Ratio R_4:$R_7 = R_5$:R_6 ? ①
Value of R_3 ? ②
Value of Cs ? ③
Speed of operation ? ④
Recovery time ? ⑤

cut off and the other conducting. The relevant tube data are shown, and R_1 and R_2 are chosen to suit these data: 10K each. Now we'll take those five questions at the right in order. For the first, is the ratio 8:1 (see 227-B); 10:1 (see 249-E); or 11:1 (see 229-B)?

Now, for the value of R_3, at 9 milliamps, should it drop 10 volts (see 225-B); 12.2 volts (see 248-C); or 22.2 volts (see 242-B)?

The value of C should be (a) as small as possible to ensure positive operation (see 238-B); (b) about equal to the effective grid input capacitance of the tube (see 231-Б); or (c) considerably larger, say ten times the grid input capacitance (see 208-B).

The remaining two questions will be answered somewhere along the line, as you will have found if you answered each question before proceeding to the next. If you read to here before answering the first, the fact that these questions are involved may help you decide some of the answers.

217-A. (From 207-A) Only a very approximate condition could be arrived at in this way. Any prediction of performance based on it would be subject to considerable error in most instances. See the other answer.

217-B. (From 233-B) Yes, the tuned-plate circuit yields the lower distortion, other things being equal, for several reasons: (1) grid loading is less, due to grid-current biasing; (2) the distortion signal developed at the plate is considerably smaller than the normal distortion of the tube at the operating level used. The distortion of the tube with this plate load can be analyzed graphically by the method shown at 149-C, from which it is found that the lower impedance (reactance) of the plate circuit at harmonic frequencies reduces output at these frequencies compared to the fundamental. But it does more than this, as shown here.

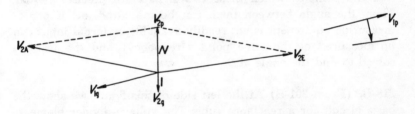

We start with an arbitrary value of second harmonic at the plate, V_{2p}. This is transformed down by the coil to V_{2g}. It is amplified, along with the fundamental. The fundamental, V_{1g}, produces an output V_{1p} at the fundamental frequency (not to scale, because this would necessitate drawing the harmonic components extremely small) and a second harmonic, generated from the fundamental input, V_{2E}. The second harmonic at the grid also results in an amplified signal, V_{2A}, at the plate, using the dominantly capacitive reactance of the plate tuned-circuit for a load at this frequency. The resultant plate voltage (second harmonic) is the combination of these two, which is V_{2p} (it has to be, because this is where we started). Since it is the relative magnitude of V_{2E} (predicted as on 149-C) that is known, the actual magnitude of V_{2p} can be derived from the relations developed around this diagram (from actual parameters). It is evident that the distortion component V_{2p} is smaller than for the same plate load as an amplifier, V_{2E}. The tuned-grid circuit has some advantages (see 235-B). Now turn to 230-C.

218-A. (From 205-A) *Correct.* Here we show the basis for the measurements. Amplitude margin can be measured from the input $(1 + AB)$ against fed-back signal (AB) by finding the point where these two are precisely antiphase. Then $20 \log_{10} 1/AB$ is the gain margin in db. Phase margin is found by meas-

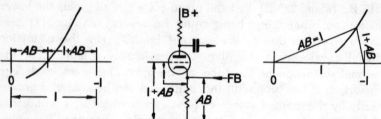

uring internal input (in this case, from grid to cathode of the input stage) against feedback signal, which gives loop gain, to find the point at which these two signals are precisely equal. Then, the angle between them can be measured, or, if phase-measuring equipment is not readily available, external input can be measured at the same point (frequency) and the triangle solved to find the angle at 0.

218-B. (From 201-B) At the left side of this figure we show the basic circuit for a reactance tube. The voltage-divider elements A and B apply a phase-shifted and attenuated voltage to the grid of the tube, which controls its plate current. The phase-shift and attenuation combination of A and B result in a plate-current characteristic that takes the form of a reactance.

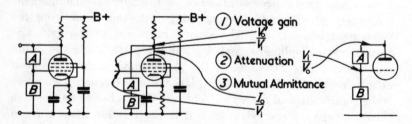

To calculate the performance of this circuit, do you (a) utilize the active voltage gain in conjunction with the attenuation, (1) and (2) (see 233-A); (b) use the attenuation with the mutual admittance (or conductance) of the tube under operating conditions (2) and (3); (see 239-A); or (c) is there another feature to be considered (see 244-A)?

219-A. (From 210-B) *Correct.* There is a distinct difference. Here, at the left, we develop the condition that makes positions (1) and (3) (at zero and 90° of the first-order rotation) produce equal-magnitude resultants. It is shown that the intermediate position (2), for 45° rotation of the first-order vectors, always has less magnitude than the other resultants. At the right, we

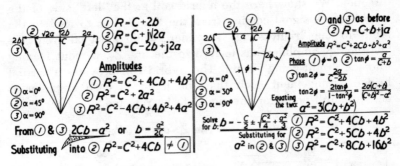

use different positions: (1) and (3) are the same, but (2) represents 30° rotation of the first-order vectors. This has the advantage that the angles identified as ϕ and 2ϕ should have that precise 2:1 relationship for linear phase-modulation. The condition is developed from the phase expressions for (2) and (3) (phase for (1) is zero, of course). Finally, substitutions are made to find the magnitude variation when this is achieved; from this it appears that the resultant is a minimum at the zero-phase position and maximum at the 90° position (3).

It is to correct this increasing deviation, as well as to allow greater phase swing in this kind of modulation, that third- and higher-order terms are needed. Does the introduction of the third-order term enable phase-linearity and amplitude-constancy conditions to be met simultaneously (see 212-C) or not (see 215-A)?

219-B. (From 214-B) Neither of these answers is exclusively correct. For transmission purposes, frequency analysis is all-important. The circuits and channels to transmit the data must handle, without serious amplitude- or phase-distortion, all the frequencies needed to convey the pulse form used. For this reason a smooth envelope to the pulse is advantageous—it requires a much smaller range of frequencies. Where the information is transmitted by radio, not only is the successful conveyance of the pulses a factor, but also freedom from interference on and from other transmisisons. See the other answer.

HYBRID COILS

220-A. A device first evolved to handle the insertion of two-way amplification in a transmission line was the hybrid coil. It now has many other uses in electronics. A pair of such coils would be used with a pair of amplifiers, one for transmission in each direction. We show here the hybrid coil at the "left" side of the amplifiers. A signal coming from the line Z_2 has to feed to the input to the "right-going" amplifier, while a signal from the "left-going" amplifier has to feed to the line Z_2, without feeding into the "right-going" input. The hybrid coil provides a virtual bridge arrangement such that the input to each amplifier is across a null point for the signal to be rejected.

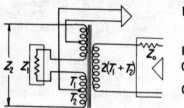

Make $Z_1 = aZ_2$ Matching requires $Z_1 + Z_o = Z_2$

So: $Z_o = Z_2(1-a)$

Input Transfer $= a + (1-a)\frac{a}{1+a} = \frac{2a}{1+a}$

Output Transfer $= \frac{1}{1+a}$ Overall Transfer $= \frac{2a}{(1+a)^2}$

Optimum: $\frac{d}{da}\left(\frac{2a}{(1+a)^2}\right) = \frac{2(1-a)}{(1+a)^3}$ ⟶ Zero when $a = 1$
   $Z_o = 0$

Here we are concerned with the efficiency of such an arrangement. To simplify consideration, the overall transformer ratio is assumed to be 1:1. A practical case can employ other ratios, with the usual conversions in impedance. This means that the line is terminated by Z_1 in series with two half-windings, reflecting a total impedance of Z_o. For matching, $Z_1 + Z_o$ should equal Z_2. For the null condition, if turns T_1 and T_2 are proportional to Z_1 and Z_2 respectively (not turns squared, but direct proportion), then both Z's will accept the same current, and the tappings, connected to the "right-going" amplifier input, will be at a null point. From these facts we derive an expression for input transfer and output transfer through the device. Multiplying the two together and differentiating with respect to the ratio a, we find the optimum is when $a = 1$, or $Z_1 = Z_2$, with $Z_o = 0$. Now which of the following statements are correct? (1) If Z_o is not zero, but small, termination can be made correct by changing Z_1 and the proportion T_1 to T_2 accordingly; (2) null at the input depends on Z_1 being equal to Z_2 (or whatever other ratio may be determined) at all frequencies. Answer: both; see 226-A. Answer: neither; see 213-C. Answer: (1) but not (2); see 228-A. Answer: (2) but not (1); see 230-A.

221-A. (From 209-B) *No*. In general, frequency modulation cannot be represented by a simple pair of sidebands or their oppositely rotating vectors. See another answer.

221-B. (From 211-A) While not strictly correct, no serious error arises from applying the equal-area rule. See another answer.

221-C. (From 213-D) Here, at the left, is the way it is done. The whole secondary is sandwiched between the primary halves, but not as a simple winding. The *a* part is divided in two and the *b* part sandwiched between them. The leakage-potential diagram

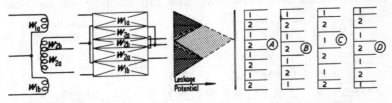

at the right of the winding cross-section shows what happens to leakage. When the whole windings are used, the solid-line diagram applies. Dividing the primary equally on opposite sides of the secondary divides the leakage-flux triangle into two smaller ones, each of half the maximum value (dotted lines show simple unsectionalized prototype for comparison). Maximum flux halved, number of turns halved (in each diagram part) and the area or winding thickness halved means the leakage inductance of each section (on the leakage flux diagram) is one-eighth that of the simple winding arrangement. Putting two in series doubles this, to one-quarter. So this sectionalizing reduces leakage inductance to one-quarter the value in a simple arrangement. When the tap on the secondary is used, the unused part of the winding is where there is no leakage-flux potential, and the dashed-line diagram applies: the leakage inductance is now lower than when the full winding is used (referred to the same turns, say the primary) as in the simple arrangement of 213-D.

Having shown the general method of deducing the effect of sectionalizing on leakage inductance, which of the arrangements shown partially at right (1 for primary sections, 2 for secondary sections) gives the lowest leakage inductance? Better still, put them in order of decreasing leakage; it is *ABCD* (see 238-A); *CDBA* (see 232-D); *CBDA* (see 241-A); or, since that's but 3 of 24 possible orders, is it one of the other 21 (see 234-A)?

222-A. (From 210-B) For very small degrees of frequency modulation, such that the arc through which the resultant vector swings can be considered to have the same curve as a parabola near its focal axis, this is true. But for larger values, even while two pairs of sidebands give quite a good approximation for either constant amplitude or linear phase modulation, there is a difference in relative values, according to which parameter is used as the basis. See 219-A.

222-B. (From 232-A) *Correct.* Here, to illustrate, we have tabulated values of Z_2/Z_1, t/T, A/a, and a comparison of the loss increases, which need explaining. The full winding will have its

$\frac{Z_2}{Z_1}$	1.21	1.44	2	3	4	6.25	9	12.25	16	20.25	25
$\frac{t}{T}$	$\frac{1}{10}$	$\frac{1}{5}$	$\sqrt{2}-1$	$\sqrt{3}-1$	1	1.5	2	2.5	3	3.5	4
$\frac{A}{a}$	21	11	5.825	3.732	3	2.33	2	1.8	1.67	1.57	1.5
Increase %	5	9	17.2	26.8	33.3	42.8	50	55.5	60	63.6	66.7
n same gage	10	20	41.4	73.2	100	150	200	250	300	350	400

maximum efficiency (minimum loss) by being wound in the same gage throughout, but the tapping efficiency is degraded. The last line of the table indicates the percentage by which the tapping resistance is increased, as compared with a winding occupying the whole space for that impedance. The line next to the last indicates the increase on the tapping when the gage is changed to fit the space. For Z_2/Z_1 from 1 to 2 the increase in loss at the tapping, using the same gage as compared with the change, is about double, but the increase is relatively small and therefore not too important. The change in gage is quite marked—a 2:1 area change per turn.

From values of 2 to somewhere about 16 (there is no definite "leave-off" point) the reduced increase in losses resulting from the use of different gages is significant and useful. At the ratio 16 the theoretical change is from 300% down to 60%.

From a ratio of 9 on up, a point is reached where it may be equally effective to use the alternative-winding approach (227-A). Remembering that the losses tabulated here are due to one winding only, evidently the advantage to utilizing the low-impedance turns as part of the high-impedance winding is negligible and the separate winding method may be better. Now turn to 236-A.

223-A. (From 215-A) In amplitude modulation the reference level is 100%, where the amplitude fluctuates between zero and twice the mean carrier level. This occurs when each sideband has half the amplitude of the carrier. The total energy in an amplitude-modulated wave is the sum of that of the component waves. As each sideband carries a quarter the power of the carrier at 100% modulation, the power is 1.5 times the no-modulation power.

In frequency modulation, level is referred to deviation. If the phase deviates by ϕ on either side of its mean phase, then the *rate* of phase deviation, which is the *frequency* deviation from mean carrier phase (when the phase deviation is zero), is proportional to the maximum phase deviation and is equal to the

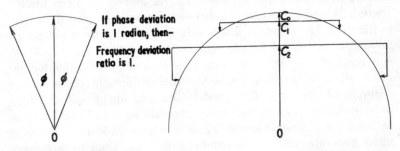

If phase deviation is 1 radian, then—

Frequency deviation ratio is 1.

modulating frequency when the maximum phase deviation is (±) 1 radian. Thus the deviation ratio is unity, which means that the maximum frequency by which the carrier deviates is equal to the modulating frequency. If the phase deviation is $\pm\pi$ radians (180°), the deviation ratio is π (approx. 3.14).

In frequency modulation the total energy is constant because the wave amplitude does not change: merely its effective frequency or phase changes. But the distribution of energy between sidebands *and carrier* changes with level. Note that the carrier level drops as deviation increases, shown here for three levels, starting at zero. Before deviation ratio reaches π, the carrier passes through a zero, or null, and the first-order sidebands cease to grow, and pass some energy to higher-order sidebands.

223-B. (From 248-A) This must have been an intuitive answer, based on other networks analyzed recently. But it should be fairly obvious that at low frequencies c causes a phase advance, while at high frequencies C causes a phase delay. Somewhere in between, the phase has to pass through zero. See the other answer.

224

224-A. (From 247-A) The vector diagram helps show what happens to harmonic frequencies generated in the circuit by the nonlinearity of the tube or transistor, from the transfer characteristics deduced on 247-A. Starting with an assumed plate signal of the harmonic considered of unity, this passes around the phase-

Harmonic Vectors	Network Type	3-Stage								4-Stage							
		Identical				Noninteracting				Identical				Noninteracting			
		Hi-pass		Lo-pass		Hi-pass		Lo-pass		Hi-pass		Lo-pass		Hi-pass		Lo-pass	
	Harmonic	2nd	3rd	2nd	3rd	2nd	3rd	2nd	3rd	2nd	3rd	2nd	3rd	2nd	3rd	2nd	3rd
	Harmonic Fundamental	3.4	5.88	.196	.065	3.45	5.2	.171	.054	2.82	4.28	.176	.053	2.56	3.24	.16	.04
	Phase Degrees	40.3	61.8	36.5	52.7	57.3	90	41.7	57.5	54.4	77.5	54.4	77.5	73½	106¼	73½	106¼
	Reduction Factor	2.71	5.48	.851	.962	3.02	5.3	.885	.971	2.37	4.18	.91	.99	2.47	3.65	.967	1.013

shifting network and is attenuated more or less than the fundamental, as well as receiving a different phase shift, and delivered to the grid. The relative phase shift (second line from bottom of table), which is the supplement of that in the table on 247-A, and relative magnitude (attenuation of fundamental divided by attenuation of harmonic) give the magnitude and phase of the reamplified harmonic, delivered to the grid along with the fundamental, identified in the vector diagram by V_g. To achieve the actual plate harmonic signal, V_p, with which we started, the tube must generate, due to the fundamental, the remaining component, V_e. If V_e is the harmonic normally generated by the tube as an amplifier, V_p will be its magnitude when used as an oscillator with the network in question. So with V_p of unit magnitude, the magnitude of V_e represents the reduction factor by which the harmonic is reduced by the network in question.

Note that the best network for second harmonic is the three-stage noninteracting (a hypothetical network), while the best for third is the identical, both of the high-pass configuration, which means that any three-stage, high-pass network will achieve lower harmonic than others. Now, where is the best takeoff point for output—at the plate (see 241-B), at the grid (see 249-B), or at an intermediate point (see 207-B)?

224-B. (From 248-B) You evidently had in mind the low-frequency roll-off point for each "stage." This does not apply here for two reasons: (1) we are concerned with frequency-fixing, not rolling off; (2) the waveform is square, not sinusoidal. Reactance applies strictly to a single sinusoidal frequency. Try one of the other answers.

225-A. (From 240-A) Here's a problem that will illustrate how to tailor leakage inductance for specific use. Here, at the left, we reproduce the filter designed at 142-A, with a different identity numbering so that the physical counterparts in the leakage inductance version can be identified. It consists physically of four

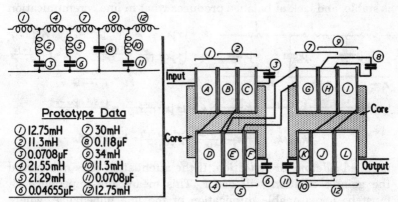

Prototype Data

① 12.75 mH ⑦ 30 mH
② 11.3 mH ⑧ 0.118 μF
③ 0.0708 μF ⑨ 34 mH
④ 21.55 mH ⑩ 11.3 mH
⑤ 21.29 mH ⑪ 0.0708 μF
⑥ 0.04655 μF ⑫ 12.75 mH

coil-assemblies, individual coils being identified by letters *A* thru *L*, while leakages are identified by numbers to correspond with those in the prototype. Capacitors, instead of having their prototype values, are all 0.05 microfarad. To get a basis for design, two bobbins, to fill a space which is 1½ inches long by ½ inch high, are wound with 1,000 turns of a gage suitable to fill the space. End flanges of both the test bobbins and those used for actual coils are 0.03 inch thick (each interspace will contain two such flanges, and there will be six to a coil assembly. Leakage inductance between the test coils measures 40 mH.

The design problem consists of finding suitable dimensions for the coil assemblies, to obtain correct inductance relationships, and specifying turns (wire gage will be chosen to suit, so the winding fills the space allocated in each case). It may be pointed out that leakage inductance for a use such as this is so versatile that there is no one "correct" design. Many dimension and turn combinations are possible, all equally correct. See if you can evolve the method, and then turn to 243-A.

225-B. (From 216-D) Relative to ground, the grids swing from 12.2 volts to 22.2 volts positive, which you can figure from the correct choice in answer to the previous question. 10 volts on the cathodes would leave the grids positive (or taking grid current to hold them "down" to 10 volts) at all times. Try another answer.

226-A. (From 220-A) Yes, both were correct. The first needs no further explanation. The second should consider what tolerance for lack of balance or equality is permissible. Provided the attenuation due to lack of balance (which would be infinite with perfect balance) is greater than the gain of the amplifiers, the system is stable, and lack of balance produces what in line communication

$$k_3 = 1 + jx \qquad z_3 = 1 + \frac{1}{jx} = \frac{1+jx}{jx} \qquad y_3 = \frac{jx}{1+jx}$$

$$k_2 = 1 + jx + \frac{jx}{1+jx} = \frac{1-x^2+j2x}{1+jx} \qquad z_2 = 1 + \frac{1+jx}{j2x-x^2}$$

$$y_2 = \frac{j2x-x^2}{1-x^2+j3x}$$

$$k_1 = 1 + jx + \frac{j2x-x^2}{1-x^2+j3x} = \frac{1-5x^2+j(6x-x^3)}{1-x^2+j3x}$$

$$k_1 \cdot k_2 \cdot k_3 = \left[1+jx\right]\left[\frac{1-x^2+j3x}{1+jx}\right]\left[\frac{1-5x^2+j(6x-x^3)}{1-x^2+j3x}\right] = 1 - 5x^2 + j(6x - x^3)$$

is called *sidetone* or *reflection*. If the attenuation does not exceed the gain, oscillation will occur. This means the impedance Z_1 must be a reasonable duplication of the line impedance, where this is not a simple resistive impedance.

226-B. (From 247-A) Here's an example of how the expression is worked out for the case of three identical R's and C's. Starting from the output end, the last section is unloaded, and its attenuation factor (k_3) is simple. Next, the value of z_3 and y_3 at the input to this section is figured as a load on the second-stage output, from which the second-stage factor (k_2) is figured. Finally, from the value of z_2 and y_2 as loading for the first stage, the first-stage factor (k_1) is determined. The overall attenuation factor is the product of the three: k_1, k_2, and k_3. Note that k_3 cancels with the denominator of k_2, whose numerator cancels with the denominator of k_1, leaving only the numerator of k_1 as the resultant product. This pattern will follow through any number of stages.

For the noninteracting networks the process is simple, although the result is hypothetical. Raise $(1 + jx)$ to a power representing the number of stages. The values in this were normalized to the "standard" circuit resistance-value. If the high-pass case is taken (this was the low-pass), jx becomes a denominator term instead of a numerator one. The value of x (using a reciprocal normalization) for $180°$ phase shift will not change, but second and third harmonics will change x (and x^2) in opposite directions. Now turn back to 247-A.

227-A. (From 228-B) The arrangement on 211-A was for a simple transformer with only two active windings. A variety of others are encountered in electronics work. First take the type where one winding's function alternates between two winding sections. This might be the primary of a class-B output trans-

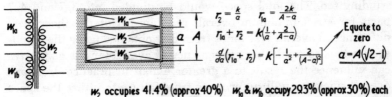

$$r_2 = \frac{k}{a} \qquad r_{1a} = \frac{2k}{A-a}$$

$$r_{1a} + r_2 = k\left(\frac{1}{a} + \frac{2}{A-a}\right)$$

$$\frac{d}{da}(r_{1a} + r_2) = k\left[-\frac{1}{a^2} + \frac{2}{(A-a)^2}\right] \qquad a = A(\sqrt{2}-1)$$

Equate to zero

W_2 occupies 41.4% (approx 40%) W_{1a} & W_{1b} occupy 29.3% (approx 30%) each

former or any transformer intended for dual function, such as one designed to match alternative, widely divergent impedances (either one or the other, not both simultaneously). The transfer takes place from only one of the alternatives to the other winding. We consider this by allowing space, equal to the one being used, for the one temporarily inactive, and solving as for the simple case. The result we find allocates approximately 40% of the space to the common winding, and 30% each to the alternative windings.

Now, how critical is this (again derived for constant mean turn length—it would be modified if variable mean-turn length is taken into account)? Figure the deviation from the optimum resulting from other practical choices, and then turn to 231-A to compare your conclusions.

227-B. (From 216-D) *Correct.* This is based on the ratio between plate-voltage swing and grid-voltage swing. The former is 90 volts, and the latter is 10 volts, a ratio of 9:1. The "bottom" resistor includes its voltage in the total, so the resistor ratio is one less, 8:1. A slightly lower ratio would be acceptable, allowing the cut-off tube to be slightly overbiased, giving a safety margin for the stable condition. On the other hand, the closer the ratio is to pre-cisely providing cutoff voltage, the more sensitive the circuit is.

As shown, the circuit does not provide for input pulses. One way to do this is lift the bottom ends of R_6 and R_7 from ground, still tied together, and insert a resistance in series to ground, across which input pulses are applied. This way the input pulse reaches whichever grid is waiting to receive it. The resistance must be small enough not to interfere with the d.c. voltage ratio calculated above, or must be taken into account in calculating it. Now turn back to 216-D.

228-A. (From 220-A) Wrong choice. Try one of the other answers.

228-B. (From 211-A) *Correct.* This means that if the mean turn length of the inner winding is, say, 3/4 of that of the outer winding, then its cross-sectional area should be 3/4 that of the outer winding too. The total space would be divided into 3/7 and 4/7 parts for strict minimum overall resistance. But the theoretical difference in overall resistance from that obtained using the equal-area rule is so small that convenience of available wire gage sizes can influence the result to a greater extent in practice. In short, overall efficiency will suffer more from failure to utilize the space fully for the combined windings (other than by stuffing it with insulation!) than it will from failure to maintain the precise space relationship. However, if the outer winding occupies 3/7 of the space and the inner one 4/7 (which comes close to the equal-weight proposition), overall resistance will be markedly higher than either equal space or the correct 3/7 + 4/7 allocation.

Good practical design uses these two rules as limits: equal area and equal proportions; between these limits the result is essentially the same as if a theoretical optimum were used. Now turn to 227-A.

228-C. (From 237-A) *No.* Check your deductions carefully and try another answer.

228-D. (From 213-D) For an approximate result here, we neglect interspace. In the better arrangement (at left) the leakage inductance when the secondary tapping is used makes the total *active* winding-thickness 8/10 of that for the whole winding; so the referred leakage inductance will also be 8/10. Reversing the order of winding the secondary (at right), in addition to the 8/10 active winding-thickness, the unused (for the moment) tapping turns occupy 2/10, which behave as a rather large inter-winding space. From the formula, interwinding space has three times the relative leakage flux as the space in which winding is actively uniformly distributed. So the effective leakage inductance when the tap is used rises this time to 1.4 times the value when the whole secondary is used. Now turn back to 213-D.

229-A. (From 232-A) This range is where use of this method will result in the more drastic change in wire gage for the smaller extra section. But the advantage in loss reduction is not so great as for some other range of impedance relationships. See another answer.

229-B. (From 216-D) Did you derive this answer from the plate voltage and grid voltage? Well, it's not the voltage, but the change in voltage between the two stable conditions that is important here. See one of the other answers.

229-C. (From 240-B) Here it is. Inputs 1 and 2 are applied to both an OR circuit and an AND circuit. The outputs from these are applied to an AND NOT circuit, with due attention to signal polarity at all points. If the OR circuit gives a pulse, it means

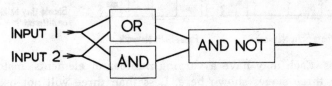

either or both inputs presented pulses at the same time. But if they both do, the AND circuit will present an output as well. So the final circuit will eliminate the AND possibility.

The elements we have discussed belong essentially to the digital-type computer, where every piece of information is of a 'yes' or 'no' type. Quantity is represented digitally in the binary system, so that every digit is either present or absent. The other type of computer, of more use for advanced mathematical computations, is the analog type. This employs function elements, to represent mathematical functions, *e.g.*, log, sine, cosine, tangent, exponential, etc. These are mechanically constructed resistors, capacitors, or inductors, designed so that linear control of input, which may be a d.c. voltage or current or a mechanical movement or rotation, results in an output that follows the desired law very closely. Systems using this type of element use extremely linear amplifier-elements, employing design principles we have covered in this book. The amplifiers may be direct coupled, with precision controlled supplies to provide high stability, so functions can be followed at frequencies "down to d.c." The applied mathematics for much of this work is outside the strictly electronics area, because it involves mechanical details.

230-A. (From 220-A) Wrong choice. See one of the other answers.

230-B. (From 246-A) Yes, it does work on self-capacitance, but this is not all. See one of the other answers.

PHASE-SHIFT OSCILLATORS

230-C. (From 217-B) This group of oscillators presents a useful exercise in investigative approach. Basically, there are two types of phase-shift networks, shown here with an associated tube circuit (transistors can equally well be used): high-pass and low-

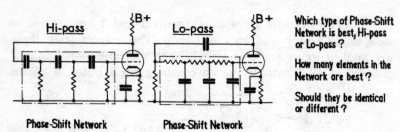

Which type of Phase-Shift Network is best, Hi-pass or Lo-pass?

How many elements in the Network are best?

Should they be identical or different?

pass. Each may have a varying number of elements, instead of the three stages shown here. Less than three will not oscillate, but above this there is no limit. The elements may use identical components cascaded, or they can have different elements in successive stages.

How would you proceed to investigate the properties of these circuits to answer the three questions posed here? After some thought, turn to 247-A.

230-D. (From 235-C) *Correct.* The larger r/R and C/c are made, the greater is the attenuation at the zero phase-shift frequency and the sharper is the change of phase and attenuation in its vicinity. However, much beyond the value unity the increase in sharpness is much slower than the increase in attenuation at that point; so, often the more practical optimum is in the region of answers 1 or 2.

There is one other type of resistance-capacitance oscillator circuit using the twin-T network, either in combination with linear positive feedback or with a phase-reversing choice of values. Approaches introduced in the section beginning at 101-A can be utilized for this type. A completely different type of oscillator is the multivibrator (see 248-B).

231-A. (From 227-A) In this comparison we cannot compare efficiencies directly; since these depend on how great are the losses, what we compare is either the losses or the total windings resistance. As a reference it is convenient to use the basic simple two-winding transformer. In comparison with this, the common winding of the ideal case is increased by 25% and the alternative winding by 66⅔%. Adding together half of these, the total increase in resistance is 35⅚%.

Two practical possibilities may be compared with this. The first is for three equal windings. This will result in an increase in total resistance of 50%. The second is for two equal windings, with the one having alternatives again divided into two equal parts. The common winding in this case has no increase, while the alternatives have an increase of 100%. The increase on the total is again 50%. There is some merit to staying close to a 40-30-30 arrangement and keeping well within the limits of 33-33-33 and 50-25-25. Now turn to 232-A.

231-B. (From 216-D) This choice will achieve the best compromise between high operation speed and short recovery time. The operating time-constant is the plate-circuit resistance (never more than 10K) working with the two capacitances (the bypass and grid-input) in series. Assume that grid input capacitance is 50 $\mu\mu$F: series effective is 25 $\mu\mu$F. So the operating time-constant is 0.25 microsecond. This will further be divided by the stage-gain ratio, which is 9, and then halved by the capacitance divider to 4.5. So the actual operating time will be about 0.06 microsecond. Recovery time is determined by the effective parallel capacitance (100 $\mu\mu$F) in conjunction with the combined resistance (R_4 and R_7 or R_5 and R_6 in parallel). If this is in the order of a megohm, the recovery time will be 100 microseconds. Making these resistors smaller in value, with the same ratio, will shorten recovery time.

231-C. (From 214-B) For referring to pulse shaping and analyzing the behavior of pulse-handling equipment, the time reference is necessary. For example, when two pulses from different parts of a computer system coincide, a certain response is necessary. Failure to maintain pulse shape, or the introduction of a time delay, can destroy the proper coincidence so that the response is incorrect or indeterminate. For this reason both terms of reference are needed. See the other answer.

232-A. (From 231-A) Now we turn to another alternative-use situation, using a tapped winding, to serve different impedances. The impedances, as in the case of separate windings, are used alternatively, not simultaneously. The turns are such that the number of turns squared is proportional to impedance. In this construction the *extra* turns, t, use a different wire gage from

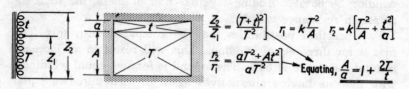

the main turns, T, such that the space allocations are a and A respectively. Making the effective winding resistance in each case proportional to the impedance it serves results in the space ratio derived.

This expedient is most effective (1) for values of Z_2/Z_1 between 1 and 2 (see 229-A); (2) for values of Z_2/Z_1 between 2 and 16 (broadly speaking) (see 222-B); (3) for values of Z_2/Z_1 above about 10 (see 249-A).

232-B. (From 236-A) *No.* With large ratios the autotransformer achieves little economy over a two-winding arrangement.

232-C. (From 237-A) Your choice was numerically correct, but the wrong way around. Turn to 213-D.

232-D. (From 221-C) *Wrong.* You apparently went by the prevailing notion of "the more sections, the better." But the correct *way* to choose sections is important. Try another answer.

232-E. (From 246-A) Yes, it does work on both, but not in any simple way. See one of the other answers.

232-F. (From 250-C) *No.* For this to be the requirement, Z_1 would have to be in series with the primary circuit. It is in shunt. Try again.

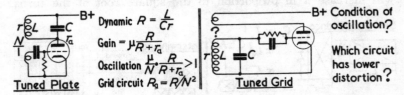

233-A. (From 218-B) *No.* These elements determine the loop gain at any frequency, but they do not relate the current drawn from the input terminals to the input voltage. Try another answer.

TUNED-CIRCUIT OSCILLATORS

233-B. Basically a tuned-circuit oscillator uses the gain of a tube or transistor to offset the losses in a resonant circuit. Design can be approached this way, but a simpler approach is usually given in terms of circuit elements and coupling. In the tuned-plate circuit (left) the L, C, and r of the tuned circuit make up a dynamic (resistive) load impedance for the plate circuit of the

Dynamic $R = \dfrac{L}{Cr}$

Gain $= \mu \dfrac{R}{R+r_a}$

Oscillation $\dfrac{\mu}{N} \cdot \dfrac{R}{R+r_a} > 1$

Grid circuit $R_g = R/N^2$

Tuned Plate

Tuned Grid

B+ Condition of oscillation?

Which circuit has lower distortion?

tube, R. This can be used to calculate gain, from the amplification factor of the tube at operating conditions used, μ. If the turns ratio, $N:1$, which is a large step-down in this circuit, is a slightly smaller ratio than the gain calculated so that the product is slightly greater than unity, the circuit will oscillate. The dynamic impedance in the grid circuit is R divided by N^2, which will be very small compared to the grid-circuit biasing resistor. The small grid current that flows every cycle to maintain bias at the point where average value of μ makes the gain equal to N will not materially load the grid circuit, and very little distortion results from the biasing action.

The tuned-grid circuit (right) is different mainly in having the high-impedance tuned-circuit in the grid rather than in the plate. To reduce the loading of the biasing resistor, this is placed in shunt with the biasing capacitor so that no signal voltage develops across it, just the d.c. bias voltage. But now, is the condition of oscillation (a) similar to that for the tuned-plate (see 236-B) or (b) quite different (see 239-B)? When you've settled that, which circuit will give the lowest distortion—tuned-grid (see 235-B) or tuned-plate (see 217-B)?

233-C. (From 235-C) *No.* The smaller r/R and C/c are made, the less definite is the phase-zero point and the attenuation characteristic at this point. See one of the other answers.

234-A. (From 221-C) Backing the law of averages: it was more likely to be one of the 21 we didn't name than the three we did. Well, you're wrong. It was one of those three.

234-B. (From 246-A) *Correct.* To see how, first consider how the cross-section dimensions of a winding affect its capacitance. From 246-A we can see the effect of number of layers on capacitance. If the number is large (in random winding there is no definite number of layers, although turns are approximately layer-arranged), then capacitance is proportional to $1/n$. Increasing turns in the same space (with corresponding change in gage) will increase n in proportion to the square root of the turns.

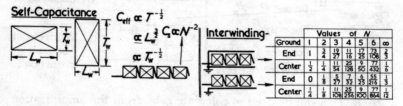

Self-Capacitance

$$C_{eff} \propto T^{-\frac{1}{2}}$$
$$\propto L_w^{\frac{3}{2}}$$
$$\propto T_w^{-\frac{1}{2}}$$

$$C_s \propto N^{-2}$$

Interwinding-

	Values	of	N				
	1	2	3	4	5	6	∞
Ground	1						
End	1	3/4	19/27	11/16	17/25	73/108	2/3
Center	1/2	1/4	11/54	25/128	9/50	77/432	1/6
End	0	1/8	5/27	7/32	6/25	55/216	1/3
Center	1/4	1/8	11/108	25/256	9/100	77/864	1/12

Increasing length of winding window (other parameters being held constant) will increase layer length in direct proportion and reduce n in proportion to the square root of the ratio change in length. The result is that capacitance is proportional to the $3/2$ power of L_w. Increasing depth of space will increase the number of layers (n) in proportion to the square root of the dimensional increase. This applies to the self-capacitance of any winding where the number of layers is reasonably large.

Now, for sectionalizing, this is equivalent to increasing T_w and reducing L_w by the same factor, the number of vertical sections, N. Substituting, we find that self-capacitance will vary inversely as N^2. This much is simple.

Interwinding capacitance is not so simple. It can only be calculated by taking the effect of each "piece" of capacitance to ground, according to the effective ground point in the winding. We have tabulated the results for values of N up to 6, for four combinations of winding arrangement, and also given the value for a theoretically infinite number of sections in each arrangement. Now turn to 201-B.

234-C. (From 248-B) There may seem to be logical reasons for working on the basis of time constant, rather than reactance, but this is not the correct answer. Try one of the others.

235-A. (From 237-A) *No.* There are two possibilities for error here: which way the ratio is, as well as its proportionality. Check your deductions and try again.

235-B. (From 233-B) The tuned-grid circuit is preferred for many applications, but this is not because it has lower distortion. It is simpler to arrange a convenient output without critically loading the tuned circuit and either stopping its oscillation or affecting its amplitude stability seriously. The tuned-plate circuit is critically dependent on the voltage gain of the stage, with the dynamic plate load provided by the tuned circuit. Any output loading will inevitably affect this relationship. Considerable coupling can be included in the plate circuit of a tuned-grid oscillator without materially affecting its operation. Turn to the other answer.

235-C. (From 245-A) *Correct.* This is found by differentiating the constant part of the arctan expression with respect to a and equating the derivative to zero. The value found will make this factor a maximum, resulting in a maximum change of ϕ_t with x.

$$\frac{d}{da} \cdot \frac{a(k-1)}{k(1+a^2)} = \frac{k(k-1)(1+a^2)-2a^2 k(k-1)}{k^2(1+a^2)^2} \quad \text{Equating to zero } a^2=1 \quad a=\pm1$$

$$\frac{v_1}{v_0} = k+j\frac{k-1}{2}\left(x-\frac{1}{x}\right) \quad db=20\log_{10}k-10\log_{10}\left[1+\left(\frac{k-1}{2k}\right)^2\left(x-\frac{1}{x}\right)^2\right] \quad \phi_t=\arctan\frac{k-1}{2k}\left(x-\frac{1}{x}\right)$$

---

② $k-1+2\frac{r}{R}=1+2\frac{C}{c}$ $\quad \frac{r}{R}=\frac{C}{c}=\frac{1}{2}(k-1)$ ④ **Optimum network ?**

The value found is $a = 1$. Substituting this into the attenuation-factor equation simplifies it to a direct form for the condition $a = 1$. This is where $r/R = C/c$. The db expression breaks down into a fixed attenuation at the critical zero–phase-shift frequency, plus a variable which passes through zero at this point. The phase-shift expression and the db expression use the same constant factor, a function of k. Making the same substitution into the value for k on 245-A shows how the fixed attenuation at zero phase-shift depends on values of r/R and C/c and enables a value of these to be chosen for any required value of k. This answers question (2) on 248-A. Now how about question (4): is there an optimum network? Answer: making $r = R$ and $c = C$; see 204-B. Answer: making $k = 2$; see 211-B. Answer: making r/R and C/c as small as practicable; see 233-C. Answer: making r/R and C/c as large as practicable; see 230-D.

236-A. (From 222-B) Another special kind of transformer is the autotransformer, where one winding with a tapping serves both circuits. Here the relationships in such a transformer are derived for input voltage and current related to output voltage and current, in terms of the turns. In the top right corner is the basic current relationship between the sections of turns, T and t, from

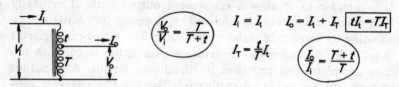

$$\frac{V_o}{V_i} = \frac{T}{T+t} \qquad I_i = I_t \qquad I_o = I_t + I_T \qquad \boxed{tI_t = TI_T}$$

$$I_T = \frac{t}{T} I_t \qquad \frac{I_o}{I_i} = \frac{T+t}{T}$$

which it appears that relationships in an autotransformer are, as far as the external circuit is concerned, identical with those in an equivalent two-winding transformer, except for d.c. connection.

View the section of turns (t) as handling the difference in voltage between the two circuits, and their common current, while turns (T) handle the difference in current and the common voltage. When viewed this way, the two parts of the winding behave exactly as a two-winding transformer, and optimum efficiency is achieved by making the winding cross-sections for T and t equal (*cf.* 211-A). Any two-winding transformer can serve as an autotransformer of one plus its normal turns ratio, simply by connecting it that way. In this it will be equally efficient.

An autotransformer has the advantage that only part of the power transferred is transformed, the rest being transferred directly without transformation, thus enabling a smaller transformer to serve larger duty applications. Is this economy greater when the ratio is (1) close to unity (see 203-B) or (2) very large (see 232-B)?

236-B. (From 233-B) To say that the conditions are similar is a little vague. For the tuned-plate the condition relates the turns ratio between the coils to the voltage gain of the tube. In the tuned-grid the voltage gain is virtually nonexistent. Sometimes a plate-load resistor will be used external to the oscillator circuit to provide an output, but across the oscillator feedback coil the voltage developed as output is quite small. Should we relate the turns ratio to the transconductance of the tube? Transconductance is the important parameter of the tube in this circuit, but coil parameters are not similar to those for the tuned-plate circuit, so the other answer would be more accurate.

LEAKAGE INDUCTANCE

237-A. (From 203-B) On 114-B the basis for leakage inductance was explained, and the leakage flux was described as leaking *between* the windings. Here we consider how the flux distributes itself through the windings, to evaluate the value of this inductance. The leakage-flux potential (like magnetomotive force in any magnetic circuit) is proportional to the out-of-balance current: it grows linearly from outside each winding to the inter-

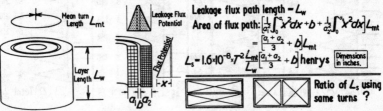

Leakage flux path length $= L_w$

Area of flux path: $\left[\frac{1}{a_1^2}\int_0^{a_1} x^2 dx + b + \frac{1}{a_2^2}\int_0^{a_2} x^2 dx\right] L_{mt}$

$$= \left[\frac{a_1 + a_2}{3} + b\right] L_{mt}$$

$$L_s = 1.6 \times 10^{-8} \times T^2 \frac{L_{mt}}{L_w}\left[\frac{a_1 + a_2}{3} + b\right] \text{ henrys}$$

Dimensions in inches.

Ratio of L_s using same turns ?

space gap. The voltage induced by the flux due to this potential is proportional to the number of turns on which each element of flux acts, which is again (assuming linear distribution of turns in space) proportional to distance from the outside of the winding in which the element is taken. So the elemental voltage is proportional to the square of the distance from the outside of the winding. Integrating and dividing by a_1 once to find the average, and again to relate the result to a constant flux acting in this distance (or area), we find the area of the total flux path can be considered as equivalent to one-third the "thickness" of both windings, added to the thickness of the interspace, multiplied by the mean-turn length. The length of the flux path is the layer length. The return path has negligible reluctance, whether in air or through magnetic material, because of the relative constriction of the active path length just described. So we can derive a practical formula for leakage inductance, referred to the turns of one of the windings, T. Note that this is due to the current in *both* windings, because the leakage cannot really be separated. The constant, 1.6 times 10^{-8}, can be verified empirically.

Now consider a winding window whose length is three times its depth: a pair of windings can be either one inside the other, or end-to-end; assuming the winding interspace is proportional to the corresponding winding dimension in each, is the ratio of leakage inductances of the two arrangements, for the same turns in the windings, 1:3 (228-C); 3:1 (235-A); 1:9 (213-D); 9:1 (232-C)? (Ratio is in same left-right order as drawings.)

238-A. (From 221-C) *Correct.* Although this combination might look least likeiy, here is the explanation. Constructing the leakage potential diagrams alongside makes it clear. Although the *A* arrangement has more sections than any other, they are wasted. At three of the seven interspaces there is no leakage potential. The same leakage inductance could in fact be achieved with two equal

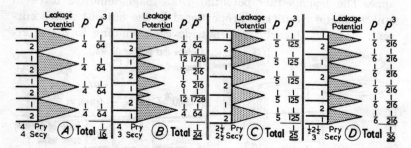

primary sections and a secondary with one "whole" and two "half" sections (at the outsides). "Half" sections, which are shown in arrangements *C* and *D*, have half the number of turns of the "whole" sections and occupy half the space (that is for series connection). In the event of parallel connection, the half-sections may use the same turns, but, using a smaller wire gage, they still occupy half the area. The *B* arrangement loses some of the potential by using equal end sections, too. *D* uses the same number of "splits" but uses half-sections at the ends, achieving two-thirds the leakage of *B*. *C* again uses equal leakage flux areas (like *D*), but is usually less convenient because both primary and secondary have half-sections, which may present practical difficulties.

Now apply this principle to find two arrangements for push-pull output transformers: in *A*, which uses class-B or class-AB, it is important for primary halves to be coupled together about an order of magnitude tighter than they are coupled to the secondary; in *B*, using class-A for maximum range, the maximum coupling between each primary half and the secondary is needed within a simple arrangement. Then check with 240-A.

238-B. (From 216-D) This question does not have a "universal" answer: it can depend on the purpose for which the circuit is to be used, specifically on the required operation speed and recovery times. This answer will give the slowest operation speed (quite critically variable for quite small changes in value of *C*) but with the very shortest recovery time. See the other answers.

239-A. (From 218-B) Close to being correct. Some treatments give this as the answer. The attenuation between A and B, combined with the active mutual conductance (or mutual admittance), does determine the current taken from the input circuit, according to the input voltage. But the only current this considers is that due to the tube, not the circuit elements. Turn to 244-A.

239-B. (From 233-B) Yes, the condition is really quite different, although in circuit configuration it looks like a simple inversion. Apart from the fact that the important tube parameter is transconductance instead of amplification factor, the coil parameters are different as well. In the tuned-plate circuit the grid loading is so light that the coupling factor (k: see 121-B) is unimportant; relative turns are what matters. In the tuned-grid circuit, relative turns are only part of the story. Mutual inductance, which involves the turns in both windings and the coupling factor, is what

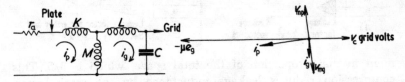

controls the oscillation condition. In the equivalent circuit here, K represents the inductance of the coupling turns, L that of the grid-circuit coil, and M is the mutual inductance between them. The vector diagram shows "how the circuit works," from which the parameters are deduced. Starting from the signal on the grid, V_c (sub c because it is the voltage across the grid-circuit capacitor), the tube generates an "open-circuit" voltage, $-\mu e_g$. This does not actually appear, but signal plate-current (i_p) does, nearly in phase with the open-circuit voltage, because the main plate-circuit resistance is r_a (plate resistance of the tube); the reactances of K and M are small compared to it. This signal current produces an inductive voltage V_{mp} in the primary coil (part of the voltage across K) and an opposing one in the secondary (grid) coil, V_{mg}. The current through L and C (close to series resonance) due to V_{mg} is i_g, which produces almost opposing voltages across L and C, of which the one across C is the one with which we started at the grid. The relevant parameters are the transconductance of the tube (bypassing μ and r_a), the mutual conductance of the two coils, and the Q-factor of the grid circuit (see 120-B). Now turn back to 233-B.

240-A. (From 238-A) Here are some possible answers to the problems posed. If yours were different, evaluate them in the way we do here for comparison. For A, primary-to-secondary coupling is simple enough, yielding a reduction to ¼ the leakage inductance of the simple one-section–each arrangement. Between primary sections, the intermixing (A is sandwiched between B one place and vice versa the other, to equalize winding self-capacitance) yields a reduction to 1/16 of the simple arrange-

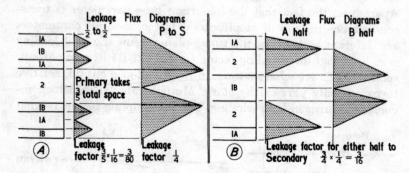

ment in that proportion of the total space, which is 3/5. This compression reduces leakage inductance by the same factor, making the final factor 3/80, which is 15% of the overall primary to secondary value and should be quite acceptable.

For B we have chosen a very simple arrangement, using two half-sections for one half-primary, and a single section for the other half. Primary-to-secondary leakage inductances will be the same for each half, and the half-primary resistances will be equal as well, in spite of any differences in mean-turn length, because of the inside-outside symmetry. Another arrangement, not quite so identical in this last respect, but giving a lower leakage-inductance factor, would be: ½-1A, 2, 1B, 2, 1A, 2, ½-1B. With seven pieces of winding, each half-primary to secondary will have a leakage factor of 1/12, which is less than half the one shown. Now turn to 225-A.

240-B. (From 212-D) *Correct.* It is the basic AND circuit with the second condition reversed, which means a pulse is passed, provided a signal is received at input 1 *and not* at input 2. Now, can you devise a combination of these basic elements to take two inputs and give an output to represent *or* . . . but *not both*? Try to figure it out; then turn to 229-C.

241-A. (From 221-C) Was this an intuitive guess? If so, it was wrong. Try another answer.

241-B. (From 224-A) *Correct.* Assuming the high-pass type network is used, this is the correct choice on several counts. It will usually be the point of lowest impedance in the circuit, where loading will have least effect. As distortion components partially neutralize at the plate and are attenuated at each stage less than the fundamental, the plate will be the point where harmonic content is lowest, as well as the signal level the highest.

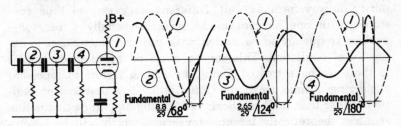

A form of distortion the previous treatment did not cover was the clipping due to grid-current biasing. This can best be considered relative to waveforms, as shown here. The dashed-line waveform (1) is repeated as a timing reference, representing the phase at the plate. Assuming clipping at the grid reflects as a flattening of the negative-going half-cycle at the plate, this will be a pulse and will not shift in phase as does the fundamental. Since the network is high-pass, this pulse, which is positive-going, will not be materially attenuated either, while the fundamental is progressively attenuated by a factor of 29 altogether. At the third stage, where the signal gets back to grid, the peak is accentuated much more than the original clipping flattened the wave. This has illustrated the phase situation. In fact, of course, this is a high degree—about 29 db—of negative feedback, which will help biasing and reduce clipping simultaneously.

The discussion on 247-A showed limits with identical-element networks and noninteracting extreme. Do these represent limits of practical cases as regards attenuation (see 249-C) or not (see 242-A)? As a clue, consider whether any other variations could be of value for some purpose not mentioned so far.

241-C. (From 250-C) This mistake is often made. The tuned-circuit Q is taken, and the external impedance is ignored. It can't be. Try again.

242-A. (From 241-B) All so far considered used sets of elements with identical time constants, whether the sets of elements were identical or widely removed in value to provide reduced interaction. We did not consider cases where successive pairs of elements have different time constants. The particular value of this arrangement is where the oscillation frequency needs to be made adjustable. Varying any of the elements from the identical case will increase the attenuation at 180° phase-shift frequency. If such variation is made without other changes, it will vary both frequency and intensity of oscillation, which will change the purity of waveform as well. Different staggering of time constants, with one element made variable—usually a resistor— enables frequency to be varied with reduced fluctuation in intensity of oscillation. This can be explored by methods similar to those we have treated, simply by adding factors to represent staggering of time constants. Optimization is a practical proposition, rather than mathematical: minimizing amplitude fluctuation requires theoretically infinite staggering, which will be accompanied by infinite attenuation at 180° phase-shift frequency; so a compromise has to be accepted that utilizes a reasonably high working-gain—something that can be achieved and maintained. Now turn to 248-A.

242-B. (From 216-D) *Correct.* The value is based on the calculated d.c. voltages at the grid for both conditions. Assuming R_4, R_5, R_6, and R_7 are made large enough and in correct ratio not to appreciably load the plate circuit (in the megohm region: R_6 and R_7 could be 150K each and R_4 and R_5 1.2 megohms each), then the grids swing from +12.2 volts at cutoff to +22.2 volts for "zero" grid. This means R_3 also has to drop 22.2 volts. As only one tube is conducting at a time, the current is 9 milliamps. This should be fairly precise; otherwise a lower ratio should be used for the grid resistors, to give a greater swing. If the cathode voltage is less than 22.2 volts, with one of the grids at 12.2 volts, this will not be cut off. If the cathode voltage is greater than 22.2 volts, the one that should be at zero grid voltage will not be, and the current will be lower than 9 milliamps. To some extent this will "self-correct." The overall swing will reduce accordingly. The B+ supply should be 222 volts, or thereabouts, to provide for 200 volts available from plate to cathode in the cutoff condition. Now turn back to 216-D.

243-A. (From 225-A) First we have to find the space we are working with. Of 1.5 inches length, 6×0.03 inch $= 0.18$ inch is taken up with flanges. In the test case the dimension factor is ⅓ of the active length (containing winding, plus the interspace, which works out to be 0.52 inch). This gives 40 mH for 1,000 turns.

Test Dimensions $1.5" - 0.12" = 1.38"$
 Overall   Flanges   Active

Dimension factor is $\frac{1.38}{3} + 0.06 = .52$ for 40mH/1000T.

First Coil Set Ratio ①:② is 9:8. Available active 1.32

Make $b = .39"$ Solve for a
$$8\left[\tfrac{1}{3}(.39+a)+.06\right] = 9\left[\tfrac{1}{3}(1.32-a)+.06\right]$$
$a = .526"$ $c = .404"$ *First column choice*

A turns ① dimension factor $\frac{.916}{3} + .06 = .365$
1000 turns makes $40 \times \frac{365}{.52} = 28.1$ mH.
12.75 mH requires $1000 \times \sqrt{\frac{12.75}{28.1}} = 675$ turns

C turns 675 turns takes .0708 μF.
.05 μF requires $675 \times \sqrt{\frac{.0708}{.05}} = 803$ turns

Matching B & D Let ⑧ use same gage as ④ allowing ⑧
1st column
$675 \times \frac{390}{.526} = 500$ turns ⑩ needs $890 \times \frac{390}{.526} = 660$ turns

First Coil Set

Widths in.			
A	.526	.512	.498
B	.390	.420	.450
C	.404	.388	.372
Turns A/B¹	675	670	665
C	803	796	790

Second Coil Set

Widths in.			
D	.452	.447	.442
E	.430	.440	.450
F	.438	.433	.428
Turns D¹/E²	890	888	886
F	858	856	854

Third Coil Set

Widths in.			
G	.400	.384	.368
H	.390	.420	.450
I	.530	.516	.502
Turns G²	1100	1091	1082
H	1690	1677	1664

Fourth Coil Set

Widths in.			
K	.404	.388	.372
J	.390	.420	.450
L	.526	.512	.498
Turns J³/L	675	670	665
K	803	796	790

Next, on each assembly we have to work out relative spacing. First, find the ratio between the two inductances in that assembly. Then assume a suitable width for the middle section, such as $b = 0.39$ inch, then, using the appropriate ratio, solve for one of the other section widths, in this case $a = 0.526$ inch. Subtracting the sum of these two from the total active length gives the third dimension. Use these dimensions to find the dimension factor for one of the leakage inductances in this assembly, in this case (1). This is applied to the test result to find the leakage inductance 1,000 turns would give in one of these "slots" to any winding filling the other slot. It is 28.1 mH. We need 12.75 mH. The square root of inductance ratio gives the turns needed for the latter.

In the tabulation at the right, we have chosen three center-section dimensions in each case and worked out the corresponding side-section dimensions. The middle one is usually a good compromise, while the other two choices represent one with a lower insertion loss (by reducing resistance of the transmission windings: although turns are very nearly the same, the space, and thus the gage used, changes), and the other represents one with greater rejection. The windings to which capacitances are connected are derived from the transmission winding reference turns by the simple square root of capacitance ratio. The transmission windings, except A and L, may use more convenient turns than those calculated, provided the sections with the same superior index are both changed in the same ratio.

244

244-A. (From 218-B) *Correct.* The vector diagram shows how *A* and *B* control the effective element contributed by the tube at the input terminals. Plate volts are divided into elements across *A* and *B*, v_A and v_B. The smaller, v_B, is also the input grid voltage to the tube. The tube's generated plate current is in phase with its grid voltage, and this (a.c.) can be divided into reactive and resistive components which are in the same proportion as *A* and *B* at every frequency considered.

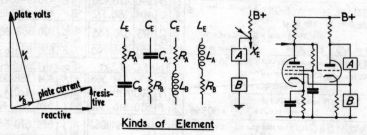

Kinds of Element

In the middle we show the basic electronic elements contributed by the tube for the four basic combinations of *C* and *R*, and *L* and *R*. Note that as plate current is proportional to the variation of v_B, and the reactive component is very nearly the same in magnitude, the shunt reactive-element has the dimension of a reactance, while the shunt resistive-element will vary as the square of the magnitude variation of v_B; this means the effective resistance component of the tube's plate current can be referred as a resistance in *series* with the reactance element represented by it.

The thing that must not be forgotten is the presence of the actual circuit elements, the plate coupling resistor and the voltage divider, across the input terminals. At the right we show how a negative inductance or capacitance can be designed by putting a phase inversion in the plate-to-grid coupling elements, *A* and *B*. Screen stabilization of the pentode's plate voltage (d.c.) is achieved just as in 179-B. In both circuits, of course, provision must be made for providing correct (and possibly control) bias (the latter·if the reactance is to be varied). This will involve extra capacitors to block d.c. voltages and feed in the control voltage, properly decoupled. Values should be such that they have negligible effect compared with the active values shown on these pages. If they do have effect, or if precision calculation is needed of the effect, the interaction methods which were described beginning at 202-A should be used.

245-A. (From 248-A) *Correct.* There must be a point of zero phase-shift, whatever the relative values of the four circuit elements. To refer the attenuation response to this frequency, it is fairly clear (if not, the formula developed verifies it; or you could use general terms until this condition for zero phase-shift

Make reactance of c at $x=1$: $\dfrac{ar}{}$

Then susceptance of C at $x=1$: $\dfrac{a}{R}$

$$\frac{V_i}{V_0} = 1 + \left(r - j\frac{ar}{x}\right)\left(\frac{1}{R} + j\frac{ax}{R}\right)$$

$$= \underbrace{1 + \frac{r}{R}(1+a^2)}_{\text{Make } k = 1 + \frac{r}{R}(1+a^2)} + j\frac{ar}{R}\left(x - \frac{1}{x}\right)$$

$$\frac{V_i}{V_0} = k + j\frac{a(k-1)}{1+a^2}\left(x - \frac{1}{x}\right) \qquad \phi_i = \arctan\frac{a(k-1)}{k(1+a^2)}\left(x - \frac{1}{x}\right) \qquad \text{③ Value of } a \text{ for maximum } \frac{d\phi}{dx}?$$

is found) that making the reactance of c equal to ar will require the susceptance of C to be a/R. Writing the attenuation expression and separating real and imaginary components, the imaginary is zero when $x = 1$, which verifies the zero phase-shift point. Then the real part can be equated to k, to stand for the attenuation at this point. This then refers the performance to the attenuation at zero-phase shift. Assuming the circuit has a requirement for k, is there an optimum for a? If you think it is $a = 1$, see 235-C; if you think making a the smaller the better, see 250-A; if you think making a the larger the better, see 249-D.

245-B. (From 248-B) *Correct.* There is no fixed rule about the relationship of the time constant to the oscillation period. Our example is derived as we show here. When the tube is conducting,

Starting voltage $200 - 120 = 80$v.

Trigger voltage 10v.   Ratio 8:1

Resistance $= 230$K. $RC = 241\,\mu$sec.

Half-period is $\frac{1}{2000}$ second $= \log_\varepsilon 8$ time constants

$\text{Log}_\varepsilon 8 = 2.0794$ Time constant $= \frac{500}{2.0794}\,\mu$sec

$C = \frac{241}{23}\,\mu\mu$F $= 241\,\mu$sec.

$\underline{1050\,\mu\mu\text{F.}}$

its plate voltage is 120. When it flips to nonconducting, it rises to full B+, 200 volts. The other way, when the plate voltage flips from 200 to 120, the grid of the other tube momentarily becomes 80 volts negative. The next flip will occur when discharge of this voltage into the capacitor C causes the grid voltage to reach 10 volts negative (so plate current commences, initiating loop amplification). This is an 8:1 discharge ratio. In every time constant the voltage ratio is e, so the ratio 8 corresponds with $\log_e 8$. From tables, $\log_e 8$ is 2.0794. So 2.0794 time constants will have to be 500 microseconds—each half-period. From this the capacitor value can be calculated. Now turn to 216-D.

246-A. In many applications of electronics the effective or active capacitance is different from its physical value. The simplest example of this is in the interwinding capacitance of a transformer, as well as the winding self-capacitance.

Interwinding Capacitance   Self-Capacitance

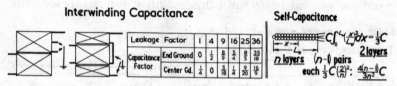

Leakage Factor		1	4	9	16	25	36
Capacitance Factor	End Ground	0	$\frac{1}{2}$	$\frac{8}{9}$	$\frac{5}{4}$	$\frac{8}{5}$	$\frac{35}{18}$
	Center Gd.	$\frac{1}{4}$	0	$\frac{5}{18}$	$\frac{1}{4}$	$\frac{9}{20}$	$\frac{16}{9}$

$$C\int_0^L \left(\frac{x}{L}\right)^2 dx = \frac{1}{3}C$$

2 layers

n layers $(n-1)$ pairs

each $\frac{1}{3}C\left(\frac{2}{n}\right)^2$: $\frac{4(n-1)}{3n^2}C$

Take first the simple two-winding arrangement, with no sectionalizing. If the end of one winding next to the other is grounded or at ground potential from a signal viewpoint (constant d.c. potential to ground) and the other winding is of low impedance, virtually at ground potential, then the interwinding capacitance is effectively *zero*. But if the center of the first winding is grounded, half the full signal voltage exists between the capacitance point and ground, resulting in half the current due to full signal voltage. Transformed to current from the full-signal point, this will be one-quarter. Connected with the other end grounded, the full physical capacitance is active. Now take the split winding, half on either side of the other: when center tap is grounded, the interwinding capacitance has no effect—it is effectively zero; when one end is grounded, *each layer* of interwinding capacitance has a reflected effect of one-quarter its physical value, making a total of one-half. Using winding-sectionalizing designed to reduce leakage inductance by the factors shown in the table, the effect on interwinding capacitance (per layer of interwinding space) is given for the two connections: (a) one end grounded, and (b) center-tap grounded. For the odd leakage-factors, one end of a full section is grounded; for even leakage-factors, the winding considered is the one with two outside half-sections (see 238-A).

Self-capacitance is that between layers of a winding and is not affected by what point is grounded. First we consider two layers and integrate the effect along the layer, relative to the physical capacitance of a layer, C. For a winding consisting of n layers, each pair of the $n - 1$ pairs will have this interlayer capacitance active, transformed down by the square of $2/n$.

Now, vertical sectionalizing can affect winding capacitance. Does this work on (1) interwinding (see 216-C), (2) self-capacitance (see 230-B), or (3) both (see 232-E), or (4) does it depend on the arrangement with which it is combined (see 234-B)?

247-A. (From 230-C) We could have given you quite a guessing game here, but there are too many variables to make the multiple-choice questioning practical here, unless this were a basic book on oscillator design. First, we figure out the transfer or attenuation expression for each kind of network. For both three and four stages we have figured out the attenuation factor (a) for that many identical elements cascaded, using the method intro-

Parameters		Three-Stage			Four-Stage			
		Identical	Noninteracting		Identical		Noninteracting	
Attenuation Factor		$1-5x^2+j6x-jx^3$	$1-3x^2+j3x-jx^3$		$1-15x^2+x^4+j10(x-x^3)$		$1-6x^2+x^4+j4(x-x^3)$	
Frequency x^2		6	3		1		1	
Attenuation		29	8		13		4	
Hi-pass Harmonic		2nd	3rd	2nd	3rd	2nd	3rd	2nd	3rd
Factor		$-\frac{13}{2}+j\frac{15}{2\sqrt2}$	$-\frac{7}{3}+j\frac{16}{9\sqrt3}$	$-\frac{5}{4}+j\frac{9\sqrt3}{8}$	$0+j\frac{8}{3\sqrt3}$	$-\frac{43}{16}+j\frac{15}{4}$	$-\frac{53}{81}+j\frac{80}{27}$	$-\frac{7}{16}+j\frac{3}{2}$	$+\frac{28}{81}+j\frac{32}{27}$
Magnitude		8.525	4.94	2.32	1.54	4.61	3.04	$\frac{25}{16}$	$\frac{100}{81}$
Phase		139.7°	118.2°	122.7°	90°	125.6°	102.5°	106.25°	73.75°
Lo-pass Harmonic		2nd	3rd	2nd	3rd	2nd	3rd	2nd	3rd
Factor		$-119-j36\sqrt6$	$-269-j144\sqrt6$	$-35-j18\sqrt3$	$-80-j72\sqrt3$	$-43-j60$	$-53-j240$	$-7-j24$	$+28-j96$
Magnitude		148	443	46.85	148.1	73.8	246	25	100
Phase		143.5°	127.3°	138.3°	122.7°	125.6°	102.5°	106.25°	73.75°

duced on 68-B with the frequency variable x included. If you have difficulty checking the result here, turn to 226-B for the detail on the three-stage identical case.

The other case (b) is a hypothetical one, using that many cascaded stages, but with values changed to avoid any interaction. This could only be achieved in practice by use of buffer stages between them, but making each successive R several times the one before it, and dividing successive capacitances by the same factor will approach this ultimate. Note that the noninteracting case results in much less attenuation for the complete network. This is found by solving for 180° phase shift (imaginary component zero) and substituting this value of x^2 into the real part to get the attenuation at this point. The high-pass and low-pass performance at harmonic frequencies is found by substituting values of x^2 that are 1/4 and 1/9 the oscillating frequency value for the high-pass type and 4 and 9 times this value for the low-pass type. From the substituted value of attenuation factor, magnitude and phase are computed.

What do these tabulated figures mean in terms of performance —particularly effect on purity of waveform? When you've tried to interpret this, turn to 224-A to see our method.

248

248-A. (From 242-A) Here is the basic network useful in another type of oscillator, one in which positive feedback is controlled so as to be in phase at just one frequency, which is determined by the network. Quality of oscillation is controlled by the

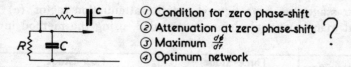

① Condition for zero phase-shift
② Attenuation at zero phase-shift
③ Maximum $\frac{d\phi}{df}$
④ Optimum network

performance of the network in rejecting frequencies other than that of oscillation. The first question to resolve is: do the network values, which we have labeled r, c, R, and C, need a specific, unique relationship to provide a zero phase-shift point? After this is answered we will tackle the other questions. If you think the answer is yes, see 223-B; if not, see 245-A.

248-B. (From 230-D) Multivibrators can be used for a variety of purposes and for each a different design may be required. A few samples will show the methods. First, assume that the function is to generate a square wave of certain frequency. Here

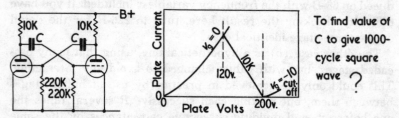

To find value of C to give 1000-cycle square wave ?

we show a simple circuit to do this, together with the relevant details about the plate-current curves of the tube type used. How does one find the value of capacitors C to give the right frequency—(1) choose values such that the time constant is half the period of oscillation, i.e., 500 microseconds (see 234-C); (2) make the reactance of C equal to the series circuit resistance (a little more than 220K): see 224-B; (3) make the time constant slightly less than one-fourth the period of oscillation (245-B)?

248-C. (From 216-D) This would provide a cathode voltage equal to the d.c. grid voltage when the opposite tube is conducting. But at zero grid voltage the tube considered would be conducting too, when it should be cut off. Try another answer.

249-A. (From 232-A) *No.* Above this point the use of completely alternative windings begins to be the most effective approach (see 227-A). Try one of the other answers.

249-B. (From 224-A) *No.* In the low-pass network, the purest signal might be at the grid, but it will be small and at very high impedance. In a high-pass network circuit, the grid is the point where harmonic content is highest. Try another answer.

249-C. (From 241-B) No, they don't. See the other answer.

249-D. (From 245-A) *Wrong.* Was this an intuitive guess? If so, it was wrong. Try another answer.

249-E. (From 216-D) Was this answer related to the 10K plate-load resistors? In any event, it was wrong. See one of the other answers.

249-F. (From 212-D) *No.* A *neither-nor* indication is really just an inversion of the *or* combination, at its output. Inversion of one input does a different thing. Try another answer.

249-G. (From 250-C) *Correct.* The best way to treat the input side of this circuit is with a current input, making Z_i a shunt admittance, rather than a series impedance. Pentodes or transistor collector-circuits usually comprise Z_i, and they must be high. Even then, for accurate computation their value must be taken into account in determining the operative Q, as must any reactance in making the final tuning. Both circuits must be tuned to the same frequency.

250-A. (From 245-A) *Wrong.* This was a guess. Either try another answer or figure it out.

250-B. (From 212-D) *No.* It might be worded *if not*, but not just *if.* Try another answer.

COUPLED CIRCUITS

250-C. The work beginning at 66-B developed a two-element, low-pass coupling network's parameters for wide-band response prediction, from a drooping roll-off to a peaking condition. The work at 71-B applied the simple one-way step to peaking and absorption circuits, which by suitable choice can become quite narrow-band. And the work at 206-A applied the interaction principle to reduce a simple resonant circuit to a form where a function of x, $x - 1/x$, replaces x in the simple low-frequency roll-off (73-B). Thus with high-Q circuits, a single tuned-circuit's response can be represented in terms of an equivalent low-pass where the cut-off frequency is a difference on either side of the center frequency.

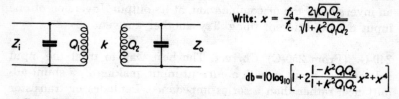

Write: $x = \dfrac{f_d}{f_c} \cdot \dfrac{2\sqrt{Q_1 Q_2}}{\sqrt{1 + k^2 Q_1 Q_2}}$

$db = 10 \log_{10}\left[1 + 2\dfrac{1 - k^2 Q_1 Q_2}{1 + k^2 Q_1 Q_2} x^2 + x^4 \right]$

Coupled circuits, of the type shown here, can similarly be represented as equivalent two-element, low-pass networks, by making the frequency substitution shown. This assumes that f_d, the difference frequency, is very small compared to the center frequency, f_c, so that $(f_c + f_d)/f_c - f_c/(f_c + f_d)$ is essentially equal to $2 f_d / f_c$, making the response of the two sidebands symmetrical. The 6-db slope, or 90° reference point, is controlled by the $Q_1 Q_2$ product, and the maximal flatness response occurs when $k^2 Q_1 Q_2 = 1$. Larger values of k lead to peaking (one peak either side of center); smaller values produce more droop. Combinations in successive stages can synthesize responses as done for low-pass in the work at 92-B. Now, obviously the loading of Z_o must be taken into account in computing Q_2; but what about Z_i (usually a tube plate-circuit or transistor collector)? Should it be near zero (see 232-F), is its value immaterial (see 241-C), or should it be very high and must be regarded as degrading Q_1 (see 249-G)?

Symbol and Subject Indexes

In the following Symbol Index only those symbols which are used consistently are listed. With 150 symbols in regular use, and with only the English and Greek alphabets to select from, there is necessarily some duplication. The choice of symbols in the text was therefore made to avoid ambiguity in common areas. The page references show where each symbol is introduced in the text.

Similarly, a listing in the Subject Index refers to the page where the subject is introduced. From this page you can explore the subject further by using the programming references. Any reference with an asterisk (*) indicates that the page contains useful data or reference material on the subject. This index also serves as a guide for studying Section 5; thus references with a dagger (†) denote the beginnings of sequences in this section.

SYMBOL INDEX

251

SUBJECT INDEX

Resonant matching, 102-A
Response
    db, 66-B, 73-B
    high-frequency, 123-A, 152-A
    low-frequency, 137-C
    phase, 73-B, 85-C, 100-A
    synthesis of, 92-B, 104-A, 250-C†
Roll-offs, 57-A, 73-B
Root mean-square value, 153-A

Scale linearity, 176-A
Screen feedback, 179-B
Screen loaded circuit, 143-A, 200-A
Sectionalizing, 213-D, 246-A†
    optimum, 221-C, *234-B
Separating the losses, 124-B
Series-impedance combination, 32-B
Series injection, 165-B, 168-B
Series network elements, 57-A
Series resonance, 46-A
Series step network, 73-B
Shaping circuits, 214-B†
Sharpness factor, 71-B, 82-C
Shelf equalizers, 73-B
Short-circuit termination, 107-B, 108-A,
    146-A
Short solenoid, 132-A
Shunt injection, 165-B, 168-B
Shunt network elements, 61-A
Shunt step network, 78-C
Sideband analysis, 209-B†
Sidebands, higher-order, 210-B
Single-layer solenoid, 125-A
Slope, negative maximum, 90-B
Slope normalizing frequency, 66-B
Space allocation, winding, 150-B
Square-wave generator, 248-B
Stability, conditional, 205-A†
Stability margins, 205-A†
Stages for feedback purposes, 197-A
Staggered time constants, 280-B
Star connection, 21-A
Step equalizers, 73-B
Step networks in feedback circuits, 198-A
Step-network terminations, 84-B
Summation, algebraic, 12-A
Suppressed carrier modulation, 215-A
Susceptance, 35-A, 50-A
Swing, affected by feedback, 164-B
Swinging choke filter, 199-A
Switching speed, 216-D
Symbolic notation, 68-B

Tapped-winding optimization, *222-B, 232-A
Tappings, disposition of inactive, 213-D
Terminating impedance, 58-A, 63-A, 84-B,
    107-B, 114-B, 151-A
Thevenin's Principle, 48-A, 54-A
Three-phase systems, 21-A
Three stages of feedback, 180-B
Time-axis analysis, 214-B†
Time constants
    LR, 30-A
    RC, 26-A, 53-A
    staggered, 180-B

Time delay, constant, 119-A
Transfer characteristics, 55-A, 134-B
Transfer current, 55-A, 134-B
Transfer functions, 187-A
Transfer power, 55-A, 132-B
Transfer voltage, 55-A
Transformer
    efficiency of, 150-B, 211-A†
    ideal, 148-B
    ratio for, 148-B
Transistor distortion, 134-B
Transistor input impedance, 134-B
Transistor transfer, 134-B
Transmission, a.c. and d.c., 17-A
Transmission line properties, 105-A
Transposition, input/output, 63-A
T-type attenuator, 72-A
T-type filter, 106-A
Tube distortion, 110-B
Tuned-circuit dynamic load, 149-C
Tuned-grid oscillator, 233-B†
Tuned-plate oscillator, 233-B
Turns determination, 117-B
Twin-π networks, 98-B
Twin-T networks, 101-A, 104-A
Twin-T vectors, 61-B
Twin-T oscillator, 230-D
Two-stage feedback, 190-B

Ultra-linear circuit, 143-A, 200-A
Unique relationships, 87-C
Universal meters, 167-A

VA (volt-amps), 56-A
Variable damping, 200-A
Vector addition, 22-A
Vector locus, 61-B
Vector rotation convention, 20-A
Vectors, 20-A
    modulation analysis, 209-B†
    impedance, 34-A
    multifrequency, 23-B
    oscillator, 233-B†
    phase-shift oscillator, 224-A
    reactance-tube, 244-A
    twin-T, 61-B
Voltage attenuation, 67-A
Voltage-divider impedance, 48-A
Voltage division, 64-A
Voltage feedback, 268-B
Voltage multiplier, 176-A, 199-A
Voltage transfer, 55-A
Volt-amps, 56-A

Wattless current, 19-A
Waveforms and metering, 153-A
Wheeler's formula, *132-A, 151-A
Width factor, 71-B
Winding capacitance, 123-A, *246-A
Winding-space allocation, 150-B
Wire-gage tables, *143-B

Y-connection, 21-A

Zero-phase oscillators, 248-A